LOST KNOWLEDGE

LOST KNOWLEDGE

Confronting the Threat of an Aging Workforce

David W. DeLong

UNIVERSITY PRESS

2004

OXFORD
UNIVERSITY PRESS

Oxford   New York
Auckland   Bangkok   Buenos Aires   Cape Town   Chennai
Dar es Salaam   Delhi   Hong Kong   Istanbul   Karachi   Kolkata
Kuala Lumpur   Madrid   Melbourne   Mexico City   Mumbai   Nairobi
São Paulo   Shanghai   Taipei   Tokyo   Toronto

Published by Oxford University Press, Inc.
198 Madison Avenue, New York, New York 10016

www.oup.com

Oxford is a registered trademark of Oxford University Press

Library of Congress Cataloging-in-Publication Data
DeLong, David W.
Lost knowledge : confronting the threat of an aging workforce / David W. DeLong.
     p. cm.
Includes bibliographical references and index.
ISBN 0-19-517097-0
1. Organizational learning.   2. Knowledge management.   3. Aged—Employment—United
States.   4. Middle aged persons—Employment—United States.   I. Title.
HD58.82.D4 2004
658.3'01—dc22   2004041577

9 8 7 6 5 4 3

Printed in the United States of America
on acid-free paper

For my wife, Sue,
who has listened to my dreams
and always said "Yes!"

Acknowledgments

A book is, in a sense, the outcome of an intellectual journey that can never be fully conveyed in words. No one produces a book alone, although the task often feels and looks very solitary. The process and the quality of the output—like most work today—is in the end a product of relationships developed over time. While researching and writing this book I have been blessed by many wonderful relationships—all supporting and, in their own way, contributing to this work.

First, I want to thank my intellectual mentors—Shoshana Zuboff, Wanda Orlikowski, Lee Sproull, and Meryl Louis—who set me on a path of discovery about the changing role of knowledge in our increasingly technology-intensive world. Tom Davenport has been a reliable friend and supporter of my research over the years. In his former role as director of Accenture's Institute for High Performance Business, Tom encouraged the initial study that led to this book. Also at Accenture, I will always be grateful to Tommy Mann and Sharon Gries, who early on recognized the problem of an aging workforce in the global energy industry and gave me the opportunity to study it.

There were scores of people who agreed to be interviewed for this research, some of them repeatedly. I am particularly grateful to Jeanne Holm at the National Aeronautics and Space Administration (NASA); John Mansfield at the Defense Nuclear Facilities Safety Board; Horace Deets, retired chief executive of AARP; Scott Shaffar at Northrop Grumman; and Sandra Bushby, formerly of the McLane Company. All of these people graciously accommodated my endless questions as we worked together to make sense of how organizations can come to terms with the threat of lost knowledge.

I am indebted to a wonderful group of reviewers who read the initial draft of this book. Dorothy Leonard, Nancy Dixon, Kent Greenes, and Allan Mackey all provided invaluable feedback and advice as this book was being created. I am very grateful for their time and consideration. My good friends Kent Lineback, Doug Weiskopf, Sara Delano, and the late Tom Richman also provided tremendous support along the way. And my Babson colleagues, Anne Donnellon and Liam Fahey, have been invaluable mentors throughout the process.

As an editor at Oxford University Press, Martha Cooley was a wonderful champion for this book when it was still just an idea. Her colleagues Niko Pfund, Terry Vaughn, Stacey Hamilton, and Mac Hawkins have been tremendous supporters of this project as it came to fruition. Robert Levers has been a terrific help in producing graphics for the book. And my resourceful research assistant, Jennifer Burgin, made this book much better through her patient and thorough literature reviews and her work on the endless revisions. Thank you, Jen.

I spent hundreds of hours reading, analyzing data, and writing in two wonderful libraries. I am grateful to the staffs of the Concord Free Public Library and the Acton Memorial Library for providing me with quiet retreats that made this lengthy project much more enjoyable.

I am continually inspired by the courage and positive outlook of my mother, Ginger DeLong, and my stepfather, Johnny Kelley, and I have also been blessed with wonderfully supportive in-laws. Bill and Millie Gladstone have been unfailingly enthusiastic about this project. What almost always goes unstated when recognizing the contributions of one's family in making a book like this possible is how inadequate words are to thank those who have sacrificed the most. There is nothing I could say that could make up for the missed dinners, the lonely weekends, and the late nights that my wife, Sue Gladstone, had to put up with in search of this dream. Writing this book would never have been possible without her ongoing love and support, and I cannot thank her enough for the gift she has given to me. This book is dedicated to her.

Finally, I want to particularly recognize my daughters, Sara and Anna, who will begin their careers at the height of baby boomer retirements. This book is an attempt to influence the future that they will inherit. To understand this world means recognizing how technology and science are transforming the role of knowledge and relationships in our daily lives. This project has, in fact, taught me a lot about relationships. Most important, it has helped me to appreciate the richness, complexity, and love of the relationships in my own family. This book is truly a product of that love.

Contents

Lost Knowledge

Introduction

You would have to have been living on the moon over the last few years not to know that baby boomers are fast approaching retirement age. This phenomenon has gotten plenty of media attention, since the post–World War II generation now ranges in age from 40 to 58 and is almost twice as big as the generation behind it, popularly known as Generation-X. A lot of these younger workers will probably be happy to see the veterans go. You know, more promotion opportunities, better parking spaces, and so on. Many baby boomers have spent their entire careers, or good chunks of them, with one company, government agency, or nonprofit organization. And, in the process, lots of them have built up a tremendous amount of knowledge about how things work, how to get things done, and who to go to when problems arise. In some cases, this practical knowledge will be extremely hard to replace because it has been developed in an era of unprecedented technological and scientific advances. For example:

- A senior nuclear weapons designer retires from the Los Alamos National Laboratory after 30 years, leaving no one in the lab who understands the design of missiles built in 1950s and 1960s, which are still deployed in military bases worldwide.[1]
- A chemist who invented a new polymer retires and soon afterward his company loses the ability to fix variations in quality when manufacturing the polymer product.
- A senior sales executive departs from her company with years of detailed knowledge about key strategic accounts and strong personal relationships with decision makers in client organizations.

As managers and professionals work in rapidly evolving scientific and technical fields, they gain tremendous experiential knowledge, only some of which is formally documented and shared. Inevitably today, employees leave without passing on enough of this valuable expertise. And, often, the only way their successors discover that they are missing key insights that their predecessors had is through mistakes, unexpected quality problems, or other costly disruptions in performance. These knowledge gaps can be very hard to pinpoint and diagnose at first because many work processes today are so intangible and complex. Even more important, because technology and work systems are increasingly interdependent, delays in problem recognition and diagnosis can be very costly. And, in the time it takes to recover this lost knowledge, organizational productivity inevitably suffers.

This book answers three questions: (1) Why should you care about the threat of lost knowledge in your organization? (2) What are the different types of scenarios where knowledge disappears and how do they affect performance? (3) Most important, what can you do to retain more critical knowledge in the face of major turnover due to an aging workforce and increased attrition among mid-career employees?

Lost knowledge has been a problem throughout human history, but its significance has taken a quantum leap in the last generation. The proliferation of computer technologies has not only produced advances in knowledge in all technical and scientific fields, but also work processes have become much more integrated and interdependent, creating all kinds of new knowledge needed to make things work. And this isn't knowledge that managers can afford to lose if they expect to sustain, much less improve, performance levels. For example, special capabilities might include:

- Safely disarming an aging nuclear weapon. (No kidding. We don't want to forget how to take those suckers apart.)
- Building and leading a cross-functional team to quickly solve a customer's supply chain problem (sounds mundane by comparison but still important).
- Creating and sustaining interagency cooperation needed to implement major government reforms.
- Maintaining legacy computer systems that still provide core operational applications.

In the future, organizations serious about improving performance are not going to have any choice. Leaders will have to address the challenges of knowledge retention if they hope to avoid the unacceptable costs of lost knowledge. The question is how to go about it. A fundamental premise of this book is that the primary reason executives avoid addressing threats of lost knowledge is that they have no idea how to attack the problem. This book will change that. It is written with a strategic orientation to serve leaders who want to understand how shifting demographics are threatening the future capabilities of their workforce, and what they can do about it. *Lost Knowledge* will help senior executives in organizations both large and small think strategically about the threats and opportunities posed by changing workforce demographics and how to formulate responses. But readers in other roles will also find help here.

Policy makers will get insights into the effects of an aging workforce and the loss of critical expertise on economic productivity. Management responses described in the book suggest where government can help support new solutions. For example, how are U.S. laws and programs currently failing to help retain and retool older workers? And how are current regulations providing financial incentives for veteran employees to retire early, taking their knowledge with them?

Line managers will learn how to diagnose and prioritize specific lost knowledge threats in their unit. The book clearly describes the options managers have for responding to different lost knowledge scenarios and, equally important, what organizational and psychological barriers leaders will have to overcome to create meaningful change.

Managers in staff functions, such as human resources (HR), knowledge management, and information technology (IT), will gain a cross-disciplinary understanding of the challenges posed by knowledge loss both for the organization as a whole and for their departmental objectives. The book provides a framework for understanding how one group's initiatives can be integrated into a broader organizational strategy that supports the development of future workforce capabilities.

Individual employees will also find help here if they are thinking of leaving a job where they have developed important expertise. Often, as an individual employee, you know best what essential knowledge you have gained in your role.

- Where is that vital document stored on the server?
- On that recent research and development (R&D) project, what costly design approaches did you learn couldn't possibly work?
- Who is the one person working for your company's vendor who knows the history of undocumented changes made on your computer system?
- What procedure in the maintenance manual have you learned to ignore because you know it's wrong?
- What is it that you always do on sales calls to retain the trust of your most valuable customer?

What would it cost your successor and the organization if this knowwhere, know-how, and know-what was to disappear suddenly when you leave? This book will lead you to think differently about the importance of the knowledge you have gained in your job and the value it has for the organization. (If your boss reads this, you might even get a raise!) Unfortunately, when many people leave jobs today, they are angry and alienated from the people they are leaving behind. Undoubtedly, many readers will feel they have not been treated well by their employers, and they have little interest in sharing their knowledge before leaving.

But, perhaps you are one of the lucky ones, and you really care about the mission of the organization you are leaving and the success of the people who take your place. Then this book will give you lots of ideas about how to begin transferring your unique knowledge before it is too late. And, if your colleagues don't seem overjoyed at your interest in sharing what you know, this book can help you understand their behavior, too.

Lost Knowledge is divided into three parts. Part I describes the macro forces in play that will make lost knowledge threats such a serious problem in the years ahead. It also shows how to identify different types of lost knowledge problems and which ones have strategic implications. A key finding of the research underlying this book is the need to recognize the interplay between retirements, recruiting, and the retention of mid-career employees. Effective workforce strategies must take all three issues into account. Finally, this part provides a framework for diagnosing current knowledge retention practices and for formulating new initiatives. One of the strengths of the framework is its holistic approach to the problem of knowledge loss. Effective knowledge retention efforts require an approach that integrates elements of an HR infrastructure and culture, along with the most appropriate transfer practices, given the types of knowledge involved. These practices should be supported by IT applications where they can be helpful.

Part II consists of five chapters that describe in detail the essential elements of the retention framework, including relevant HR processes and practices, a broad range of transfer approaches for explicit, implicit, and tacit knowledge, as well as supporting IT applications. There is also a chapter on strategies for recovering knowledge once it has left your organization.

Part III addresses the specific challenges of implementing retention initiatives. One chapter provides lessons from some organizations, such as Sandia National Laboratories, Northrop Grumman, the Tennessee Valley Authority, and a division of the energy company BP, which have already begun addressing the challenges that lost knowledge poses for future workforce development. Other chapters give advice on launching new retention programs and overcoming barriers to organizational change, which pose special problems for management. Another premise underlying this book is that many organizations are going to be overwhelmed with threats of lost knowledge, as gaps in skills and capabilities grow more serious, due largely to baby boomer retirements. Leaders will have to make difficult decisions in the future about where and how to focus their investments in retention activities. Thus, the book ends with a chapter on how to approach knowledge retention as a strategic problem. This chapter will guide executives in thinking about the tough choices that lie ahead.

Lost Knowledge is a solution-oriented book, but it's not a cookbook. In fact, recipes are one of several things that you won't find here. Because every organization represents a different context for knowledge use, don't look here for a definitive "solution" to your lost knowledge problems. Nor is there a strict formula for developing a knowledge retention strategy. The book does, however, identify most of the variables you will need to consider, and it provides guidance for how to undertake a process for designing and implementing your own approach to retention. Ultimately, however, the answer will have to come from inside your organization.

Also, you will not find rigorous benchmarking or quantitative comparisons of different sites in this book because contexts defining threats of lost knowledge and the potential responses are always unique. The exploratory research reported here is broad-based and thoughtful, but it is not scientific. If you wait for quantitative studies before taking threats of knowledge loss seriously, not only is it going to be too late, but also the results will most likely be irrelevant to your situation.

One thing that makes *Lost Knowledge* both timely and useful is that it is based on more than 200 original interviews in dozens of organizations around the world. Examples and quotes drawn from these interviews are used throughout the book, and readers should assume they are the source of all materials unless otherwise footnoted. The threat of losing knowledge can be politically sensitive or embarrassing in many organizations, so sometimes interviewees have asked that their comments be kept anonymous as a condition of participating in the research.

This book has an ambitious goal. That is, to speak about the problem of lost knowledge in a way that is relevant across sectors and across functions. Others no doubt will choose to dive deeper and focus more narrowly on the retention challenges for specific industries and functions. But there is a larger need at the moment, which is to define the landscape of what is shaping up to be a very serious problem in many organizations and to provide managers with frameworks to begin addressing issues in their context.

There have been a number of excellent books in the last few years describing the demographic shock waves that are about to hit the industrialized world.[2] This book is not one of them. Nor is *Lost Knowledge* another book on the general problem of "managing knowledge," which has received a lot of attention in the last decade.[3]

Retaining organizational knowledge is a complex challenge that cannot be addressed solely with a knowledge management solution. Meeting this challenge means improving career management practices, phased retirement programs, and succession planning, as well as creating a culture that retains valuable employees, among other things. Ultimately, this book argues that knowledge retention is a matter of survival because lost knowledge directly threatens the existing capabilities that many organizations need in order to sustain their current performance levels, much less to innovate and grow. Unlike the pursuit of opportunities to manage knowledge better, executives have no choice when it comes to knowledge retention. They must act or they will lose critical competencies they depend on already. *Lost Knowledge* will show you how you can make a difference in shaping future workforce capabilities by taking action today.

PART I
The High Cost of Losing Intellectual Capital

In a knowledge-based economy, effectively developing and applying intellectual capital is the key to creating value. Thus, the potential costs of losing knowledge should be intuitively obvious. But knowledge is a multi-dimensional concept and its value is determined by circumstances, so diagnosing lost knowledge threats is more complicated than it first appears. This section describes different types of situations where knowledge can be lost and shows how to identify where the loss of intellectual capital hurts organizational performance. This section also provides a framework for designing a knowledge retention strategy.

1

The Landscape of Lost Knowledge

On July 20, 1969, astronaut Neil Armstrong stepped onto the moon and uttered the immortal phrase "That's one small step for a man, one giant leap for mankind." Armstrong's achievement, a feat replicated by 11 other U.S. astronauts who followed him, represents possibly the greatest technological achievement in human history.

More than $24 billion was invested by the National Aeronautics and Space Administration (NASA) over 10 years to land astronauts on the moon. At its peak, 400,000 people were working on the Apollo project. And Armstrong's feat was no lucky accident. By 1972 five more Apollo missions proved that NASA could safely explore the moon and had learned a tremendous amount about space travel. So why haven't humans been back to the moon in more than 30 years? Well, to be sure, there have been other priorities in the U.S. space program. Exploring distant planets with unmanned space craft, conducting Space Shuttle experiments, and building the International Space Station have consumed much of NASA's $15 billion annual budget in recent years. And ongoing budgetary constraints and the loss of the Space Shuttle *Columbia* in February 2003 added to the uncertainty about NASA's long-range goals.

But, even when government officials talk about returning to the moon, few mention the simple and startling fact that the U.S. space agency has forgotten how to get there. The $50 billion-plus price tag put on returning to the moon[1] quietly ignores the fact that NASA has forgotten how they did it in the first place. That's because sometime in the 1990s NASA lost the knowledge it had developed to send astronauts to the moon. In an era of cost-cutting and downsizing, the engineers who designed the huge *Saturn 5* rocket used to launch the lunar landing craft were encouraged to take early retirement from the space program. With them went years of experience and expertise about the design trade-offs that had been made in building the Saturn rockets. Also lost were what appear to be the last set of critical blueprints for the Saturn booster, which was the only rocket ever built with enough thrust to launch a manned lunar payload.[2] One NASA manager confessed, "If we want to go to the moon again, we'll be starting from scratch because all of that knowledge has disappeared. It would take at least as long and cost at least as much to go back."

Of course some experts would say, "Who cares? If NASA goes back to the moon in the future they will use different technologies and different materials." That may be true, but it ignores two important questions. How did a world-class organization like NASA lose the capacity to replicate one of the greatest achievements in the history of mankind? And what supporting knowledge and technologies have also been lost or seriously degraded? For example, even if NASA's engineers could build and launch a *Saturn 5* rocket again, they have forgotten how to fly it.[3]

Drivers of Lost Knowledge

The story of lost knowledge at NASA is symbolic of a new challenge that threatens to undermine the evolution of the so-called "knowledge economy."[4] To make sense of what happened at the U.S. space agency, we must recognize two major forces that are shaping the workplace today: (1) an aging population and (2) the increasing complexity of knowledge needed in technologically advanced societies. The first of these drivers is well known. It is no longer news to most managers and policy makers that we are entering an era of major demographic changes, reflected most noticeably by an aging workforce. In the United States, the post–World War II baby boom generation has begun to retire from the workforce. This generation of 76 million people born between 1946 and 1964 is much bigger than the succeeding Generation-X cohort of 46 million people born between 1965 and 1980. The generation currently entering the workforce, sometimes known as Millennials, the NetGeneration, or Generation-Y, was born between 1981 and 1999. It includes about 76 million people.[5] A similar demographic pattern exists throughout the industrialized world—a large aging workforce is being followed by a younger generation that is smaller because of lower fertility rates. Although the United States will not see a decline in overall population, there will be a significant shift in the makeup of its workforce.[6] The Bureau of Labor Statistics, for example, projects that between 1998 and 2008 workers 45 and older will increase from 33% to 40% of the workforce. This represents an additional 17 million workers in this age group. Meanwhile, workers age 25–44 will drop from 51% to 44% of the labor force in the same time period. That is a decline of 3 million workers from the pool that would be expected to succeed those retiring (see figure 1.1).[7]

There is some debate about whether these major demographic shifts will actually produce a significant labor shortage in the society as a whole.[8] But concern about widespread labor shortages, which means the inability to fill

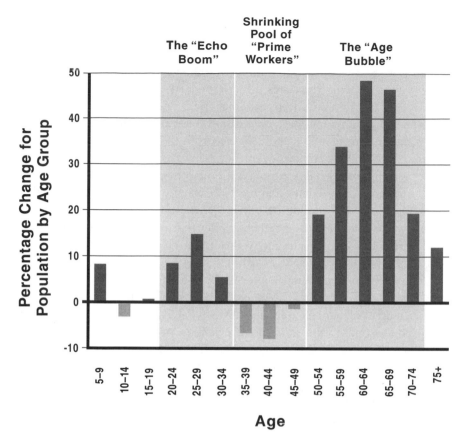

FIGURE 1.1. **Changing Distribution of the Workforce 2003–2013**
By 2013 the number of workers in the United States age 35 to 44 will shrink almost 10 percent, while the number of workers age 55 to 64 will grow by almost 40 percent. *Source*: Global Insight, Inc.

jobs at prevailing wages, is not the same as replacing a lot of highly skilled employees with much less experienced people. Whether or not labor shortages develop, there is little question that many experienced workers will be leaving their jobs in the next decade. And that giant sucking sound you will hear is all the knowledge being drained out of organizations by retirements and other forms of turnover.

These attrition patterns will be at least as bad in other industrialized countries, too. Like the United States, baby boomers make up 30 percent of Canada's total population, but its workforce is aging even faster. By 2011, Canada's median age is expected to be 41.0 years, compared to 36.5 in the United States. By 2010, the 45–64-year-old group will represent 37 percent of

Canada's workforce, up from 30 percent in 1990, and the proportion of "older" workers will continue to climb for about 20 years as baby boomers move toward retirement.[9]

In Europe, the aging population combined with a significant falloff in fertility rates actually translates into a 1 percent decline in overall population during this decade. After 2010, that trend will accelerate over the next 40 years with Germany, Italy, and Spain all experiencing population declines ranging from 14 to 25 percent, according to the United Nations Population Division.[10] A similar, even more dramatic pattern is unfolding in Japan, which already has a population with a median age of 41 and a very low birth rate.[11] These demographic patterns are producing both an aging labor force and a shrinking one. In 25 years, for example, Germany will have a workforce that is 20 percent smaller than in 2000 and a retired population that is 50 percent larger. Very similar changes will occur in Japan and Italy.[12]

These macro-level changes in overall population numbers translate into new labor force patterns that are of concern to economists and policy makers. But as industrial nations transition into what has become known as the knowledge economy, the practical implications for management of a rapidly aging workforce and a shrinking pool of highly skilled younger workers has not been fully explored. To do this, we have to look at how these demographic trends are playing out at the organizational level. Executives today are facing some really scary numbers.

Take the U.S. Defense Department's civilian workforce of 675,000 people, for example. Between 2002 and 2008, 75 percent are expected to retire. And about one-third of all secondary schoolteachers in the United States are expected to retire by 2008. Meanwhile, at NASA the number of engineers and scientists older than 60 outnumber those under age 30 by almost three to one. And 25 percent of this workforce will be eligible to retire within four years. The oil and gas production industry can expect to lose more than 60 percent of its employees by 2010.[13] And the aviation industry also has many people eligible for retirement. One major airline, for example, recently lost more than 1,200 veteran maintenance technicians to early retirement. That's more than 25,000 years of specialized experience fixing some of the world's most sophisticated airplanes that's gone out the door. Try not to think about that the next time you're rocketing down the runway.

Energy is one sector that expects to be particularly hard hit by retirements.[14] In many global oil and chemical companies, for example, estimates that large numbers of the employees in a particular function will become retirement eligible in the next decade are not uncommon. Here are some examples:

- "Within the next five years, at least 50% of our engineers across the company will be retirement eligible. This function is made up of predominantly white men in their 50s."—HR leader, diversified U.S. chemical company
- "There's an overwhelming number of people in their 50s (45%) in our production areas."—Personnel manager, diversified Japanese-based chemical company
- "We expect a 16% retirement rate over the next five years."—Global recruitment and HR planning manager, European-based petrochemical company

Of course, not every organization is looking at such dramatic losses. And executives recognize that a modest level of turnover is good for every organization, creating promotion opportunities for younger employees and a chance to bring in fresh ideas. Still, for a growing number of organizations the impacts of an aging workforce have become a serious concern, and the problem is complicated by its patchwork quality. One thing confusing the picture is that the impact of demographic changes is going to affect industries, organizations, and professions differently. In the United States, for example, the federal government, energy, education, manufacturing, health care, and aerospace and defense sectors will be faced with very high rates of retirement eligibility in the next few years.[15] But, even in individual organizations, retirement patterns will vary by division, plant, or work unit. This makes it more difficult for leaders to create organization-wide initiatives to address the problem. "The average age in some plants is rising a lot and in others it's dropping," said one Shell Chemicals manager. "It depends on where you are in the cycle. It also depends on when units came up and when you laid people off. We've got one plant where the average age is quite young and in others it's the opposite." In reality, retirement rates within any organization can vary significantly by function, work group, and geographic location.

Regardless of which units are hurt, however, the average age and level of work experience in many sectors is going to drop significantly in the next decade. "We could lose as much as 50% of our total population in the next 5 to 10 years, where the average employee has 25 years of experience," said the senior executive of one major oil company. "And, even if we can hire replacements, in 10 years our average work experience will drop considerably. That probably has an impact on our NPV."[16]

Of course, human resource experts, demographers, and politicians have begun making all kinds of claims about how current demographic trends will affect the workforce. Some predict labor shortages. Others argue that organizations will have to make major changes in personnel policies, compensation, and work design to entice older workers to stay on past traditional retirement dates. Still others predict more older workers will be staying in the workforce, requiring changes in personnel policies and compensation plans.[17] What all of these prognosticators have in common is they don't really know what is going to happen in your organization.

The problem of managing through these major demographic changes is actually much more complicated than just coping with retirements. At the other end of the talent pipeline, a younger cohort of technicians, analysts, engineers, research scientists, plant operators, and salespeople, for example, are joining organizations today with a different set of values and expectations, which creates new recruiting and employee retention issues. Recruiters looking for aviation mechanics, chemical engineers, librarians, and physicians, for example, are worried about the shortage of applicants in these professions in the coming years. Workers simply have more options when making career choices today.[18] And, until the economic downturn that began in 2001, younger workers were changing jobs much faster than their baby boomer parents. The recession that marked the early years of the new millennium temporarily improved prospects for recruiting and greatly slowed turnover in most organizations. But this is only a temporary phenomenon.[19] The demographic trends are immutable. The workforces in industrialized countries are changing dramatically, and that spells trouble for organizations that depend on highly trained and experienced professionals and managers to create value.

The Changing Nature of Knowledge

Changing workforce demographics, however, are only part of the problem. What is not as well understood is that there is a second factor that will make the operational and strategic impacts of this looming brain drain potentially much more serious than business and political leaders realize. In the last 25 years, the industrialized world has experienced unprecedented advances in technology and scientific domains, made possible in large part by the proliferation of information technologies.[20] Individual scientific domains, such as chemistry, physics, and genetics, along with engineering and technical fields, such as aeronautical, electrical, and network engineering, have become increasingly specialized and complex. Knowledge-intensive work today is much more interdisciplinary, often requiring the integration of expertise across a wide range of subjects. In the pharmaceutical industry, for example, drug discovery today requires collaboration between experts in fields such as molecular biology, biochemistry, pharmacology, genomics, and bioinformatics.[21] And, to take another case, managing environmental cleanup projects requires knowledge of chemical, thermal, and fluid dynamics, along with expertise in specialized treatment processes for different pollutants, federal and state regulations, dispute resolution, and complex project management techniques. Operating in interdisciplinary environments like these, professionals and managers inevitably develop important practical knowledge about related disciplines, not to mention relationships with other experts who they can turn to. The cumulative knowledge gained by working with others in an environment that integrates complex specialties creates kinds of expertise that are very hard to replicate.

An understanding of the structure and content of complex computer systems and networks is another type of intellectual capital that has become critical to effective performance in many roles. But this type of knowledge has proved frustratingly difficult to capture and share. For example, as a database manager for three years, Mark Hargrove was responsible for running a complex series of computer programs every month to update some 30 million records of his company's credit card customers and potential customers.[22] When Hargrove decided to leave the company, he spent six weeks training his replacement, Joan Locke, a young database analyst. He wrote out detailed descriptions of the computer jobs that had to be run, the quality control procedures required, as well as tips on how to make the process run smoothly. Locke began running the monthly update when Hargrove left, but the programs did not run correctly because she overlooked key steps in the myriad of detailed instructions left by her predecessor. "I mean how much documentation can you absorb?" asked her boss, the director of database operations.

In addition, the new database manager was missing certain knowledge that Hargrove had failed to document. He had forgotten, for example, to make explicit the file naming standards used in the system. This meant the next computer program in the update process was expecting a certain file label from the previous job, or it would not run. These breakdowns in knowledge sharing between Hargrove and Locke cost the department almost $100,000 in extra charges for rerunning computer jobs and paying overtime penalties in other departments whose activities were disrupted when the database update process was not completed on time. Perhaps most damaging was the credibility and goodwill the database team lost with its marketing department because of the suddenly unpredictable update process. It took considerable extra effort to rebuild previous levels of trust between the two groups. This story typifies the difficulties of transferring knowledge about complex computer systems. It is played out repeatedly in IT-centered work. But the costs of this type of lost knowledge do not appear on any balance sheet. They are hidden, but no less real.

Knowledge about specific information technology systems and networks is abstract and dynamic, and it reflects a set of complex interdependencies that are difficult to keep in mind. At the same time, knowledge about how technical systems work is also inflexible, rule-based, and rooted in historical design decisions that may not be documented. And when these hard-to-remember rules are violated, the results can be very costly, such as when a new database manager fails to respect file naming standards for each computer program. Today, this is the type of knowledge needed to maintain the infrastructures of most large organizations in the industrialized world. And a lot of this know-how is walking out the door.

Thus, the challenge facing many organizations is not only the loss of some of their most experienced employees, but also many of these professionals and managers are taking with them new types of critical expertise and experiential knowledge that didn't exist a generation ago. In the context of the new economy, future leaders are likely to face not simply a labor shortage, but a knowledge shortage, as organizations bleed technical, scientific, and managerial know-how at unprecedented rates. And what is the effect on productivity of losing all this expertise? Examples range from silly and expensive to life threatening and downright scary.

- A technician making control boards on a radar equipment assembly line at Texas Instruments took early retirement, and immediately parts coming off the line began failing quality assurance (QA) tests for some mysterious reason. A team of expensive engineering consultants can only validate that the unit is producing boards built to specifications. Finally, with the assembly line down, exasperated managers brought the retired technician back, and she quickly diagnosed the problem as faulty documentation of an assembly procedure. This veteran technician had always ignored the incorrect instructions because she knew how to produce a control board that worked. But before this knowledge is recovered the unit lost over $200,000 in sales revenues and almost lost its next contract with a major customer.[23]
- When an ethylene reactor exploded at a petrochemical plant on the Texas Gulf Coast an investigation found that the unit's engineer and the operators in the control room at the time of the accident had all been on the job less than a year. Retirements and turnover had left the plant with inexperienced personnel, and not surprisingly, the explosion was attributed to operator error. Having less experienced people working in increasingly sophisticated computer-controlled production operations increases the risks of serious and costly mistakes.
- After Boeing offered early retirement to 9,000 senior employees during a business downturn, an unexpected rush of new commercial airplane

orders left the company critically short of skilled production workers. The knowledge lost from veteran employees combined with the inexperience of their replacements threw the firm's 737 and 747 assembly lines into chaos. Overtime was skyrocketing and workers were chasing planes along the line to finish assembly. Management finally had to shut down production for more than three weeks to straighten out the assembly process, which forced Boeing to take a $1.6 billion charge against earnings and contributed to an eventual management shakeup. Lost knowledge was certainly not the sole cause of Boeing's production problems, but it was a major contributor.[24]

A lot of managers in the years ahead are going to be talking about labor shortages and the difficulties of recruiting top talent, particularly specialists, like geoscientists, radiology lab technicians, nuclear physicists, and aviation engineers. But the difficulty of finding replacements for experts leaving organizations or finding new recruits to support projected growth is only part of the problem. Concentrating on staffing overlooks the real price organizations often pay when they lose highly skilled professionals and managers to retirement or mid-career job changes. The knowledge these veterans take with them has immediate, though often hidden, impacts on productivity. So the problem for management is not just one of headcount and finding another body to fill the role. It is a matter of retaining or replacing the sophisticated, context-dependent knowledge that resides with the employee who is leaving. In other words, focusing on the threat of lost knowledge instead of staffing shortages provides a more accurate perspective on the real impact of turnover in the knowledge economy.

Unfortunately, research shows that even when leaders in industry and government recognize the problem, most do not know what to do about it. They need an answer fast, however, because the hidden costs of lost knowledge are becoming a huge drain on organizational productivity and, in some cases, a threat to sustaining competitive advantage. And the problem is going to get worse.

Impacts of a Brain Drain

This book is about both a problem—lost knowledge—and a solution—knowledge retention. The two concepts are intimately related, but they are not exact opposites because an organization can never retain all of the knowledge it could lose, nor would it want to.

Lost knowledge and knowledge retention are broad abstract concepts that have little value unless they are carefully defined and illustrated to show their relevance to organizational effectiveness. The next section will explain these concepts more carefully as they will be used throughout the book.

What Is Lost Knowledge?

Humans have been creating and losing knowledge for thousands of years. Knowledge about languages, cultures, arts, and technologies has always been at risk. For example, knowledge of a great deal of Egyptian history was lost about 400 AD when Egyptians began using a version of the Greek alphabet, giving up their own writing system known as hieroglyphics. Scribes in the ancient culture had used hieroglyphic writing for more than 3,000 years to record the words and deeds of their leaders and for inscriptions on temples and stone monuments. But the meaning of this picture writing was lost to historians and archeologists until 1799, when a French officer in Napoleon's army discovered a stone tablet near Rosetta, Egypt, close to the Nile River. This tablet, known as the Rosetta stone, carried the same inscription in both Greek and Egyptian hieroglyphics. It allowed scholars to decipher its hieroglyphs and to eventually recover the ability to read Egyptian hieroglyphic writing, opening the door to knowledge of an advanced culture that previously had become inaccessible.[25]

In a 1993 speech, the U.S. Librarian of Congress, James Billington, said, "One ghostly image haunts all of us charged with preserving the creative heritage of humanity: the specter of the great, lost Library of Alexandria."[26] The destruction of this library is another famous example of lost knowledge. The library was the first known attempt to collect all of the world's recorded knowledge, and scholars still dispute what led to its mysterious disappearance by 300 AD. During this period, Alexandria, Egypt, was one of the greatest cities on earth, and the library was the centerpiece of Greek civilization. It was here that Euclid developed his geometry, Archimedes formulated basic principles of physics, and Eratosthenes determined the Earth's circumference with amazing accuracy. At the time of its destruction, the Great Library probably contained more than 400,000 papyrus scrolls, including original manuscripts of the Greek tragedians Sophocles, Aeschylus, and Euripides. Scholars still dispute exactly when and how the library was destroyed, but its destruction remains possibly the greatest example of lost intellectual and cultural knowledge in history.[27]

Of course, not all knowledge lost to history was recorded. Knowledge of technology and craftsmanship has sometimes disappeared with those experts who developed and applied it. For example, Damascus steel, the world's first high-carbon steel, was forged for centuries by skilled blacksmiths in India. The steel was used to make incredibly sharp and strong swords and knives used by warriors in Persia and Arabia. But by the 1700s the art of making Damascus steel disappeared for reasons still not entirely clear. Only recently have metallurgists rediscovered the key elements of the process used, which may enable more modern applications of this special steel in industry.[28]

For more than a century the world's greatest violinists have insisted that the instruments made by famous Italian violin-making families in the seventeenth and eighteenth centuries, such as Stradivarius and Guarneri, are of higher quality than those made today. These rare instruments routinely sell for more than $1 million. But while skilled violinists can distinguish qualities in the sound of individual violins, scientists have been unable to measure those differences. In other words, there is a debate about whether important knowledge has actually been lost.

Still, a recognition of "the Stradivarius secret" persists, and researchers have tried for over a century to rediscover what the master craftsmen in the Stradivari family knew about making violins. For years, some speculated it was the varnish used. Meanwhile, others argued that soaking the wood in water was Stradivarius's secret. Whatever the answer is, many musicians believe that knowledge has been lost that prevents violin makers today from creating instruments equal to those made hundreds of years ago.[29]

While the notion of lost knowledge obviously can be applied in many situations, in this book the concept is used in a narrower context. As applied here, "knowledge" is the capacity for effective action or decision making in the context of organized activity.[30] Thus, lost knowledge means the decreased capacity for effective action or decision making in a specific organizational context. Here are some examples:

- Leaders in the U.S. nuclear weapons industry are concerned about losing the knowledge needed to safely design and test nuclear weapons because of the retirement of so many veteran nuclear scientists and engineers.[31]
- A semi-conductor design team fails to retain its notes and other documentation of progress made when its project is shelved. As a result, when the project is restarted a year later, the new team must re-create all of the work previously done.
- When a veteran marketing manager leaves General Mills, the knowledge that is lost about the product's customers and how to market effectively to them costs the company millions of dollars, according to the firm's director of staffing and recruitment.[32]

Lost knowledge can occur at a broad organizational/functional level, such as the potential loss of a nuclear-testing capability. It also occurs on a work unit/small group level, as illustrated by the semi-conductor design team, and on an individual level, as shown by marketing managers at General Mills. This book focuses on situations where an organization has had the capacity for effective action or decision making in a particular function, team, or individual role and has demonstrated this ability repeatedly. But that capability is now seriously threatened or is no longer available because of retirement, turnover of younger employees, reorganization, reassignment, or lack of access to knowledge archives. The latter is usually due to either poor record keeping or obsolete electronic storage.

Lost knowledge as defined here does not include a firm's inability to replicate something that it has done only once. For example, Ford Motor Company was unable to re-create the success of its Taurus design team, a failure that has been proposed as an illustration of lost knowledge.[33] Nor does it include failed attempts to transfer "best practices" from one part of the organization to another.[34] Certainly, the ability to share expertise across organizational boundaries is a critical activity in knowledge-intensive work. But the inability to transfer best practices into new organizational contexts or to replicate a capability demonstrated once suggests barriers more related to innovation, environmental fit, and luck, which are very different than sustaining or regenerating a capability the organization has demonstrated repeatedly in a particular setting.

Any discussion about the phenomenon of "knowledge" requires some clarification about its relationship to the concept of "information." Lots of very smart people have tried to articulate the differences between these two concepts.[35] The difficulty of this task underscores the fact that knowledge and information are often overlapping constructs whose relevance is determined by the situation. Information is data that is structured so that it is transferable, but its immediate value depends on the potential user's ability to sort, interpret, and integrate it with their own experience. Knowledge goes a step further and implies the combining of information with the user's own experiences to create the capacity for action. Employee turnover certainly can result in lots of information being lost. But this book addresses the problem of "lost knowledge" because the capacity for action is a more valuable organizational asset than access to information, although in practice it is sometimes hard to differentiate the two.

Finally, there is bound to be tremendous confusion in any discussion of lost knowledge unless we recognize that there are at least four distinct types of knowledge interacting at all times. And the loss of any one of these types can affect performance.[36]

- *Human Knowledge*: This constitutes what individuals know or know how to do. Human or individual knowledge is manifested as skill (e.g., the ability to develop a marketing plan, give feedback to subordinates, or program your wireless phone) or expertise (e.g., deep understanding of complex chemical reactions, the limitations of specific networking software, or the complexities of policy implementation). Human knowledge is generally described as either explicit or tacit knowledge, but this oversimplification can be misleading, as will be discussed in chapter 5.[37] Human knowledge may also be sentient, that is, located in the body, such as knowing how to type or ride a bicycle. Or it may be cognitive, that is, largely conceptual and abstract.[38]

- *Social Knowledge*: This form of knowledge exists only in relationships between individuals or within groups. It is often called "social capital." An executive with an extensive network of personal relationships with clients or a high-performing team of research scientists both reflect the presence of social knowledge embedded in those relationships. Social knowledge is largely tacit, shared by group members, and develops only as a result of working together. Its presence is reflected by high levels of trust and an ability to collaborate effectively.[39]

- *Cultural Knowledge*: This type of knowledge reflects a collective understanding of how things are done in a particular organization, that is, how to think and how to behave if you want to be accepted as a member of a particular group. While social knowledge, as previously defined, describes intellectual capital residing in specific relationships, cultural knowledge describes collective knowledge that is shared more broadly across an organization. If a top salesperson retires, he or she takes away a valuable set of relationships with clients, but the departure does not affect the cultural knowledge of the unit. If, however, most of the sales force left at once, then this collective knowledge could also be affected.[40] The loss of cultural knowledge can become particularly salient in organizations experiencing very high levels of turnover.

- *Structured Knowledge*: This type of knowledge is embedded in an organization's systems, processes, tools, and routines. Knowledge in this form is explicit and rule-based. A key distinction between structured knowledge and the other types is that structured knowledge is assumed to exist independently of human knowers. Thus, it is clearly an organizational resource.[41]

What Is Knowledge Retention?

Knowledge retention consists of three activities—knowledge acquisition, storage, and retrieval (see figure 1.2).[42]

"Knowledge acquisition" describes the practices, processes, and routines used to move knowledge into a state where it is kept available for future use.

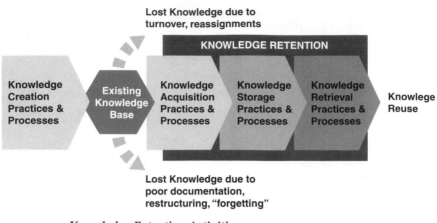

FIGURE 1.2. Knowledge Retention Activities

This can mean one expert teaching another person or group how to perform a complex task, capturing detailed problem-solving instructions in a database, or embedding important company practices in an employee orientation program.

"Storage" represents the processes and facilities used to keep knowledge and information until it is needed. Storage entities include individuals, groups, culture, work processes, routines, and systems, such as a database.

"Retrieval" includes behaviors, routines, and processes used to access and reuse information and knowledge in new situations, such as searching an expert database, calling a colleague, remembering a past experience, brainstorming with a group about past experiences, or searching a document database.

These three activities have been used to characterize "organizational memory,"[43] which has become a popular concept in recent years among academic researchers and consultants.[44] But the notion of "organizational memory" remains relatively vague and not very useful for practicing managers who need to address the problem of lost knowledge. Knowledge retention is effectively the act of building organizational memory. There are several reasons why this book focuses on retaining knowledge instead of building organizational memory. Lost knowledge, in effect, means that organizational memory has been degraded. But the latter does not describe a way to counteract the problem. Retaining knowledge more effectively is the way to do that. Knowledge retention is more action-oriented. Organizational memory describes an artifact that may or may not be drawn on to influence future performance.[45]

Knowledge retention also describes a solution to a critical problem that affects performance. Organizational memory is a more benign concept describing a phenomenon that exists independent of environmental changes (e.g., increased retirement). Finally, knowledge retention is a grounded, practical way of attacking the real threat of lost knowledge. Organizational memory, however, is a more theoretical concept that has been subject to relatively little empirical analysis.[46]

Conclusion

In sectors such as government, manufacturing, energy, health care, education, and aerospace, knowledge retention will become an overriding concern in the years ahead. But, in organizations with younger workforces, reducing the costs of lost knowledge will evolve into an objective that supports long-term growth strategies, or is simply part of an overall knowledge management strategy. The point is that knowledge retention may be a matter of survival or a secondary concern for your organization today. But for virtually every organization—large or small—reducing the costs of lost knowledge is going to become an increasingly compelling issue. And the price of ignoring this threat will grow exponentially in the years ahead, contributing in some cases to major operational disruptions, the loss of competitive advantage, and even tragic accidents.

Leaders who fail to confront this threat will increasingly be held accountable for jeopardizing the future viability of their organizations. In the long term, you cannot compete effectively in the knowledge economy unless you are serious about knowledge retention.

2

Diagnosing the Strategic Impacts
of Lost Knowledge

Recognizing that lost knowledge may be a threat to organizational performance is an essential first step. But designing effective solutions also requires a clear understanding of what forms these threats can take. This chapter describes different types of lost knowledge problems and shows how they can impact an organization's strategy. The chapter ends by outlining five barriers that must be overcome to implement effective knowledge retention solutions.

A Typology of Lost Knowledge

Sociologist Diane Vaughan notes, "The invisible and the unacknowledged tend to remain undiagnosed and therefore elude remedy."[1] Grouping all incidents or threats of lost knowledge together helps keep them invisible and makes it very difficult to get any traction in addressing them. You need to understand the four dimensions of lost knowledge problems in order to think more effectively about what intellectual capital your organization needs to retain. Lost knowledge:

- Can occur at individual, group, or organizational levels
- Have either anticipated or unanticipated effects
- Have tangible or intangible impacts
- Create immediate or delayed costs

Different lost knowledge scenarios will call for different solutions. Here are descriptions of the four dimensions.

At What Level Is Knowledge Lost?

As mentioned earlier, knowledge can be lost at the individual, group, functional, or organization level.

- A veteran chemicals purchasing executive leaves with detailed knowledge of supply sources, history of negotiations, contract details, and relationships with key suppliers. His successor lacks the market knowledge to counter 10 percent price increases immediately levied by suppliers.

- An engineering group fails to document changes made in the structural configuration of a nuclear weapons laboratory, and the group members leave over time. As a result, accurate knowledge of the lab's current engineering configuration is lost and future changes to the building's ventilation system become much more costly.
- FAA radar technicians have been retiring in large numbers, taking with them lots of practical knowledge needed to repair old radar systems still in use.

These examples show how knowledge can be lost at different levels of the organization. Of course, knowledge lost at the individual, group, or functional level can have implications for the organization as a whole. Not surprisingly, the perception of lost knowledge problems will be heavily influenced by your role and position in the hierarchy. Senior executives are more likely to be concerned with the strategic implications of losing knowledge across entire functions or areas of the business, particularly when those losses threaten the organization's performance. A major chemical company wants to expand in Asia, for example, but top management is worried about losing the experienced chemical engineers it will need to open new plants.

Middle managers and supervisors, however, are more likely to be concerned about losing the intellectual capital of small groups or specific individuals. A particular individual's knowledge is more likely to be valued by immediate colleagues, so retaining it is a local concern, even though it may have broader impacts.

Are the Effects of Lost Knowledge a Surprise?

The costs can be tremendous when the impacts of lost knowledge are unanticipated. After a maintenance technician retired from a plant producing soybean oil, large batches of oil suddenly started to go bad during production. It took the company two years to discover what the retired technician knew that made the difference. This veteran employee had learned that he needed to change the fifty-cent seals on the machines that pressed the oil every week, instead of every eight weeks as dictated by the maintenance manual. Unexpectedly losing this experiential knowledge cost the company millions of dollars in lost product and sales revenues. One of the goals of knowledge retention is to reduce the frequency of these costly surprises that disrupt productivity.

In many situations, however, entities can anticipate the loss of critical knowledge. The U.S. Department of Energy (DOE) recognized that the retirement of veteran workers at its Rocky Flats nuclear weapons facility would significantly increase the costs and risks of its recent cleanup efforts. DOE knew that these workers, who had lived with the dangers of plutonium and other toxic waste for years, were best qualified to pinpoint hazards to environmental cleanup crews. Anticipating the potential cost of this lost knowledge encouraged DOE to accelerate its schedule, helping to save what was estimated as billions of dollars in cleanup costs.[2]

Are the Effects of Lost Knowledge Tangible or Intangible?

Losing knowledge may have impacts that are very tangible and financially quantifiable, or the impacts can be intangible and hard to measure. For example, the manager of an oil drilling platform in the Gulf of Mexico shuts down his operation for safety reasons when he cannot readily locate the design engineers who would know how to fix a fracture in a critical pipe. When making the decision, he knows the shut down will cost the company several hundred thousand dollars.[3]

In contrast, the pending retirement of a disgruntled R&D lab manager for a vaccine manufacturing company had executives very worried because he would take so much knowledge with him. Working in the firm for 20 years, he was the company's primary expert in microbiology, and he had an extensive network of external contacts that he used to acquire information about the latest technologies and relevant scientific advances. In addition, this crotchety veteran had extensive experiential knowledge of the firm's operating systems, and he knew how to get things done across organizational boundaries, such as obtaining a new computer for his department in a week through informal channels. Replacing this lab manager would be extremely difficult, and company leaders knew his departure would have a significant, though intangible, impact on organizational productivity.[4]

In many cases the costs of lost knowledge are intuitively obvious but very hard to quantify. This is most often seen with the loss of social capital, such as the retiring executive who has long-standing personal relationships with key suppliers or customers. Another common situation is where the gradual degradation of knowledge in a particular function makes it very hard to predict when and how the knowledge loss will manifest itself, but the impact could be serious. This is what happened in one chemical company where the knowledge in a group that maintained special valves continued to decline as veterans retired. The problem never got management attention until an explosion was attributed to a faulty valve. One obvious challenge for management is making the costs of lost knowledge more visible.

Are the Costs of Lost Knowledge Immediate or Delayed?

Sometimes when intellectual capital disappears the effect on performance registers almost immediately, producing quality upsets in manufacturing, faulty outputs in computer-related work, or lost capabilities for delivering services. A group of consultants had developed a successful new service offering for telecommunications customers, which included a unique way to diagnose inefficiencies in billing and collection processes. But the four consultants who created the new service unexpectedly left the firm without documenting the details of the offering.[5] The immediate result was that the firm could no longer sell and deliver a service that had represented a promising new stream of revenues.

One of the most insidious things about losing knowledge is that its impacts can often be delayed but still are very costly. In early 2000, one refinery of a global metals producer experienced major quality problems when a recently rebuilt processing tank came back on stream. Management was very concerned because the refinery's other tank had to be rebuilt the next year. A similar quality problem had occurred 15 years ago when the tanks were last repaired. But failure to capture what was learned then about getting the tanks back on line cost the company more than $10 million in 2000 when it was unable to fill orders for long-standing customers and temporarily had to sell some of its product at a lower cost. Important tasks that are only performed intermittently are at particularly high risk because of the knowledge that can be lost, or "forgotten," in today's high turnover environment. In each case, the effect of losing the knowledge is delayed, which makes it more difficult to see specific lost knowledge as the cause of a current problem. And recovery of that knowledge is even more unlikely.

Learning from Different Types of Lost Knowledge

Understanding the landscape of lost knowledge is an essential step for diagnosing what is at risk. The four dimensions described suggest different places to look for problems. For example, you may know about the threat posed by increased retirements in one function, but are you overlooking the areas where a smaller number of R&D scientists are likely to leave with knowledge that is even more threatening to your strategic objectives?

Are you looking at potential lost knowledge costs for all levels? Specifically, are there costs at individual and group levels that have serious implications for organizational level performance? For example, losing a veteran accountant or HR manager may be temporarily disruptive, but not as costly as losing a key salesperson managing international accounts. Also, have you considered lost knowledge impacts that might be delayed over years? Or is the threat so severe that you can focus only on mitigating the costs of imminent knowledge loss? That was the case when Delta Airlines suddenly found it only had a month to take action during its downsizing in 2001. Delta had to find out which of its departing veteran employees represented the most critical knowledge losses and take action to retain what they could.

Finally, are you paying enough attention to the intangible costs of lost knowledge—those impacts that are particularly hard to quantify, like the loss of key personal relationships needed for selling or negotiating? Are there ways you could make these costs more visible to encourage preemptive action? And are there better ways to anticipate the immediate costs of losing certain individuals so operations are not disrupted by unexpected knowledge losses?

These four dimensions help define the landscape of lost knowledge problems, and understanding them is essential for diagnosing threats in your own situation. But you can't make effective decisions about where to invest in retaining intellectual capital unless you also identify where lost knowledge directly threatens the implementation of the organization's strategy. There are at least five ways this can happen.

When Is Lost Knowledge a Strategic Threat?

In practice, of course, lost knowledge routinely disrupts activities in hundreds of ways everyday, slowing down operations, distracting employees from important activities, and causing them to redo relatively mundane tasks.

- Where did our team put that file on the server?
- What is the history of that policy decision, and what happens if we change it?
- Who is it at that vendor who is so good at straightening out purchase orders?
- What did we agree to at our staff meeting last month?

Some of these situations are just annoying, and many are unavoidable when organizations experience turnover or individuals struggle with decision overload in their daily activities. Some lost knowledge can be very costly, such as the new chemicals purchasing manager who lacks the network of industry contacts to counter his supplier's sudden price increase shortly after he takes the job. Or the new database analyst who costs his company $400,000 by mailing to the wrong segments when he misinterprets the outputs of a computer model ranking potential customers in deciles. Knowledge that affects the daily operations of every organization is continually being lost. The trick is figuring out beforehand, which knowledge—if it's lost—will undermine your organizational strategy.

There are at least five major ways this can happen:

• Reduced capacity to innovate
• Ability to pursue growth strategies threatened
• Reduced efficiency undermines low-cost strategies
• Losing knowledge can give competitors an advantage
• Losing specific knowledge at the wrong time increases vulnerability

Identifying these situations ahead of time will help you to focus on the knowledge retention initiatives that will have the greatest impact on long-term performance.

Reduced Capacity to Innovate

Firms pursuing an innovation strategy should be particularly concerned about losing employees with knowledge essential for the development of new products and services. Losing experience and expertise when senior people retire, particularly in R&D, can slow down and reduce the quality of innovation, which is central to many firms' business strategies today. "You just can't be as innovative with young Ph.D.s. The experience really matters," said the HR manager for an R&D unit in a European basic chemicals company. It may be hard to make an explicit connection between a unit's innovative capacity and the knowledge of its staff, but it is still possible to estimate the financial consequences of losing the knowledge most needed to bring new products or services to market.

For example, one retiring research scientist was an expert in processing data produced by special computer systems that monitored chemical extrusion processes. "If you don't get this data processed properly, you might as well throw the system away," he said. This researcher's specialized knowledge helped the company increase throughputs in certain processes, delaying the need to invest tens of millions of dollars in expanding its plants. But his knowledge of extrusion processes and how to analyze the performance data was also critical in developing new specialized products that created additional revenue streams. It would take his replacement almost a year to come up to speed before being able to produce outputs valuable to the company.

Thus, the only way to sustain the pace of these innovations was to rehire this retiree as a "consultant" to retain his knowledge. Otherwise, the introduction of new products would have been delayed. Analyzing the real costs of losing access to an individual's or a group's specialized knowledge will often show potential impacts on a firm's innovation capacity.[6]

Ability to Pursue Growth Strategies Threatened

Companies pursuing growth strategies that do not rely solely on acquisitions will find that losing knowledge through retirements and turnover can seriously undermine their ability to support expanded operations. One petrochemical company executive explained:

> The bubble of experience that is retiring has been around for at least five years and, frankly, nobody got it. There's an arrogance that says, "We're a great company. We can hire anybody we want. We can fix the problem just by hiring people." But there's little thought about what you lose by just hiring new people. Now our hand has been forced by our growth desires. The experience is going and we can't support the growth.

The issue of supporting growth is closely linked to problems in recruiting both the young professionals and experienced hires who are needed to staff expanded operations. Many international organizations expect recruiting high quality professionals for global operations to be a major issue in the years ahead, whether it is geophysicists needed for oil exploration, chemical engineers needed to open new plants in developing countries, or people experienced in selling or managing in other cultures. Losing specialized knowledge like this can slow down growth plans. This should be no surprise.

But increased retirements also make the task of assimilating new employees more difficult because the availability of potential mentors is greatly reduced. This affects the number of new hires you can absorb to support expansion plans. When pursuing aggressive growth strategies, you need to realistically evaluate how the organization will resource new programs and operations. In the process, you also must take into account the extra burden lost knowledge will place on strategy implementation.

Reduced Efficiency Undermines Low-Cost Strategies

Lost knowledge can also have an important impact for organizations focused on cost-cutting and productivity improvements. "What you really lose through people leaving is efficiency—knowledge of how to get a job done faster and better. But, of course, that's hard to quantify," said a retired research director, who had returned to work for his company as a contractor.

Of course, in many situations that require advanced skills simply adding more human resources is not a viable solution. Manufacturing executives have sometimes learned this lesson when trying to staff highly automated plants in developing countries. "The dilemma is you can't just throw labor at these plants," said one experienced manager. "You need a smarter, experienced skill base." Therefore, if you expect to sustain past performance improvements, you need to ask two questions: What knowledge, if lost, would undermine our productivity gains? And what knowledge must be retained to support continued performance improvements?

Another problem that can significantly undermine a low-cost strategy is more frequent and more costly errors. For example, no one likes to talk about it, but having less experienced people working in increasingly sophisticated computer-controlled manufacturing operations increases the risks of serious and costly mistakes. The explosion in a U.S. chemical plant, described in chapter 1, is such an example. Given that the engineer in charge and the operators in the control room at the time of the accident all had less than a year of experience in the unit, it's not surprising that the explosion was attributed to operator error. "We have so many people who are not familiar with our units, you have to wonder if we're not going to see more of this," confessed one executive. And even when errors are not caused by inexperience, diagnosing and fixing them often takes more time when veteran employees are no longer around to help. This is what the Federal Aviation Administration (FAA) found when many experienced maintenance technicians retired, said one FAA union official.

Errors in R&D are also likely to increase as experience declines. "Typically, what happens is people have to make all the same mistakes the retiree did," said a former research scientist. When evaluating the effects lost knowledge can have on your company, you need to assess where reduced expertise is most likely to leave your organization vulnerable to costly mistakes. Certainly all mistakes cannot be avoided. But estimating the potential risk and cost of these errors can help determine where knowledge retention efforts are more likely to pay off.

Losing Knowledge Can Give Competitors an Advantage

The sales vice president (VP) for a major distributor of industrial equipment was widely known and well respected throughout the industry. He had extensive personal relationships with decision makers in many major customer organizations, which gave his company a competitive advantage in this cost-driven distribution business. Thus, the chief executive officer (CEO) was very concerned because he knew the upcoming retirement of his sales VP would give competitors an opening to steal away major accounts. Are there areas where your organization has a competitive advantage because of specialized knowledge? Losing knowledge that has been a source of advantage is one strategic threat.

Another variation on this problem is losing knowledge that your competitor is able to retain. For example, one global chemical company suffered a serious decline in its plant design and construction capabilities. This firm used to be the best in the industry, but it has fallen back in the pack. Why? "One root cause is the loss of key engineers and our failure to retain their knowledge," explained one manager. "The use of contractors is also part of the problem. We've been transferring knowledge to them, but that doesn't encourage its reuse." You could be in trouble if competitors become better over time at retaining knowledge in specialized areas that are keys to implementing your strategy. You need to identify these essential capabilities and figure out how your organization is going to develop and retain them better than your competitors.

When valuable employees leave your organization, it is also important to know where they are going. Are they going to competitors? The head of HR for a major specialty chemical company said, "We scan the market continually to understand the likelihood of being able to acquire top talent from our competitors. That's a game we're used to. Pinching from our competitors is always a win-win situation for us." Not only does this strategy enhance his own organization's capabilities, but it also depletes his rivals, making it harder for them to compete. Are there areas where you are vulnerable to losing key personnel to competitors? Are you doing everything you can to prevent this from happening?

Losing Specific Knowledge at the Wrong Time Increases Vulnerability

Some years ago, one of DuPont's most talented mechanical engineers helped invent some high-pressure compressors essential for running big polyethylene reactors. These huge reactors gave DuPont a competitive advantage in the industry. But, like any new technology, the compressors broke down regularly and this one mechanical engineer was critical to getting them back on line. "We had a lot of scary incidents with those compressors at first," recalled one manager, retired from the plant. "If that engineer had ever left in those days, we would have been in big trouble because if there was ever a big explosion the company might have left the polyethylene industry, which is such a good business for them today." In the years that followed, the compressor technology matured and maintenance procedures were well documented, so the engineer eventually retired without incident.

The value and structure of knowledge is continually evolving. Today's leading edge expertise is often tomorrow's core knowledge that will be embedded in standardized processes.[7] In certain parts of your organization there is relatively new knowledge that is both essential to your strategy and more vulnerable to loss today than it will be in a few years. Do you know where that knowledge is? Are there practical things the organization could be doing to move that knowledge from its more vulnerable state to a more stable position? Of course, some knowledge will always be vulnerable to loss, like the expertise of your most brilliant R&D scientist or your top salesperson. But being conscious of where you are most vulnerable to lost knowledge will help identify areas where action could be taken.

Retirement Interacts with Recruiting and Retention

There is, however, another important way to understand how knowledge loss threatens strategic objectives. And that means recognizing the interactive effects of retirement, recruiting, and employee retention on overall workforce capabilities. Specifically, increased retirements, which result in lost knowledge, will put special pressures on two critical HR levers traditionally used to develop and sustain workforce capabilities.

New Challenges in Recruiting

One reason retirements are a major concern for many traditional organizations is because recruiting younger workers is going to be increasingly difficult in many sectors and in many countries. Economic downturns may temporarily relieve this problem, but that effect will be short-lived, given long-term demographic trends.[8] Here are some examples of the recruiting challenges that have been experienced in recent years:

- Even as thousands of petroleum engineers and geologists near retirement in the oil and gas production industry, there are record low numbers of students enrolled in petroleum engineering programs in the United States. With the industry's hiring rate lower than its attrition rate, analysts estimate that the industry will have just 40 percent of its current knowledge and expertise by 2007.[9]
- Among medical specialties in the United States, there are notable shortages of physicians in oncology, radiology, cardiology, and orthopedic care. For example, for every five openings nationally in cardiology, there is only one physician available, according to the American College of Cardiology.[10]
- "Last year we needed twenty-five chemical engineers in one country. But of the total pool of graduates there who had the capabilities needed to work in a global operation, there were maybe eighty, and we got

only three," said one European-based HR executive for a global chemical company.

As if the shrinking labor force in many countries isn't enough of a problem, there are a variety of other reasons that organizations are likely to have trouble recruiting:

- A long-term orientation toward downsizing and cost-cutting has meant many firms and government agencies have done relatively little hiring for years and lack the more sophisticated recruiting networks and processes needed today.
- Some sectors suffer serious recruiting problems. Nursing, for example, has had well-documented troubles attracting qualified candidates.[11] Young people often see some traditional "smoke stack" industries like chemicals as environmentally unfriendly. They also suffer by comparison to other opportunities available to recent graduates. "We're trying to hire people to come work in a dull, boring, steel and mortar company, where they have no opportunity to be a millionaire by age 30," lamented one chemicals executive.
- Work sites of more traditional industries may be located in rural areas that are less attractive to young people.[12] Recruiting top talent to central Michigan, the Gulf Coast of Louisiana, or Eastern Europe can be tough.
- The increasingly diverse population of job candidates, primarily in the United States, is likely to be reluctant to join more traditional companies that still have white, male-dominated cultures.
- There is much more competition for top-rated engineering and science graduates who receive offers today from a wider variety of potential employers, such as investment banks, large consulting firms, and high technology companies, as well as organizations that have traditionally hired these graduates.
- Finally, as companies expand their global operations and develop increasingly complex computerized production processes, they need to hire more sophisticated and skilled employees. One European R&D manager described how his firm's needs had changed, saying, "Unlike the past, being a scientist today is just not enough. We need researchers who are able to communicate, which also means being able to listen, to see through things, and get into the plants. They must be able to sell their ideas and relate to others." All of these factors add to the uncertainty of a more competitive recruiting market, and this situation will be exacerbated by increased retirements.

And, even when companies and government agencies can attract promising new hires, considerable resources are required to assimilate them. But retirements have stretched those resources even thinner by removing potential mentors. One union official representing FAA employees explained how the significant reduction in technical maintenance staff means newly hired technicians rarely get to respond to a radar system outage with a more experienced colleague. As a result, it takes new technicians considerably longer to diagnose and fix the system's problem and their general learning about the FAA work environment is slowed considerably.

One manager in a major petrochemical company explained the problem of integrating new employees this way: "We're going to run into a bottleneck in the future because there is a limit to how many new people we can bring in. We don't want to lower our standards in the quality of the people we hire, and we want to develop them into employees we can use long term. The question is how many people we can bring in and assimilate at once?"

One executive at Chevron Texaco also recognized the resource issue around assimilation saying, "It's a struggle to sustain long-term mentoring. We have wide spans of control. So when you bring two new people in where there are fourteen direct reports that's a potential productivity hit for the manager."

The irony is that getting new employees into the organization is a key to transferring knowledge from the older to the younger generation. "Problems of knowledge transfer can't be divorced from supply management. If there's nobody there to tell the story to the knowledge dies," says John Sumser, CEO of Interbiznet.com, a firm that monitors the electronic recruiting industry.

"Generation Gaps" Increase Focus on Employee Retention

The challenges posed by the aging workforce contribute to a second problem guaranteed to give any HR strategic planner nightmares. Many experienced managers are very concerned about increased attrition among younger workers and experienced hires. Most traditional industries and government agencies have historically been blessed with low rates of voluntary attrition among professionals and managers. This is still generally true in Japan, where people rarely leave organizations voluntarily before retirement. But in Western industrialized countries there is widespread recognition that younger employees have significantly different values than their baby boomer bosses[13] and are much more impatient and willing to leave their companies for a better opportunity elsewhere.

"Generation Y is different," said one staffing director. "What we've got to understand is people want to come in to learn and grow. And the faster they do that the better. Today we hire students who took college classes in Six Sigma. The culture shift for us is we've got to challenge people more when they come in, and give them more opportunity to grow. They don't want to wait to apply their skill sets. They're ready. But our culture says: 'Wait, your turn will come.' So people leave to apply their skills somewhere else."

This values clash between older and younger workers has serious implications as organizations try to expand their capabilities for the future. Because unless companies reconcile the differences between generations, this values conflict will result in increased attrition among younger workers. And losing promising young employees is an even more serious problem when retirement rates are high because this attrition requires additional resources to find already scarce replacements. Thus, increased retirement rates put even greater pressure on organizations to address the problem of turnover among Gen-X and Gen-Y employees. To accommodate the changing expectations of younger workers, some companies are reexamining their cultures to see what must be changed to improve retention. "We need to be listening to the people we bring in," said one HR manager. "All of us need to start listening to those new voices."

The retirement of veteran scientists, technical specialists, engineers, and other professionals will also contribute to another retention-related issue. These losses will necessarily lead to an increase in "experienced hires" needed to replace the veterans. One major company has already seen the number of mid-career hires jump from 10 percent to 35 percent of its total new hires. But experienced professionals and managers, who have been socialized elsewhere, are more likely to challenge their new firm's culture, to question the way things are done, and to leave if they don't like their new work environment. "The toughest thing for us is the integration of mid-career employees into our culture, which impacts retention," said one manager. "Historically, retention has not been an issue for us. But now we're seeing people we hire come for four or five years, build a tool kit, and then leave." The issue is how welcoming is an organization's culture to employees who join in mid-career. This will become a more serious concern in the future, as organizations have to replace more and more retiring professionals with "outsiders."

When thinking about the strategic impacts of changing workforce demographics, organizations need to design an integrated approach to address three human resource challenges. Let's call them the three R's—retirement, retention of mid-career employees, and recruiting (see figure 2.1). Trying to tackle only one or two of these will seriously undermine the skills and knowledge needed to achieve long-term business objectives. Organizations that focus only on recruiting, for example, will not be successful in sustaining— much less growing—workforce capabilities unless they also deal with the elements in their culture that encourage things like turnover and knowledge hoarding.

FIGURE 2.1. Integrating the Three R's

Barriers to Knowledge Retention

Before pursing this integrated approach, which will be outlined in chapter 3, here are five barriers likely to undermine initial efforts to improve knowledge retention in your organization. It's worth understanding these barriers so you know what you are in for.

- Lost knowledge costs are usually hidden.
- Leaders don't know where the organization is vulnerable.
- No one owns the problem of lost knowledge.
- There is no slack for knowledge-sharing activities.
- Management must do more than just capture knowledge.

Lost Knowledge Is a Problem Whose Costs Are Largely Hidden

While some executives intuitively recognize the threat of losing intellectual capital when people retire, many have a harder time seeing the problem. "Obviously, there is a cost, but it's not recognized," lamented one research scientist. "Cuts, like early retirements, have often been made without serious consideration of how things are going to run with fewer people."

Organizations that are better positioned to address the challenges of retaining knowledge from an aging workforce seem to have senior executives who intuitively recognize the problem and are willing to invest resources in addressing it. Chapter 10 will suggest ways to make lost knowledge costs more visible for those who need to build a business case to fund knowledge retention initiatives.

Uncertainty about Where the Organization Is Most Vulnerable to Lost Knowledge

"First, you must identify where the real risks are of not having the knowledge or expertise the organization needs," said Henk Bonouvrié, HR manager for Akzo Nobel's Chemicals R&D Institute. "Then you try to analyze the chance those risks will develop." Often managers cannot get support for pursuing knowledge retention efforts because there is no shared perception of where the greatest risks are for the company. A more strategic approach to workforce planning can help firms identify these risks to see where the organization is most vulnerable to the loss of specialized expertise. This problem of identifying priorities will be addressed in chapter 10.

No Clear Ownership of the Problem

Another barrier to addressing knowledge retention is the lack of responsibility for the issue. People in "knowledge management" roles were interested but often seemed preoccupied with other initiatives. IT managers believe they own the capability and enabling technology to drive knowledge capture systems. And HR often controls the processes for recruiting and retaining people. But it is functional and line managers who must create the values and culture that support behaviors needed to share, capture, and apply tacit knowledge derived from experience. In practice, then, improving knowledge retention must be a line management concern because that is where the challenges of transferring knowledge are best understood. But even these stakeholders are often uninterested. One manager from a diversified chemical company noted:

> The VP of engineering operations gets it. He understands we're losing our knowledge base incrementally, and if we don't do something about it we'll be in trouble. But his directors are saying, "Yeah, it's a problem, but other things are more of a priority." They're minimizing it because their vision is more short term. And they're close to retirement, too, so for them it doesn't matter.

One battle top management will have to fight in the years ahead will be gaining middle management support for knowledge retention initiatives. Most of these managers have been conditioned so long by the demands of cost-cutting to meet short-term goals that they won't respond to messages that appear to conflict with that objective. Another challenge will be the cultural barriers to knowledge sharing that have grown up as a result of extensive downsizing. The idea that knowledge is your power base and that hoarding knowledge will keep you employed is a difficult belief to overcome, but its presence cannot be ignored. Issues of sponsorship and resistance will be taken up in chapters 10 and 11.

No Slack Left for Knowledge-Sharing Activities

Even when the problem of knowledge retention is recognized, the resources needed to allow younger employees to learn from older ones are virtually gone. "We're never going back to the protégé/mentor model and the cast of thousands where less experienced people all have mentors," said a business information manager in DuPont's engineering organization. "We can't afford that in time or money, and we can't get that many people." One challenge for cost-driven organizations is going to be figuring out how to improve knowledge sharing in an environment where interactions between retiring professionals and managers and their replacements are very limited. This problem will be addressed in chapter 4.

Capturing Knowledge Is Not Enough

Finally, as mentioned earlier, transferring knowledge within an organization is useless unless those acquiring it have the ability to learn from others and make better decisions. Some organizations are finding that their younger employees lack the problem-solving skills—and sense of empowerment—to make decisions based on knowledge passed on by more experienced employees. "There is always more than one cause to a complex event. So what you want is managers who know how the hell to think," said a manager at Shell Chemical. Companies concerned about knowledge retention also need to evaluate the quality of the problem-solving skills their younger employees have. Retaining knowledge is of no value unless those who will have access to it also have the ability to interpret and use it effectively.

Conclusion

Understanding what strategic threats could be posed by lost knowledge is an essential step before pursuing knowledge retention initiatives. And recognizing barriers to success highlights where you will need to pay special attention when designing solutions. But your perspective on the broad range of possible knowledge retention initiatives will depend heavily on your organization's experience with lost knowledge. The next chapter begins by describing three common starting points.

3
A Strategic Framework for Action

Imagine an organization where highly skilled veteran employees and managers are routinely retiring or leaving their jobs, taking with them valuable knowledge that affects organizational performance. This pattern is obvious to every experienced manager. Yet employees don't talk about it with senior management. Leadership continues to take pride in the company's short-term performance and easily dismisses those who raise questions about the future and the difficulty of replacing those who are leaving. Yet the organization's employees are smart. In the safety of their own departments they bemoan the loss of valuable colleagues and struggle to fill in the experiential knowledge that is gone. They know the organization is losing knowledge at an alarming rate, but no one dares to raise the issue to top management. What would leaders do about it anyway?

Is this a fairy tale? Unfortunately, no. This scenario has been all too common in many organizations during the last decade. There has been a conspiracy of silence about lost knowledge and its costs. Employees don't speak up about it because they don't think it will make any difference. And speaking up may actually be costly because it only reminds senior management of how powerless they feel to address the problem, since there are no obvious solutions.[1] But this situation is changing rapidly, and today many organizations increasingly find themselves unable to ignore the problem, as they face one of three scenarios.

Confronting the Immediate Threat of Lost Knowledge

For example, the September 11th terrorist attacks and a sluggish worldwide economy made severe downsizing inevitable for Delta Air Lines in the fall of 2001. When Delta offered an attractive severance package, 11,000 employees volunteered to leave the company, including about 1,200 aviation maintenance technicians, many with 20–30 years of experience at Delta. While it was good that employees would be leaving voluntarily, Delta had learned from previous experience that these reductions-in-force (RIF) hurt business performance if they were not managed carefully. After a RIF in 1994, dispatch reliability had gone down noticeably, costing the airline both cancellations and customers. Delta's management had to find a solution quickly to minimize the loss of knowledge that would be leaving the airline within two months.

Dealing with an immediate threat of lost knowledge that has serious implications for performance is just one of three common scenarios that are forcing executives to look for knowledge retention solutions. Each situation has different consequences for the development of a knowledge retention strategy. After describing the types of scenarios facing many leaders today, this chapter will outline a framework for knowledge retention. All of the elements in the framework are essential for minimizing the long-term loss of organizational knowledge. They include key aspects of your HR infrastructure, as well as knowledge transfer practices and supporting IT applications.

Here is another example of how lost knowledge can suddenly become a big concern for management. In 1997 Northrop Grumman, a major defense contractor, needed to design a long-term support strategy for its B-2 bomber program. Many of the veteran engineers in Northrop Grumman's military aircraft unit had gained extensive experience working on as many as half a dozen programs in two decades at the company. But because of the declining number of new military aircraft programs, engineers hired in the last 15 years had worked on only one or two programs.[2] Northrop Grumman was downsizing as the division tried to develop its B-2 bomber support strategy, and many veteran engineers took the severance package offered. The knowledge these highly experienced employees were taking with them threatened to reduce Northrop Grumman's ability to effectively sustain the new long-term support strategy. Management knew it had to find ways to transfer much of this experiential knowledge to its remaining workforce.

Responding to an Emerging Human Capital Crisis

A growing number of organizations have recognized that, given the current age demographics of their workforce and historical retirement rates, they are inevitably going to face a significant loss of human capital in the years ahead. This is the second scenario that forces managers to think about knowledge retention. Organizations in this situation have more time to deal with the threat of lost knowledge than Delta Air Lines did, but the challenges they face are often viewed as more organization-wide than those focused on short-term problems.

The Tennessee Valley Authority (TVA) had been downsizing since the late 1980s in the face of increased competition and the need to control costs. But in 1998, the second-largest utility in the United States recognized that the median age of its 13,000 remaining employees was 48. Since most TVA employees historically retired well before age 60, management knew the utility could expect significant attrition in the next 5 to 10 years. TVA was bound to lose many of those it depended on to run its nuclear, coal-fired, and hydroelectric power plants efficiently and safely. And the knowledge embodied in some of these veteran engineers and operators would be very hard to replace.

The transfer of knowledge to new generations of leadership is a major area of concern for many organizations worrying about their long-term human capital needs. Like many successful firms, the McLane Company was built by a veteran cohort of executives who have invested most of their careers in creating the dominant logistics provider for the grocery, convenience store, and food service industries in the United States. But in 1997, this $10 billion subsidiary of Wal-Mart Stores recognized that it was going to face a leadership crisis in the decade ahead. Four of McLane's seven top executives would retire by 2005, taking with them an incredible store of knowledge they had gained in growing and managing their distribution and logistics business. The company has had to find ways to transfer decades of experiential knowledge to its next generation of leaders.[3]

NASA has an incredible record of accomplishment in space exploration. But it is probably the most publicized example of an organization forced to confront the problem of a rapidly aging workforce. "Almost 40 percent of JPL's [Jet Propulsion Laboratory's] science and engineering workforce is currently eligible for retirement," said Jeanne Holm, chief knowledge architect for NASA, in the spring of 2002. "In just four years, half of NASA's entire workforce will be eligible. Many of these people are the most experienced project managers—the people who worked on Apollo (the mission to the Moon) and built the first space shuttle. Yet, we have few programs designed to bring their wisdom into our institutional memory."[4]

There were murmurs that the loss of knowledge at NASA because of retirements contributed to the Columbia Shuttle disaster in February 2003.[5] Although this would be extremely difficult to prove, and was an unlikely path for investigators to pursue, the fact that retirements were mentioned so quickly as a possible factor contributing to the tragedy is evidence of how sensitive NASA insiders have become to knowledge retention problems.

Retention as Part of a Knowledge Management Strategy

There is one other scenario that forces management to think about knowledge retention. With the emergence of the knowledge economy, organizational knowledge has become recognized as a critical resource. In many firms, intellectual capital is now considered as important as financial capital.

Increasingly, organizations are trying to manage these knowledge assets to support their strategic objectives. Firms like General Electric and Ford maintain elaborate processes for transferring "best practices" between plants to improve productivity. The U.S. Army routinely uses After Action Reviews to help support a dynamic system for capturing and reapplying lessons learned to "learn faster than the enemy." Professional service firms like Accenture and Cap Gemini Ernst & Young maintain extensive knowledge bases that leverage consulting expertise from one project to the next. In the last decade, the concept of "knowledge management" has come into wide use to describe the development of tools, processes, systems, structures, and cultures explicitly applied to improve the creation, sharing, retention, and use of knowledge critical for effective decision making and action.

A commitment to managing knowledge more effectively almost always requires better knowledge sharing among individuals, groups, and operating units to improve organizational learning and overall performance. But initiatives to enhance sharing also make the costs of losing intellectual capital more visible and, thus, increase the importance placed on knowledge retention. The World Bank, Corning, and Best Buy are three organizations that recognize the importance of retention in the context of a broader knowledge management strategy.

The World Bank provides loans, policy advice, technical assistance, and knowledge-sharing services to reduce poverty and support economic development to more than 100 developing countries. Since 1996, the Bank has been committed to being the clearinghouse for knowledge on leading development practices. "What we as a development community can do is help countries—by providing financing, yes," said World Bank president James Wolfensohn. "But even more important, by providing knowledge and lessons learned about the challenges and how to address them."[6] Thus, by 1999, the Bank had launched a knowledge management strategy to fight poverty by systematically sharing expertise with client countries, and public and private partners.[7]

But this focus on knowledge sharing has also made the cost of lost knowledge more evident. For example, staff who returned from working in field offices or who completed special projects had extensive knowledge about how to get things done in local social and political settings. But there were no processes for capturing that knowledge and making it available to their successors.[8]

Corning Incorporated, a leading producer of fiber optics, is another example where retention is part of a broader knowledge management strategy. Corning is a firm built on innovation. To maintain its high rate of innovation in research, development, and engineering, the firm wanted to improve its capacity for organizational learning and knowledge sharing. But as Corning launched a series of knowledge-sharing initiatives in the 1990s, it became apparent that the loss of critical R&D knowledge was undermining efforts to improve sharing. When the company offered an early retirement package in 1998, it lost an estimated 2,000 years of experiential knowledge from the central R&D organization alone. Then, between 1999 and 2001, the company's workforce doubled, so that half of all employees had been with the firm less than four years.[9]

Corning's R&D workforce has since been cut back again in the recession that followed the September 11th terrorist attacks. These great swings in workforce demographics, losing experienced researchers and taking on many younger workers in a brief period, have raised concerns about how losing knowledge could inhibit innovation.

In the late 1990s, Best Buy, the largest consumer electronics retailer in the United States, was pursuing an aggressive growth strategy. But, like most retailers, the firm suffered from very high turnover among sales associates. This meant Best Buy was losing knowledge that had been acquired by employees before they left, and stores were continually trying to find ways to train new sales associates more quickly. Rapid growth further exacerbated Best Buy's staffing problems because its more experienced employees were often promoted to new positions, which disrupted the continuity of knowledge in its stores.[10] Best Buy launched a knowledge management initiative in 2000 to address capability issues threatening its growth strategy. From the outset, the retention and reuse of knowledge was an important objective of the firm's knowledge management strategy.

The chances are you can identify with one of these scenarios. You may be worried about the immediate threat of critical knowledge loss, a jump in retirements and mid-career turnover, or lost knowledge may be undermining your knowledge-sharing efforts. Or it may be some combination of all three problems. But, no matter what brings the threat of lost knowledge to management's attention, possible responses often seem complicated, costly, and uncertain as to their effects. The challenge is how to design solutions that will effectively address the three contributors to lost knowledge—retirements, more competitive recruiting, and higher turnover among younger employees. The next section outlines a framework for coordinating the development of such initiatives. Setting priorities and deciding where to start will be discussed in chapter 10.

A Framework for Retaining Organizational Knowledge

The threats posed by changing workforce demographics were not created in a year and will not be solved overnight. The most effective knowledge retention strategies will require a customized, multifaceted approach and a long-term commitment. For some firms, the challenge of knowledge retention will start out looking like a fire drill, as it did at Delta Air Lines when they tried to capture know-how from veteran employees leaving in a few weeks. Other organizations, like TVA, NASA, and Shell Oil Company, recognized they had a little more time but knew they had to begin taking action or they would face serious problems with lost knowledge in the years ahead.

There are four types of initiatives that intentionally or unintentionally are shaping your current retention strategy (see figure 3.1). Each type also represents a set of levers organizations can use to stem the loss of intellectual capital and to build long-term workforce capabilities. This framework will help evaluate the systems, policies, and practices currently in place in your organization that directly affect knowledge retention. It can also be a tool for identifying and prioritizing new initiatives. The four types of initiatives, which will each be dealt with in subsequent chapters, are outlined briefly below.

HR Processes, Policies, and Practices

There are at least five areas that create the organizational infrastructure for knowledge retention. They are usually managed or heavily influenced by the HR function.

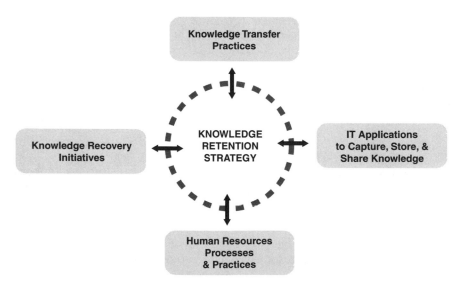

FIGURE 3.1. Framework for Organizational Knowledge Retention

Systems for Evaluating Skill/Knowledge Base

The first step in understanding where an organization is most at risk for lost knowledge is having a detailed process to track current skill inventories and future needs for all essential professional and management roles in the organization. This helps management identify future knowledge gaps that are likely to emerge, given retirement eligibility and historical retirement patterns. This type of system also supports extensive succession planning for professional, as well as managerial positions. The McLane Company, for example, launched a series of leadership development initiatives in 1998 when its "bench strength analysis" showed that it was going to have a gap in personnel qualified for VP roles across its 18 divisions. Tracking current skill inventories allows more effective resource allocation around knowledge retention initiatives.

Career Development/Succession Planning Processes

To complement the skills inventory system, extensive career development and succession planning processes are needed to retain employees—or at least slow turnover—and build long-term workforce capabilities. If a skill management process monitors the current and future state of resources needed, a career development program helps build the knowledge and competencies professionals and managers need to prepare for future roles. And succession planning and career paths show employees the opportunities that lie ahead. Experience has shown, however, that formal career development and succession planning programs are not sufficient for building long-term workforce capabilities.

Building a Retention Culture

The quality of your career programs may send an important signal about your organization's real commitment to its employees, but it is functional and business unit managers who create the day-to-day working environment that ultimately determines the rate of employee retention and has the greatest influence over knowledge-sharing behaviors. Thus, culture is critical. Probably the most difficult task facing leaders worried about knowledge loss is how to change their organization's values, norms, and practices (i.e., culture) to better support the retention of employees and their valuable knowledge. Organizations trying to sustain and improve performance need to create a working environment that minimizes attrition of high performing employees, since turnover and knowledge retention are closely connected. They also must strive to create a culture that makes knowledge acquisition, sharing, and reuse part of everyday practice. Even organizations who began paying attention to knowledge retention issues early on are still struggling with the culture problem. The goal of achieving an ideally effective retention culture remains elusive, but chapter 4 will provide illustrations from a number of organizations whose early activities point to positive steps that can be taken in this area.

Phased Retirements Programs

Early retirements became standard practice in many sectors over the last 20 years, since lots of organizations found it a relatively painless way to downsize. But, as knowledge retention and recruiting problems become more acute, organizations will have to look for ways to extend the tenure of their most valuable veteran employees. The most common practice today is known as "flexible phased retirement," which means allowing older employees to create more varied and shorter work schedules. Unfortunately, a range of legal barriers restricting pension payments still makes it difficult for private sector companies in the United States to implement formal phased retirement programs. Experts, however, expect these laws to be eased over time.

The problem of keeping experienced managers and professionals on the job is especially complicated for global firms, which must contend with a variety of mandatory retirement laws that are continually changing. For example, some European countries are currently considering the modification of mandatory retirement rules, which can create succession planning headaches for companies operating there. In Japan, meanwhile, the mandatory retirement age has been 60, but executives are expecting it to be raised to 65 to help ease the country's labor shortage.[11] These changes can add additional complexity to the challenges of knowledge transfer and succession planning.

Reinventing Recruiting Processes

The last element under HR initiatives is the recruiting process itself. Many organizations are revamping their efforts in this area today, recognizing the major changes in the employment market described earlier. The competition for professional talent in the years ahead is going to be so fierce that companies are now recognizing the need to rethink their presence on college campuses, their image among potential candidates, and what they actually have to offer those they want to hire. Firms that aren't proactively rethinking and investing in their recruiting efforts are likely to find it harder and harder to catch up. Recruiting is included in this framework to re-emphasize the interdependence of both ends of the human capital supply chain in knowledge retention. The effectiveness of a firm's recruiting efforts in an increasingly tight labor market will have a significant impact on the resources a firm has for transferring knowledge and its ability to do so. However, because recruiting has only indirect impacts on activities normally associated with knowledge retention, and because it has been covered so thoroughly by other researchers, it will not be addressed in detail in this book.[12]

Knowledge-Sharing Practices

Infrastructure processes, policies, and practices are critical for supporting long-term knowledge retention needs, but firms also need to institutionalize an elaborate set of practical knowledge-sharing practices that can become embedded in the day-to-day work environment. Of course, the first step in developing these practices is to inventory and evaluate those that the organization already has in place. Organizations will vary significantly in their uses of the many potential knowledge-sharing practices, each of which serve different purposes and have different strengths and limitations. Five of the most widely used ones are:

- *Interviews/Videotaping*: Delta Air Lines, Corning, the World Bank, and Sandia National Laboratories are among the growing number of organizations that have used this approach to capture valuable experiential knowledge that would otherwise be lost to the organization. Interviews are often the only option left for capturing knowledge when key employees are about to leave.
- *Training*: For transferring explicit knowledge, training can be a useful part of a knowledge retention strategy for certain jobs. Delta Air Lines, for example, incorporates lessons from veteran aviation mechanics into its training materials. Of course, a limitation of training is that it does not support the transfer of tacit knowledge, which may be the more costly resource to lose.
- *Storytelling*: A growing number of organizations, such as NASA, the World Bank, and IBM have recognized the value of storytelling for converting tacit knowledge into explicit knowledge. But, like every method, storytelling also has limitations.
- *Mentoring*: One-on-one coaching or apprenticeships would seem to be a logical choice for transferring important tacit and implicit knowledge from experienced employees. But, in practice, many organizations today find this method difficult to sustain because they are so resource constrained that it is hard to get experts to take the time to adequately train their successors.

- *Communities of Practice*: Building informal networks of employees who share similar interests and problems can be another important way of transferring and, thus, retaining knowledge. Shell Oil Company has made extensive use of these types of networks to help share knowledge. All of these approaches will be explored in more detail in chapters 5 and 6.

Information Technology Applications to Acquire, Store, and Share Knowledge

IT resources can be an important part of any knowledge retention strategy, but executives must be careful not to view technology as the solution to their knowledge retention problems. IT applications are only enablers. They cannot meet knowledge transfer objectives alone. To retain knowledge for the organization, line executives must make certain that IT applications are part of a comprehensive effort that also changes practices, processes, and behaviors. Many of the technology applications used to improve knowledge retention are still in the pilot stage. Here are four types of systems that can support these objectives:

- *Expert locator systems*: Insurance giant CNA and BP have both developed this IT application, often referred to as corporate Yellow Pages, to help link less experienced employees with experts.
- *Applications to accelerate learning*: These systems are built with technologies that intensify collaboration and e-learning capabilities. The U.S. Navy is using specialized collaboration software to accelerate knowledge transfer from its more senior procurement managers to less experienced colleagues in the acquisitions community. NASA has developed e-learning programs to develop the skills of current aerospace workers and to encourage others to pursue careers in the industry. And one global metals producer is using software that directly supports problem solving on the plant floor to enhance knowledge transfer across generations of employees.
- *Capturing knowledge*: Dow Chemical has created a Web-based searchable repository for easy access to all critical documentation of research projects dating back to the 1930s. Northrop Grumman uses a lessons learned database to retain technical knowledge about the history of structural problems with the F/A-18 fighter/attack jet program. Finally, Berlex Laboratories, a biopharmaceutical company, is using an electronic notebook system to help retain the knowledge of its research scientists working in R&D facilities around the world.
- *Mapping human knowledge*: Shell Chemical has built a talent manage-

ment database that gives the company an overview of its skills inventory. And the development of social network analysis software now enables organizations to make visible key patterns of social interaction that underlie most critical knowledge transfer.

Knowledge Recovery Programs

Every organization will inevitably lose some critical knowledge. Managers can anticipate and respond to this situation in three ways.

Programs for Effectively Utilizing Retirees

The easiest knowledge recovery tactic to employ when expertise walks out the door is hiring recent retirees back as contractors or consultants. Retirees not only have the skills needed but they also know the culture and organizational history, and have the extensive social networks necessary to get their jobs done, even when they are different from those they left. Given the looming shortage of specialized technical and engineering talent in many sectors, bringing retirees back as contractors is going to be a widely used short-term tactic for knowledge recovery in the years ahead.

Indeed, one of the most consistent findings in this research was the extent to which organizations in some sectors, like chemicals, and the federal government have already become dependent on bringing recent retirees back to work on a part-time basis. Using retirees as contractors, however, is a double-edged sword. It helps retain access to irreplaceable expertise, but it can also create a false sense of security that the organization still controls specific knowledge.

Outsourcing Lost Capabilities

In some situations, retaining knowledge adequate to sustain acceptable performance levels is going to prove unrealistic. In those cases, looking at new business models may be the only choice executives have. Outsourcing noncore capabilities has been a trend in parts of both the private and public sectors for years. But some organizations are going to face another round of outsourcing decisions when it becomes apparent that the loss of substantial expertise in specialized areas is too difficult and costly to replace or sustain.

Regenerating Lost Knowledge

Increasingly, management is going to recognize that it has simply lost a critical capability that it can't or won't recover by rehiring former employees or through outsourcing. Sometimes this knowledge loss will occur when top management makes conscious decisions to downsize or relocate offices and, as a result, employees with unique knowledge leave the organization. More often, knowledge will be irretrievably lost either through poor documentation and storage practices or through the retirement of highly skilled experts who fail to pass on their know-how. Regenerating essential knowledge that an organization can no longer access is a costly and frustrating effort, but in some cases it must be done.

Ultimately, every organization's approach to knowledge retention will be unique. But, by necessity, it will include some combination of the elements described in this framework. No matter where your organization starts, beware of the dangers of attacking knowledge retention with solutions that are too narrow. The most common mistake inevitably will be implementing technology applications alone, thinking that they will solve the problem. Effecting long-term knowledge retention in a serious way requires a much more holistic approach.

PART II
Evaluating Knowledge Retention Practices

The next five chapters provide examples of knowledge retention solutions outlined in the retention framework described in chapter 3. None of these solutions by themselves will keep your organization from losing critical knowledge. The elements of this framework are interdependent. HR policies need to be aligned with knowledge sharing practices, which often need to be supported by IT systems.

The examples of retention solutions described in the following chapters are merely intended to spark your imagination so you can begin thinking about what might be possible in your organization. Each element in the framework could be a book in itself. Indeed, many books have been written already on career development programs, communities of practice, collaborative software, and so forth. But no one has discussed how these solutions need to be combined to address the growing threat of lost knowledge.

In some chapters, you may find yourself saying, "We're already doing that." Indeed, many of the solutions described here are well known in HR, IT, or knowledge management circles. But, usually, they are not being applied with knowledge retention in mind. And, most certainly, they are not being integrated with other solutions to provide a holistic response to lost knowledge threats.

This section invites you to rethink your organization's current processes, policies, and practices with respect to knowledge retention in areas most critical to your strategic objectives. Are they helping your organization retain the types of knowledge it needs to be successful? And to what extent are these processes, policies, and practices compatible with each other?[1] Is your organization's strong succession planning process disconnected from your mentoring programs? Do you have good IT systems to capture knowledge, but a culture that discourages reuse? (Welcome to the club!) Understanding the interdependence of possible solutions is an important aspect of thinking strategically about knowledge retention.

Integration is the key to an effective retention strategy. For analytical purposes, these solutions must be presented individually, but you should be continually thinking about how they can be interconnected and aligned in your organization. The issues of integration will be addressed in more detail in chapter 12.

4
Developing an HR Infrastructure
for Knowledge Retention

- When Northrop Grumman was downsizing in the mid-1990s, the company's military aircraft division lost a lot of veteran engineering talent that would have been valuable in the firm's long-term support strategy for its B-2 bomber program. But Northrop Grumman had no process in place to take into account the expertise of individual employees who might be leaving. Leaders needed a more effective way to manage the division's skill base.

- Four of the McLane Company's seven top executives were scheduled to retire by 2005, taking with them a lifetime of experiential knowledge gained in building the company into an international distribution and logistics leader with 14,500 employees in the United States alone. Several years ago, McLane's management recognized they needed more elaborate career development and succession plans to support this leadership transition and to minimize the loss of hard-earned knowledge that would be crucial for sustaining performance in the highly competitive distribution and logistics business.

- Early proponents of knowledge preservation at NASA discovered that it was not difficult to sell senior management on IT-based initiatives, such as lessons learned databases and expert locator systems. But experience with these technology solutions quickly showed that what was missing was cultural change that would encourage the values and practices necessary to reduce the costs of lost knowledge. Unfortunately, the cross-agency cultural changes needed to make retention efforts effective would require a much larger budget and more time to execute than new IT applications.

- Anticipating the retirement of up to 40 percent of its workforce in the next four years, a large utility company has undertaken a diversified knowledge retention program. One of the challenges it faced was how to encourage particularly valuable employees to keep working with the company even after they became retirement eligible.

These scenarios reflect four common problems that organizations must address to retain knowledge and develop workforce capabilities in the long term. Each one reflects a question that executives should be asking:

1. What is our organization's current skill and knowledge base, and how will it need to change, given our strategy?
2. How do we do replacement planning for key employees? And, how do we make certain their successors have been adequately prepared to fill those critical positions?
3. Does our culture support behaviors needed for ongoing knowledge retention?
4. How can we encourage highly skilled older employees to stay longer?

Organizations need an integrated set of human resource capabilities to address these issues (see figure 4.1). There are, of course, many variations on these processes, policies, and practices, but they are the foundation of every effective knowledge retention strategy. The solutions illustrated in this chapter describe some "better practices" in the four areas characterized previously. They will help you diagnose the state of your organization's HR infrastructure for supporting knowledge retention and workforce development.

Systems for Evaluating Skill/Knowledge Bases

In 2003 a Conference Board study of 150 companies found that 63 percent did not have an inventory of their skill base.[1] But no organization can systematically evaluate current lost knowledge threats, or its future needs for knowledge development, without a detailed picture of current capabilities. Northrop Grumman and Shell Chemical are two companies that recognized the need for action in this area.

Northrop Grumman's Discipline Management Process

In 1997, when the work for one structural analyst on Northrop's B-2 bomber program was largely completed, the veteran employee received a layoff notice that was dictated by HR rules that were almost 20 years old. These downsizing criteria included no strategic judgment about his talent or knowledge. Instead, the layoff decision was determined by how much work was left in the program, the employee's seniority, and the location of his worksite. When the analyst got his layoff notice, it was up to him to find work elsewhere in the company. But, when he was unable to locate another suitable project, he left the huge defense company for another firm, even though he was one of Northrop's best structural analysts.

This scenario repeated itself over and over in Northrop's military aircraft division in the late 1990s as the firm went through several major downsizings. By 1999 management realized they had lost considerable expertise that

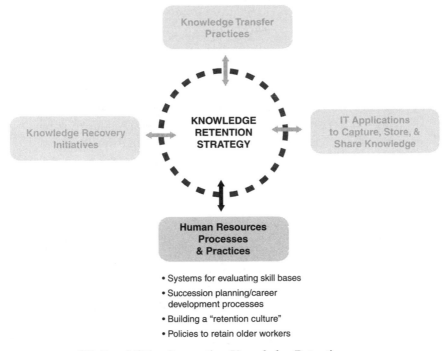

FIGURE 4.1. HR Capabilities Supporting Knowledge Retention

could have been retained if the division had a process to manage talent more effectively. This would have enabled better decisions about how to redeploy experienced engineers and, in the process, retain their knowledge.

To address this problem, the business unit introduced a discipline management program that better identifies and manages the skill base of the division's 2,000 engineers. The main technical functions are broken down into 35 disciplines, such as software engineering, systems engineering, structural analysis, and subsystems. A discipline manager is assigned to each area and is responsible for all hiring, firing, and movement within the discipline across all projects in the business unit. Typically a senior manager who also has department or product team responsibilities, discipline managers are responsible for knowing all of the talent within their skill area, so they can make more effective personnel decisions when staffing a new program or downsizing. For example, when staffing up the new F-35 Joint Strike Fighter program, if the program manager needed a structural engineer, this requirement would be submitted to the discipline manager who would look across the organization to find the best talent fit out of the hundreds of engineers in that field. The discipline manager takes a strategic perspective in terms of the company's overall priorities. If a senior engineer is needed to get the new project started, that person may be moved from another program if not being optimally used there. Knowledge management director Scott Shaffar explained:

> It's a judgment call. Today there's a lot of negotiation and discussion that takes place in making staffing decisions. It took lots of effort to change the HR rules that surrounded our old project management structure. But the payoff is we're a lot smarter today about knowing where our talent is. That gives us a better chance of using them more effectively and keeping the best people around.

Shell's Technical Skills Management Process

When managers at Shell Chemical needed to staff a new project in Asia recently, they knew almost immediately who would be the best candidates throughout the global organization for each technical position. They even knew who would be most likely to accept a transfer. Like Northrop Grumman, Shell Chemical has recognized that it can't develop, retain, and deploy its highly skilled professionals—and their critical knowledge—without a robust process to track the current status of the organization's skill base. Shell implemented its global technical skills resource management process to ensure an adequate level of technical resources to support its long-term globalization objectives. For example, this process helps the company make sure it has enough experienced manufacturing control engineers in current operations, as well as enough in the talent pipeline to meet the future needs of the business.

To implement the process, Shell named global skill resource managers who are responsible for ensuring the overall health of one of seven skill families, such as process engineers, project engineers, and manufacturing control engineers. Skill families are made up of skill pools that have common or similar skills and knowledge requirements. For example, the manufacturing control family includes three skill pools—analyzers, instrumentation, and manufacturing control systems.

Global skill resource managers identify critical jobs in their skill family for which there should be global interest in sustaining performance and which also represent important positions for developmental reasons. The global managers' job coverage planning role means making sure Shell Chemical has an adequate pipeline of talent to meet the current and future needs of the business. Their focus is more on the long-term issues and requirements of the skill family, but they also spend time getting to know the people in the skill family and learning about their individual career interests and expectations. To do this, global skill resource managers are responsible for visiting periodically with every employee in their skill family to learn: (1) What are their specific skills and abilities? (2) How mobile are they? Are they willing to transfer to another Shell site? (3) What are their career interests? And, given the opportunities in Shell, what would they like to do next? If an employee is not sure about their career direction, the skill resource manager can educate them about potential options in Shell.

While the global managers are concerned with one skill family, local skill resource managers focus on the short-term needs of Shell Chemical's 11 worldwide manufacturing sites and its two major R&D centers across all seven skill families. Part of the local skill manager's role is to meet regularly with each technical employee at their site to assess the individual's current and future career interests. They act as coaches about skill development and the types of jobs an individual might pursue next, given their career goals. With this knowledge, the local skill resource managers work closely with the global skill resource managers to understand the overall condition of the skill families and to plan for immediate and longer term talent needs of the company. Shell has developed a database of this individual level information so the organization can identify who will be candidates for particular openings in the years ahead.

The technical skills management process has had several benefits for Shell. Management used it when staffing a new project in China. "Having a global process helps us identify the talent across our entire organization and where it can best be used at any point," said Cary Wilkins, manager of global HR processes for Shell Chemical's manufacturing organization. Equally important, it has reduced management's anxiety about critical knowledge gaps that might be emerging in Shell's workforce. "When you don't understand the depth of a particular skill area, you are going to imagine the worst," said Wilkins. "You hear all these little stories, but with this process in place we found the facts didn't support our fears."

But, most important, by knowing what skills the workforce has, where they are located geographically, and who is willing to move, which is especially critical today, Shell's leaders can think globally about managing their workforce against the needs of the business. This strategic advantage only comes from having a clear understanding of your organization's knowledge base.

Comprehensive and practical processes that monitor existing capabilities will improve the quality of management decisions about organization-wide skill development and, at the same time, reduce the likelihood that your best people are the ones laid off. Note also the involvement of discipline managers at Northrop Grumman and skill resource managers at Shell emphasize the importance of building the process around people. Monitoring the evolution of your organizations' knowledge base is not an exercise in building a database that employees are expected to update. Although technology can certainly be helpful, monitoring your skill base must be a human-centered process because it takes experienced managers to interpret the complex mix of skills and knowledge each employee has and to build trust in how the process is being used.

The most difficult aspect of implementing this kind of organization-wide process is convincing managers to take a more global view of HR decisions. In some cases, the new skill management process will replace a system that was working fine in some local sites. But with the new system, managers sometimes will be asked to make decisions that are in the best interests of the larger organization, even if they are detrimental to a local site. Knowledge retention, when linked to organizational strategy, means sometimes making HR decisions that appear suboptimal at the local level.

Succession Planning and Career Development Processes

Having a detailed inventory of your organization's capabilities is a good start. But there is much more to do. Once leaders have identified those employees with the most critical knowledge or hard-to-replace skills, they need a way to allocate resources developing and retaining these people. This requires sophisticated succession planning and career development processes, which should be integrated into a long-term succession management system.[2]

Historically, most organizations have limited succession planning to leadership roles, but managers increasingly recognize the need to extend the practice down in the organization to cover other essential professional and managerial roles. The increased reliability on complex technical, scientific, and professional knowledge makes succession planning essential for a much broader set of positions in many organizations. Shell Chemical, for example, examined the vulnerabilities it faced in process engineering and asked who will be ready to replace our key managers in this critical skill area as they retire over the next several years. Succession planning has also taken on increased importance in many government and private sector organizations who are facing unprecedented turnover among their most experienced senior leaders as baby boomers retire.

Analyzing McLane's Bench Strength

At the McLane Company, four of seven top executives were expected to retire by 2005. The challenge facing the company's leadership was how to transfer decades of experiential knowledge gained in building the company. McLane maintains an elaborate tracking program that provides detailed accounting of the firm's management "bench strength" who will be needed 5, 10, 15, and even 20 years out. For example, McLane's "5-year bench" is those regional VPs who are expected to be able to move up to executive vice president (EVP) in that time. Business unit presidents who are expected to become EVPs are viewed as the "10-year bench," and so forth.

In 1998 top management recognized the company was going to have a leadership gap in the next 5 years if it did not find a way to speed up the development of its divisional vice presidents to take over the company's 3 business operations and 32 operating divisions. The problem was exacerbated by the looming retirement of McLane's most experienced senior officers. Sandra Bushby, McLane's former director of organizational development, explained:

> Key people will be retiring over the next two to three years, so everyone understands the business problem. I turned in a proposed succession plan to formalize the process of transferring knowledge from our departing senior leaders. We needed to download their knowledge to the RVPs [regional vice presidents], so they would be ready to move up. And we needed to download what the presidents knew to their VPs, so they could take over the business units. Clearly, there was need to transfer and retain knowledge at the divisional levels. Unfortunately, that wasn't a problem the divisions knew how to solve.

McLane has developed a comprehensive set of programs for transferring strategic, operational, and cultural (i.e., values) knowledge to a new generation of employees. But to continually update knowledge transfer needs, the firm has also increased the frequency of its bench strength analysis to twice a year to identify potential knowledge gaps at all levels of the organization. For example, recent evaluations revealed that a specific vice president being groomed for a president's position lacked experience opening new divisions. The analysis also raised broader concerns about a sales force deficient in relationship marketing skills, and dispatchers who were not developing the skills needed for promotion to transportation manager roles.

One objective of the regular bench strength analysis is to identify knowledge gaps that are systemic, such as that found in the sales force, versus those that are an individual skill issue, like the VP. This insight helps dictate the solutions used to improve knowledge transfer. Pointing to a key shift needed in succession planning, Horace Deets, former executive director of AARP, said, "We focus a lot on executive succession planning, but we don't focus on critical skills succession planning. We don't look at who are the key people we really depend on. They could be an engineer, an IT person, or a salesperson. Leaders need to ask: What are we going to do if we lose this person whose departure would be a real loss for the organization? Then we need to ask: What are we doing to keep this person challenged and happy? That's where the career development process comes in."

Career Development Processes

Although often talked about interchangeably with succession planning, career development processes actually address different questions: What are the career paths open to individual employees in the organization? What capabilities do they need to acquire to qualify for specific roles? And how can an employee acquire those skills? Skills inventory and succession planning processes are designed to address the organization's needs for getting the right capabilities in place. But career development processes are intended in large part to serve employees' personal needs for knowledge acquisition and skill development, as well as helping the organization prepare individuals for future roles. Succession planning identifies skilled managers and professionals whose capabilities must be replaced, as well as those with the potential to fill critical roles. But the career development process provides a roadmap for building the capabilities that need to be transferred to the next generation.

There are many versions of career development processes. Two criteria that differentiate those processes are how broadly they are applied to the workforce and their level of integration with developmental courses and experiences. To help reduce attrition, Sun Microsystems introduced a career counseling program that was available to anyone working at the company. It encouraged employees to explore career aspirations and create development plans with the help of assessment instruments and workshops. The program also helped participants make specific career choices, given the opportunities within Sun.[3]

Siemens, Europe's largest electronics and electrical engineering firm, has a global personnel development process that requires an annual dialog between managers and their employees. Part of the conversation is intended to clarify expectations around the employee's next career move from his or her current position. The manager and employee are expected to develop a mutually agreeable answer to this question. If the next career move is expected to occur in less than a year (either within Siemens or leaving the firm), then there is a standard process similar to a succession plan that they must follow to find a replacement and begin the process of transferring knowledge.[4]

Other career development processes are focused on a smaller group of high potential employees who have been identified as essential to sustaining the organization's skill base. Sometimes recognition of the need for these programs comes only after costly experiences caused by inadequate skill development.

Management Development at Wasatch Life Insurance

In 1996 Wasatch Life Insurance Company's operations suffered from a shortage of experienced management talent.[5] As the organization went through a period of rapid growth, mid- and senior-level managers were promoted or retired before skilled replacements could be developed.

The loss of leadership skills among frontline managers at Wasatch Life had serious implications for the business. Customers were buying variable annuities at a furious pace, but the firm lacked skilled management to run its struggling back-office operations. As a result, thousands of documents, such as premium payments, beneficiary changes, and policy cancellations went unprocessed. Customer service was pummeled by angry customers, and the company had to "eat months of interest payments" that were not accurately calculated for customers. In addition, employee morale sunk to new lows and turnover increased in the already tight labor market.

To address the problem Wasatch Life created a new process to develop management and leadership talent internally. Candidates must apply to the year-long program and go through a rigorous screening process before being accepted. Leaders at Wasatch Life know that whenever the economy is growing fast it is more likely to lose skilled managers who are lured away to other opportunities. Thus, it needs to be continually developing potential replacements so it can avoid costly service breakdowns that can come with sudden departures. "If we don't take care of our key talent, they're going to go," said one of the company's HR managers.

Leadership Development at Sandia Labs

Although less concerned about mid-career turnover, because of the nature of its business, Sandia National Laboratories[6] has faced its own unusually difficult leadership transitions and knowledge retention challenges. The United States has not designed or tested any nuclear weapons since 1992. This means the next generation of senior managers in the nuclear weapons program will have limited experiential knowledge about building and monitoring these weapons. To address this problem Sandia launched a leadership development program several years ago to begin aggressively training its mid-level managers for more strategic roles in the nuclear weapons business. At the same time, Lab management recognized the need to develop the next generation of "nuclear weaponeers." No kidding, that's what they call them. These weaponeers have to be ready to conceptualize, design, and build new weapons should the need arise. Thus, Sandia created a nuclear weapons interns program that over four years began training a core group of engineers from both inside and outside Sandia in the details of weapons development. In the process, the future weaponeers were given lots of exposure to the history of the weapons program by past leaders who returned to teach particular classes. Management wanted those who might be called to design weapons in the future to be able to take full advantage of the lessons learned from previous weapons systems so this knowledge could be incorporated into future designs. A former HR manager in the weapons program summed up Sandia's career development efforts, "Strategically, we understand the critical skills we need to sustain the nuclear weapons program, and we use that understanding to plan around recruiting, employee development, and retention."

When lost knowledge threatens long-term organizational performance, succession planning and career development processes play an important role in addressing the problem. Succession planning, as done at the McLane Company, can help expose emerging gaps in leadership before they affect performance. If used regularly, this type of process will also help identify successors early enough to provide more time for knowledge transfer. Recognizing the increased reliance on specialized technical and scientific knowledge, succession planning should be extended down in the organization wherever practical to cover key professional roles and middle management positions to reduce the unexpected costs of turnover in these areas. Also, it is a mistake to just assume that middle managers are handling succession planning within their units. Given the increased interdependence of so many functions today, the loss of one key person's knowledge can have serious ripple effects well beyond the department. Thus, leaders need to continually engage lower-level managers in discussions about their alternative staffing plans.

While succession planning can help preempt knowledge loss for the organization, career development processes may be one of the most effective retention tools for key employees. Career development processes can increase retention in tight labor markets by signaling to individuals that the organization is interested in their personal development. Keeping highly skilled employees challenged and focused on realistic future opportunities with the organization is an important source of commitment that is needed to support long-term knowledge-sharing behaviors. At the risk of stating the obvious, professionals and managers who are alienated by a sense that the organization cares nothing about their personal development are unlikely to behave in ways that support knowledge-sharing and retention objectives. Given resource constraints, however, career development initiatives must be focused first on managers and professionals who have been identified as having the skills and knowledge most critical to your organization's future.

One of the lessons from those, like Wasatch Life, who have benefited from an employee development program is the need to customize these offerings to suit individual needs and capabilities. One-size-fits-all doesn't work in career development. In some situations, threats of lost knowledge may mean development opportunities for successors need to be accelerated, as they were at Sandia Labs.

In other situations, an aging workforce may actually reduce promotion and development opportunities if a large cohort of older workers hangs on in late career positions reluctant to retire. When succession planning makes these situations obvious, leaders must look for creative ways to engage high potential mid-career employees so they don't leave when frustrated by the temporary lack of upward mobility. One executive explained:

> The key is matching the needs of the business with the needs of the individual. For example, we have a bunch of technical people who want to be managers, but right now we need more bench engineers. We think what these people are telling us is they want an opportunity to demonstrate their leadership capabilities. So we have started to look for ways for them to manage a project or a process. There are other ways of creating leadership opportunities without creating a whole new cadre of managers.

Building a Retention Culture

When NASA administrator Sean O'Keefe assumed leadership of the U.S. space agency in December 2001, he found an organization that was both highly fragmented and whose overall capabilities were seriously threatened by an aging workforce. O'Keefe immediately recognized that changing the organization's culture would be an essential part of any overall plan that would address the agency's strategic human resource issues.

Changing NASA's culture meant breaking down the political and operational barriers that had encouraged the agency's 10 space centers to operate largely independent of each other. But there were serious obstacles to doing this as other executives in the agency had learned. When leaders tried to implement an organization-wide knowledge management strategy, they quickly recognized the challenges of NASA's siloed culture. One former chief information officer (CIO) recalled, "Competition among centers for projects and funding can be an engine for creativity, but it also sustains a culture of privatizing knowledge. Scientists and engineers sometimes don't include material in their reports that might compromise their competitive advantage."[7]

By-products of this siloed organization were a lack of an agency-wide strategic plan, a limited ability to track personnel across the agency, which contributed to skill shortages, unhealthy competition between the centers, and non-integrated business and IT systems. Of course, creating a culture that emphasized collaboration and teamwork among all the NASA centers would have many benefits in addition to addressing strategic HR and knowledge retention issues. But O'Keefe recognized that culture change was an essential element in creating an organization that could capture and leverage existing knowledge as it went through a major workforce transition.

In late 2002 O'Keefe launched the "ONE NASA" initiative, which was described this way: "A ONE NASA approach emphasizes a unified strategic plan, a strong commitment to teamwork, tools and capabilities for greater collaboration across the Agency, and more efficient systems within the Agency. ONE NASA's focus is cultural change."[8]

This change, of course, is a multi-year effort that involves initiatives in many areas. Among the projects supporting culture change are: (1) NASA's Knowledge Sharing Initiative, which provides mechanisms to help the agency's senior project managers pass on their tacit knowledge and lessons learned from years of experience in the organization; (2) new HR policies that require technical "experts" to make up to 20 percent of their time available to other projects, instead of being dedicated 100 percent to one program; (3) completion of an integrated financial management system that for the first time gives the agency a single financial system for all 10 centers; and (4) a ONE NASA Web portal that creates a unified public face for the agency.

The U.S. space agency is one of a growing number of organizations finding it necessary to confront how their existing culture discourages knowledge retention. Culture influences all aspects of an organization's performance, of course. But in an era of changing workforce demographics, leaders must pay particular attention to their culture's effects on both employee and knowledge retention. Of course, retaining employees can help retain critical knowledge, but employee retention and knowledge retention are not the same thing. Some highly paternalistic cultures produce attrition rates that are actually too low by creating an environment where most employees can and do stay with the organization long term, regardless of their performance. Low turnover, however, does not mean that knowledge is necessarily being shared and retained in critical areas.

An ideally effective "retention culture," on the other hand, consists of values, norms, and practices that encourage high-performing and highly skilled employees to stay. Such an ideal culture would also encourage knowledge retention by rewarding behaviors such as mentoring, coaching, and information sharing. Thus, "retention culture" is shorthand for both how a culture influences who stays and who goes in an organization, as well as how it encourages behaviors related to knowledge transfer. These behaviors include a willingness to share, as well as regularly seeking out and reusing existing knowledge. Retention is just one of many dimensions along which an organization's culture can be assessed. Others might include quality, agility, teamwork, accountability, and so on. But with the likelihood of increased attrition due to changing demographics and values in the workforce (e.g., less loyalty), retention takes on much greater significance as a measure of your culture. There are several ways to spot a culture that values retention.

High Levels of Trust

First, a culture's support for knowledge retention can be gauged by levels of trust in the organization, which is often reflected in a shared sense of purpose. Employees are much more likely to want to share their knowledge if they feel emotionally committed to the organization's mission. For example, employees near retirement at NASA, TVA, and Corning were often anxious to participate in knowledge retention initiatives because of their emotional investment in the ongoing success of the entity.

Asking professionals and managers to share the intellectual capital, which is a primary source of their value to the organization, requires considerable trust on the part of the employee. Decisions to share what they have learned will be determined by whether the organization has earned that trust by demonstrating respect for its employees. No one is talking about guaranteed employment anymore. But when the inevitable layoffs have come, have they been handled in ways that show respect for individuals affected, so that survivors are not left feeling that hoarding knowledge is the key to survival in the company.

When downsizing in late 2001, Delta Air Lines asked more than 50 high-performing employees who were leaving voluntarily to explain different aspects of their jobs and to share key contacts and other essential details before they left the company. Afterward, each division had a luncheon hosted by the unit's senior vice president to recognize and thank those who participated in the knowledge transfer process. This kind of gesture helps sustain trust levels with remaining employees and builds support for future knowledge preservation activities.

Support for Individual Development

In addition to trust, a culture should also be assessed for the degree to which it encourages individual development (e.g., do you have a "developmental" culture?). Larry Senn, chairman of Senn-Delaney, an experienced culture change consulting firm, said the aging workforce is leading many CEOs to be more concerned about their organization's bench strength. "Unless you can create a developmental culture," said Senn, "where employees see their jobs as passing on information and coaching others on effective behaviors, then you won't develop sufficient bench strength, key people will leave, and you are bound to lose some of the key knowledge that made you successful."

A simple way to test whether your culture adequately supports individual development is to ask: Do your employees believe the company is being managed in a way that considers their interests as well as those of the shareholders? The answer to this question needs to be "yes," if management expects people to behave in ways that will help the company retain critical knowledge when they leave. Knowledge-sharing behaviors flourish only in an environment where there is a sense of mutual commitment between the organization and its employees.

This commitment starts when the organization demonstrates an interest in the employee's long-term success. Air Products & Chemicals shows this commitment to its new-hires by introducing them to the company through its career development program (CDP). This is a good example of how culture is shaped and enacted through standard organizational systems and processes. New-hires with engineering and IT degrees, along with a few M.B.A.s and Ph.D.s, participate in three job rotations averaging 10 months each. Although Air Products arranges the first assignment, CDP participants must find their second and third assignments themselves. And the firm encourages these young professionals to take positions in areas they might not otherwise consider. So a process engineer will take an assignment in project engineering or manufacturing to broaden his or her understanding of the business.

Air Products' career development program reinforces its commitment to individual development in several ways. The program has been in place for more than 40 years, so many of the firm's top executives participated in it, and they have consistently supported hiring 50 to 75 new professionals every year, even when business is bad. This consistent flow of new talent through the CDP has reduced the demographic age gaps other organizations have experienced due to hiring freezes. Equally important, CDP has created a workforce that is highly self-directed in changing roles and taking on new responsibilities, since they were socialized that way from the start. "CDP results in greater employee retention and development because people find ways to change careers without leaving the company," said Doug Moyer, the program's manager.

Skandia Insurance Company offers another example of how to support its core belief in the importance of individual development. A few years ago, this Swedish-based firm found an increasing number of its talented mid-career employees were quitting. Exit interviews showed these workers were feeling burned out as they tried to balance work and family demands, while also going back to school to improve their skills. To address the problem, Skandia introduced a "competence account," which allowed its employees and the firm to fund a 401(k)-like account, which would finance sabbaticals for personal development. For employees who are considered "at risk," Skandia triple-matches the individual's investment in the program as a way of encouraging workers who are falling behind on the skills curve to catch up. In its business, Skandia defines "at risk" employees as those who: (1) have only a high school education; (2) have been with the company more than 15 years; or (3) are over age 45. Workers in these categories are considered most likely to need to have their skills refreshed. Currently, 50 percent of Skandia's 1,700 employees in Sweden take part in the program, which is one way the company demonstrates its commitment to individual development.

High Levels of Integration and Collaboration

In practice, cultural barriers to knowledge retention often take the form of a silo mentality, we/they turf issues, decisions favoring local interests over the entity as a whole, and not recognizing and sharing information others need to succeed. A culture that does not reprimand behaviors that undermine integration is promoting knowledge loss and reducing organizational productivity.[9]

By-products of a lack of integration were evident at NASA's Jet Propulsion Laboratory shortly after knowledge-sharing initiatives began. Employee resistance led to a study to understand what aspects of the culture encouraged or discouraged knowledge reuse among engineers and scientists in the agency. "One finding was that we couldn't use the 'reuse' term because it was viewed as less prestigious," said Jeanne Holm, NASA's chief knowledge architect. "Employees want to say they figured it out themselves. That's one of our cultural problems and our strengths. So when we talk to people we don't talk about 'reuse' of knowledge. Instead, we call it 'adaptation' or 'adoption' of process or technologies." Understanding how your culture shapes attitudes toward knowledge retention will inevitably require interpreting idiosyncratic practices like this.

Aligning Culture to Support Retention

Values, such as trust, individual development, and integration cannot be developed and sustained unless the organization's systems, processes, and practices are aligned to support them. For example, even in an organization where there are high levels of trust and employees are interested in sharing their knowledge, nothing will happen unless there are practices in place to enable knowledge transfer. The general manager (GM) of a metals refinery learned this lesson when one plant brought its shift teams together to use a reasoning-based software application for problem solving. Suddenly, veteran employees were readily sharing their experiential knowledge with younger workers. The GM found that senior operators he assumed were unwilling to share knowledge just needed a forum to do so. Cultures that support behaviors related to knowledge retention need regular practices to do so.

They also need a common operating environment, which is a policy that energy giant BP has pursued relentlessly in its effort to become a leading knowledge-based company. Sustaining a strict standard for computer, software, and communication technologies doesn't ensure knowledge will be shared, but it can remove an important barrier to knowledge transfer.

Finally, compensation and reward systems must be designed to support knowledge-sharing behaviors. Quaker Chemical recognized this was essential when top management tied the firm's bonus system to employee participation in its electronic knowledge-sharing system. Companies can't expect to make significant changes in behaviors related to knowledge retention until reward systems—both formal and informal—are aligned in support of the desired behaviors.

In fact, the most critical characteristic of a culture supporting retention is that its norms and practices be completely aligned with the performance values needed to inspire knowledge sharing. Compensation systems that encourage knowledge hoarding, promotion practices that penalize the development of deep technical expertise over fast promotions into management ranks, and cost-cutting activities that discourage investments in learning are all practices that contradict top management's espoused commitment to learning and innovation. When employees see a disconnect between the values touted by leadership and the values actually reflected in management practices, they conclude that the espoused values of knowledge sharing and learning are not taken seriously by the organization, and management's credibility is undermined.[10]

Thus, an essential step in creating an environment that supports knowledge retention is to do a culture audit to diagnose the fit between your organization's current values and practices to see where they are misaligned. In the long run, failing to design management systems and processes that support trust, individual development, and integration will be a costly mistake for organizations concerned about knowledge retention.

Culture Change: The Bigger Picture

Realistically, the need for culture change is not going to be driven by the threat of lost knowledge or by the desire to retain knowledge. Instead the goals that motivate leaders to undertake culture change will be broader, such as the need for greater efficiency or integration, or the need to learn faster than the competition, or to leverage existing knowledge to support growth and innovation. Changing norms and practices to support these larger goals can also encourage behaviors that support knowledge retention. Sustained top management support is a prerequisite for any large-scale culture change. If you don't have that support and you need to change your culture, then realistically you should scale back your knowledge retention objectives. In all likelihood, your organization will face one of five scenarios.

1. Senior leadership is already proactively supporting major culture change and is willing to provide similar support for a range of knowledge retention-related initiatives. Faced with the deregulation of the U.S. electric utility industry, TVA needed to become much more efficient in its operations. Chairman Craven Crowell, however, recognized that major performance improvements would require significant culture change. This change included seven performance values TVA wanted its employees to embrace, including integrity, respect for the individual, teamwork, innovation, and honest communication.[11] This major culture change effort encouraged new behaviors that provided an excellent foundation when TVA began implementing a new knowledge retention process.

2. Senior leadership is already proactively supporting major culture change, but is not particularly concerned about threats of lost knowledge. This will make organization-wide retention initiatives difficult to implement, but limited programs with local sponsors are likely to be more successful if the culture has already become more oriented to knowledge sharing and learning.

3. Senior leadership won't provide sustained support for culture change. (Lip service in the form of a few speeches doesn't count.) But executives do recognize the need to address threats to existing workforce capabilities. NASA started off in this situation, until Administrator Sean O'Keefe took up the mantle of culture change. Realistically, any knowledge retention initiatives implemented without serious attention to behavioral changes will have limited impacts. But, in the practical view of Kent Greenes, SVP and chief knowledge officer of SAIC, a huge research and engineering services firm, "You've got to meet the organiza-

tion where they are and work with the opportunities you're given." Nevertheless, expectations must be set accordingly if the need for behavioral change is not addressed.

4. Senior leadership won't support culture change and is unconcerned about the costs of lost knowledge. This is the most difficult starting place, assuming that knowledge loss is really hurting organizational performance and that behavioral changes are needed. Any knowledge retention programs in this case must begin as local, grassroots efforts that demonstrate meaningful results and prove their value in order to gain more widespread credibility.

5. To cover all the possibilities, there will be a few lucky organizations that already have an effective knowledge-sharing and retention culture in place, but these situations will be rare. When culture change isn't needed to encourage retention behaviors, then the only management decisions are what specific processes, policies, and practices are needed to improve retention.

Policies to Retain Older Workers

Aligning knowledge retention objectives with the organization's culture is an ongoing task. But, from an HR perspective, there is one other critical component in any comprehensive knowledge retention strategy. The policies and practices your organization has in place to entice highly skilled older employees to keep working beyond retirement eligibility will be a key to minimizing the costs of lost knowledge. Agilent Technologies faced this problem.

Agilent is a portfolio of high-tech businesses that spun off from Hewlett-Packard several years ago. Agilent has a mature workforce with many highly skilled employees who are probably thinking about retirement as they become eligible. Even though the company has been diversifying into new biochemical and communications markets, Agilent does not want to lose much of the core knowledge gained in its traditional test and measurement equipment businesses. "We can't afford to have all our engineers retire at age 55," said Karen Scussel, vice president for HR operations. "So the question we are asking is, 'What are some things we can do to entice employees who have critical skills that we need to stay?' "[12]

Although early retirements became standard practice in many sectors over the last 20 years, as knowledge retention and recruiting problems become more acute, lots of organizations will need to find ways to extend the tenure of their most valuable older employees. As some researchers have predicted:

Sometime soon, probably between 2005 and 2010, managers will come to realize there are not enough skilled younger workers entering the labor force to replace the older ones leaving through retirement. When that happens, they will likely do a rapid about face—from encouraging early retirement to discouraging it. They will soon begin asking the question: What can we do to retain, reengage, and retool older workers?[13]

When designing policies to retain employees nearing retirement, executives must answer several questions. First, who is management trying to retain? Do they want to encourage virtually any older employee to stay on with the organization? This may be the case in firms with a strong performance ethic where management is not worried about prolonging the careers of employees who long ago "retired-on-the-job." Or broad retention efforts may make sense in industries, such as utilities, facing major skills shortages across the board. It is just as likely, however, that leadership is worried about retaining a particular type of employee, for example, senior project managers, chemical engineers, nurses, and so on. Or even specific individuals throughout the organization who have been identified as having unique and critical knowledge. Each situation will suggest different solutions.

The second decision is: Does management want policies that support flexible phased retirement options or the rehiring of retirees as contractors or consultants?[14] Both can be effective ways to retain access to essential employee knowledge. But each approach also has advantages and disadvantages. In early 2004 the vast majority of organizations using programs to retain access to veteran employees preferred to rehire them as contractors (or consultants) after they formally retired.

This approach has been preferable because it sidesteps the labyrinth of laws and pension regulations that make part-time work for older employees difficult to administer. (These legal issues will be discussed below.) But rehiring retirees as contractors, which will be covered in detail in chapter 8, also has drawbacks. Legally, retirees must go through a period of separation from the organization before returning as contractors or consultants. According to one study, that separation averages over five months before the retiree returns to work. In addition, former employees are legally barred from returning to the same position held before retiring. And, of course, retirement may turn out to be more fun than expected, or a better opportunity may come along, so that former expert is suddenly no longer available. Despite these considerations, many organizations do rehire retirees with valuable experience, either because their skills are so hard to replace or their knowledge of the organization makes them a cheaper alternative than hiring and retraining replacements.

Flexible Phased Retirements

An AARP study found that 8 out of 10 baby boomers expect to work at least part-time in their retirement years. Other studies have shown that many older employees would prefer to stay longer with their current organizations if management could provide more flexibility in job design and benefits.[15] They go by different names, for example, phased retirement or flexible retirement programs, but the solutions for retaining older workers inevitably involve a mix of alternative job design options, such as reduced responsibilities, reduced work hours, flex time, and job sharing.

In recent years, relatively few private sector companies in the United States have provided phased retirement programs for older workers. The practice has been more common in the public sector and in university settings. This is, in part, because of a variety of legal obstacles involving federal tax and age discrimination laws, as well as restrictions created by pension plans, which have often been designed to encourage early retirement.

One major utility company, however, has tried a phased retirement initiative. The firm's "Conditional Part Time Employment Program" gives line management an important tool to help in retaining employees where there is the potential for critical knowledge loss. An employee who qualifies for the program can work part-time, typically 20 hours a week or less, drawing part-time pay, but retaining full benefits and continuing to accrue pro-rated annual leave. Although this program was implemented largely to address the company's concerns about transferring knowledge from its aging workforce, all of the utility's employees are eligible, for example, new parents, those taking care of aging relatives, and so on.

Employees interested in the program must get permission from their manager before participating. On a case by case basis, management evaluates the impact of the individual's request on the business and on other employees. "The benefits to the company are an important part of this," says one company executive. "We clearly state that our goal is retaining employees and knowledge and creating a more productive workforce."

One example of how the new program could be used is reflected in the story of an engineering manager who retired recently after 30 years with the utility. He was very knowledgeable and a good mentor, but he was also financially ready to retire. "If we had had a program like this already in place, perhaps we could have retained that manager for another year to mentor and train people," said a company executive.

The utility has put in place a risk assessment process to identify specific employees who are most likely to retire soon and who also have critical experiential knowledge. Thus, management can use the new conditional part-time program to approach specific employees about creating more flexible work arrangements as part of a process to transfer their knowledge before they leave the organization.

The risk assessment effort helps management identify the specific knowledge that needs to be transferred before an individual leaves. And the part-time program gives the utility an effective process for buying time to transfer the veteran's knowledge. But one executive noted:

> This type of effort can't be done with a cookie cutter approach. It depends on what the knowledge is that we need to retain. You might cover it over six weeks of brown bag lunches with a group of engineers. Or if it's a turbine specialist who has gained that knowledge over 15 years, you might need a junior person to shadow them for a year. But if we can negotiate this conditional part-time employment with a potential retiree, then at least we know how much time we have. As part of this program, they are still a company employee, and we know what we have to accomplish in that year. But, if they retire, we may not get them back as a contractor.

This company's experience raises several important points about phased retirement programs. Most of these programs have historically been offered only informally, which means managers negotiate customized arrangements with specific employees. But informal programs are, by necessity, limited in scope. If skill shortages become more dramatic, there will be increased pressure in many organizations to formalize these programs. This can encourage broader use of phased retirement options and reduce uncertainties about whether a part-time employment relationship adheres to federal laws and pension plan rules.

Another important point illustrated by the utility's program is the need to link employee retention programs directly to knowledge retention tactics. It's one thing to encourage veteran employees to work longer. But that's just delaying their inevitable departure, which will still cost the organization valuable knowledge unless there are complementary programs in place. Thus, the decision to participate in a phased retirement program should include a specific plan for transferring as much critical knowledge as possible to others in the organization during the employee's remaining tenure. Many of the tactics for transferring knowledge will be discussed in the next two chapters.

Action Steps to Retain Older Workers

There are at least four actions that management can take when considering specific ways that employees approaching retirement can be encouraged to keep working.

1. *Align your organization's pension calculation with your objectives for employee retention.* If retaining employees is important across the board, make sure your retirement program is not encouraging people to leave too early. Sandia Labs changed their retirement plan a few years ago because pension benefits peaked at age 55, which discouraged Sandia's nuclear weapons experts from staying on at the Labs. Under the revised plan, employees do not qualify for maximum pension benefits until age 62. An executive recalled, "One person in my group was about to turn 55, when we changed the pension calculation. The day it went into effect, he came into my office and said, 'You just got me for five more years.' "

2. *Educate older workers about retirement planning.* Ironically, employees often retire early without fully understanding the financial implications of their decision. About two-thirds of baby boomers are way behind in saving for retirement. "They dream of retiring in their late 50s or early 60s, but the numbers just don't add up," said Bill Arnone, a partner in Ernst & Young's human capital practice. It turns out that offering seminars to provide employees with the financial facts about retirement can be a great incentive to keep them on the job. "The more older workers know today about financing their retirements, the less likely they are to leave early," said Arnone.

3. *Publicize phased retirement as an option, either as a formal or an informal program.* This means thinking through who should be offered such programs, as well as the legal and compensation implications. Health insurance benefits are likely to be a great concern to potential participants and that must be addressed. These programs don't have to be offered to all employees. You may want to retain senior R&D scientists but not accountants, for example. Lawrence Lorber, a partner in a New York-based law firm Proskauer Rose LLP, explained, "You have to draw a rational line between those you offer it to and those you don't." He added that phased retirement offerings based on a job category rather than age are not likely to violate the Age Discrimination in Employment Act, which is designed to protect workers 40 and over in the United States.[16]

   Legal compliance and compensation rules aren't the only considerations, of course. Management also needs to think through the kinds of work opportunities and employment arrangements it wants to offer. Should phased retirement options include responsibilities for mentoring or other forms of coaching and developing younger workers? How many hours a week or month are required? Is the individual just expected to train a successor or to share his or her knowledge more broadly with others in the organization?

   Ultimately, an organization's culture and the history of management/employee relations will strongly influence what options can be pursued to retain veteran workers. Even if the entity is receptive to HR innovations, a phased retirement process will still require full support of top management, the firm's pension committee, as well as legal counsel. If, however, the organization has little history with alternative work arrangements and if new policies about how employees retire seem threatening, then management may be better off just setting up a program to rehire retirees as contractors or consultants.[17]

4. *Diagnose the organization's attitude toward older workers.* It is one thing to offer programs that entice veteran employees to stay with the organization. But a major barrier to the success of these initiatives will be the organization's cultural attitude toward older workers. If you want high-performing employees to stay, they must feel that both their experience and work contributions are valued by management. Research shows that it is not unusual for veteran employees to feel their experience is not recognized and that they are not generally respected by younger colleagues. Retaining valued older workers is going to require supervisors and managers who, though often younger, are sensitive to generational differences and respect the motivational needs of veteran employees.[18] A good place to start is to create an ongoing dialog with groups of older employees to surface issues about how they are treated by the organization.[19] What an organization's culture says about how older workers should be treated is subtle, but it will be important in determining how long highly skilled veteran employees choose to stay with an organization.

Historically, companies have treated retirement as a one-time, all-or-nothing event, but recent studies clearly show that older workers no longer view it that way. As they wind down their working years, baby boomers are either going to find more flexible and appealing work arrangements in their current organizations or they will go elsewhere. In many cases, they will take with them experiential knowledge that will cost their employer dearly. It will be up to leaders to adapt their organizations to the changing dynamics of retirement.

While informal phased retirement programs have been satisfactory until recently, the large, long-term wave of boomer retirements in knowledge-intensive organizations will force many leaders to rethink the need for more formal programs to retain experienced workers. No doubt the pressures will grow to change legal obstacles and pension regulations.[20] If these changes are in your organization's best interest, you should start lobbying now. Employees tend to think ahead when planning their retirement date. Once set, it will be harder to get them to change their minds to think about more gradual

departures. Thus, the sooner an organization has phased retirement programs in place, the more likely it will be able to entice valuable older workers
to stay on the job.

Conclusion

A few years ago, chemical giant DuPont launched an organization-wide program to "re-engage" its employees. The firm's leadership was worried that it
was losing the loyalty of its highly skilled workforce. Top management
thought investing more heavily in employee development and promoting
new long-term career paths would re-energize employee commitment. In
practice, however, one DuPont executive conceded that from the outset he
knew the initiative was inadequate to stop the loss of experienced employees.
"The competition was simply too intense," he said. "But the company's executives saw no alternative. They had to make an effort."[21]

This is an important story because it speaks to the difference between
"making an effort" and "making a difference." Whether it is losing employees to a super-heated global economy or to retirement, organizations confronted with an aging workforce are not going to sustain critical capabilities
simply by making minor changes to their HR infrastructure. Retaining essential intellectual capital in the years ahead will require a concerted long-term
effort to align HR processes, policies, and practices with the new realities of
workforce demographics.

Of course, phased retirement programs will be an essential part of any
infrastructure needed to support employee and knowledge retention. But
like the other elements covered in this chapter, programs to retain older
workers do not specifically address the dynamics of knowledge transfer.
How critical experiential knowledge is actually acquired, shared, and reused—often across generations—is the subject of the next two chapters.

5
Improving the Transfer
of Explicit Knowledge

- Some veteran employees at the World Bank have spent years in developing countries implementing long-term projects where they have learned all kinds of invaluable lessons about how to cut through red tape in local government offices and which government officials can be relied on. But what happens to this knowledge when these field staff members retire? That's right. It's gone! To do something about this, members of the World Bank Africa Regional Unit's knowledge and learning group have begun initiatives to interview veteran staffers returning from long field assignments. Text and video clips from these interviews can be accessed on the Bank's intranet.
- In the 1990s NASA entered the era of "faster, better, cheaper" space exploration, which meant many more projects were undertaken, just as the agency began losing its most experienced project managers to retirement. To stem the loss of valuable intellectual capital, NASA has launched a knowledge-sharing initiative within its community of program managers to help train younger managers, who were being promoted faster as the demand for new project managers grew. Storytelling is a primary vehicle being used to transfer knowledge in this effort.
- Quest International's innovative specialty flavors and fragrances business depends on highly skilled flavorists and perfumers. To transfer this knowledge to younger employees, senior experts at the Netherlands-based company are given responsibility for mentoring two or three junior application specialists. Quest uses this "buddy approach" to make sure veterans guide younger colleagues and help them gain experience.
- Leaders in the U.S. Federal Highway Administration (FHWA) recognize that staff turnover and restructuring are a major cause of lost knowledge needed to promote safety and improve the nation's highway system. With a relatively large percentage of its technical and operational staff soon eligible to retire, FHWA is actively promoting the use of communities of practice to share knowledge between veteran and less experienced staff members in specialties such as quality coordination, roadside safety, and compliance with the National Environmental Policy Act.[1]

The heart of any knowledge retention strategy should be the knowledge-sharing practices an organization uses to transfer experience and expertise so it can be applied by others in the firm. There are many potential practices that contribute to knowledge acquisition, sharing, and reuse. These methods can generally be classified as providing either direct or indirect knowledge transfer. Practices that support direct knowledge transfer involve more personal interaction between the knowledge source and the recipient. These include face-to-face meetings, after action reviews, mentoring programs, communities of practice, and storytelling. Information technology has enabled some of these interactions to become more virtual through video conferencing, e-mail, or threaded discussion groups, but exchanges are still characterized by frequent interactions.

Practices that support more indirect knowledge transfer usually involve some kind of mediation between the knowledge source and the ultimate recipients. This means knowledge is captured from a source and somehow edited, formatted, and stored for later access by potential users. These intermediate steps are significant because they often mean the recipient doesn't know the knowledge source and can't question or verify the knowledge being transferred. This has important implications for the types and amount of knowledge that can be transferred and, hence, retained. Indirect practices include interviews,[2] documentation, such as written reports or lessons learned databases, and training when it is not being conducted by the original knowledge source (see figure 5.1). Both direct and indirect practices can be helpful for creating a general knowledge-sharing environment, but the question for many executives is which ones are most useful for addressing specific knowledge retention needs? This chapter will first outline some basic principles underlying effective knowledge transfer to support retention. Then it will describe the use of indirect transfer practices. Chapter 6 will cover more direct transfer practices.

Dynamics of Knowledge Transfer

If you are concerned about lost knowledge, you are probably confronting at least one of the three scenarios described in chapter 3. You are either facing an immediate threat of losing intellectual capital or you are worried about a looming HR crisis and the retirement of many key employees in the years ahead. Or a broad-based knowledge management strategy is being undermined by the organization's inability to retain knowledge, much less leverage it. Regardless of the situation, the first step is to understand the types and location of critical knowledge most at risk.

Knowledge is commonly classified as residing in either individuals,

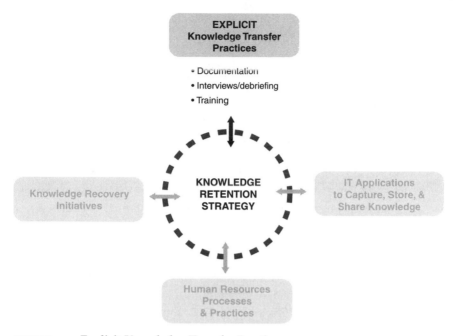

FIGURE 5.1. Explicit Knowledge Transfer Practices

groups, or the organization as a whole. One immediate consideration is what type of knowledge transfer situation you are facing. There are four general situations: (1) individual to individual (usually expert to novice); (2) individual to group, either to broaden availability of specific knowledge or to preserve knowledge until a successor is named; (3) group to individual—transferring knowledge to a new member; or (4) group to group, where the objective is to preserve one group's knowledge over time, or to broaden access to specific knowledge, often labeled a "best practice."[3] Each particular scenario will influence your choice of transfer practices.

Knowledge is also frequently classified as either explicit or tacit. This distinction, however, is an oversimplification and is misleading when the objective is knowledge retention. Knowledge that is explicit is easily codified and can be shared independent of its human source, or it can be embedded in processes or systems. This type of knowledge is often captured, stored, and shared in electronic or paper documents. Tacit knowledge, on the other hand, "includes cognitive skills such as beliefs, images, intuition and mental models as well as technical skills such as craft and know-how."[4]

Tacit knowledge is often described as what we know but cannot articulate, the classic example being how to ride a bicycle. But this explicit/tacit dimension is too general to be useful to managers trying to decide what knowledge transfer practices would be most effective in their situation. Characterizing all knowledge that is not already codified in documents or databases as "tacit" does not recognize that knowledge that is not explicit can exist in at least four different states. Understanding these distinctions is necessary to decide how best to transfer knowledge that may otherwise be lost. The four types are:

1. *Implicit rule-based knowledge*: The increased complexity of organizational life today means our minds are loaded with knowledge that could readily be made explicit and codified if we just had the time and inclination to do so. When an assembly technician knows that the best way to produce a radar control board contradicts what the manual says, that is not tacit knowledge. It's simply rule- or fact-based explicit knowledge that has not been articulated. This is better described as "implicit" knowledge.[5]

2. *Implicit know-how*: This is another type of unarticulated knowledge that an individual or group can readily communicate, but it doesn't necessarily lend itself to codification because of the contextual complexity involved. For example, when the expert in urban planning projects at the World Bank was interviewed about his experiences in Brazil, he could articulate which government officials were most helpful and who was ineffective. This type of knowledge, while not normally made explicit, can readily be transferred, if the expert is asked the right questions.

3. *Tacit know-how*: This is true tacit knowledge in that it is very difficult for the expert to verbalize, much less transfer to others. This is "how do you ride a bicycle?" type knowledge. A veteran salesperson knows when to close a deal. An experienced R&D scientist knows when a particular new product idea is worth pursuing. Or a senior aerospace production engineer knows how to put together a tiger team to address a critical problem. In each case, the expert's knowledge is borne of experience, and it is incredibly hard to articulate because it is so complex and situationally defined. Thus, transfer methods used must be different than for implicit rule-based knowledge and implicit know-how.

4. *Deep tacit knowledge* is really the "cultural" knowledge defined in chapter 1. It is the collectively shared beliefs, mental models, and values that determine what individuals view as important and even what they define as relevant knowledge. This knowledge is the most difficult to access, and it is usually transferred unconsciously through a set of practices that are unique to every organization. For example, Corning has a philosophy about managing resources that its leaders refer to as "flexible critical mass." When the company wants to address a major problem in R&D, for example, it might start a couple dozen projects work-

ing with different materials. But Corning places a high value on knowing when to cut loose less promising projects, so executives will quickly narrow the organization's focus to concentrate resources on those few projects with the most potential. The firm's top management recognized that flexible critical mass was a management approach central to the company's success and they were anxious that a tacit understanding of this philosophy be passed on to the next generation of management. An important difference between "tacit know-how" and "deep tacit knowledge" is the latter is collectively shared, while the former may reside in only one person.

Understanding the distinction between explicit, implicit, and truly tacit knowledge is essential if you are going to make effective decisions about knowledge transfer practices. But, in addition to recognizing different types of knowledge, there are five principles that also should be considered when deciding which transfer tactics an organization should be using or when evaluating practices already in place.

1. *Knowledge transfer practices should benefit current performance, as well as future capabilities.* While the orientation should be toward supporting future knowledge needs, to gain support in today's resource-starved work environments, retention initiatives should also demonstrate practical benefits for current problems. Communities of practice at the U.S. Federal Highway Administration help staff members address issues today, while also transferring knowledge for future use. This current/future balancing act will no doubt create some difficult dilemmas for far-sighted executives who recognize the long-term costs of failing to retain specific technical, scientific, or policy knowledge even though the short-term payoff is unclear. No doubt our grandchildren will be cursing us for knowledge management decisions made early in the twenty-first century on issues such as tracking toxic nuclear waste and other invisible environmental health hazards. Knowing about what waste has been stored and where will remain relevant for decades or even centuries, but cost-driven decisions made today could make that knowledge unavailable to future generations.

2. *Diagnose the motivational barriers to knowledge transfer. Specifically, evaluate the willingness of veteran employees to share knowledge and of less experienced employees to access and reuse it.* The success of knowledge transfer programs depends on the participation of both sources and recipients. To be motivated to participate experts need to be convinced that their knowledge is really valued and will have an impact on future decision making. At the same time, their successors need to be able to easily access this critical knowledge and to be made aware of the costs to the

organization of ignoring these resources. As will be discussed later in the chapter, many of the early problems with knowledge retention efforts can be traced to the difficulty of access and a lack of interest in knowledge that has been retained. Addressing the dynamics of motivation is a key to success that will be addressed in chapter 11.

3. *Tactics (e.g., interviews, mentoring, and so on) should be chosen to produce a specific desired result, given your budget and the time available to capture critical knowledge.* The effectiveness of particular approaches to keep knowledge accessible to individuals or groups cannot be assessed unless management is clear about its objectives in a specific context. Are you trying to keep the explicit and implicit knowledge of one scientific expert available to his or her group? Or is the goal to pass on implicit knowledge about a specific technical system to an individual? Or is it tacit know-how about leading projects that needs to be passed on to the next generation of program managers? From a knowledge transfer perspective, these are very different objectives and they require different solutions.

The location of the knowledge as it currently exists (individual or collective) and its quality (explicit, implicit, or tacit) has a tremendous influence on transfer options, as do the time and resources available. But often managers will choose a transfer approach without carefully thinking through the desired results for knowledge sharing and retention.

4. *Knowledge transfer practices should focus on "learning forward" not just on capturing war stories.* The goal of retaining knowledge is always related to creating value through access and reuse, not just capturing intellectual capital, which is a waste of resources. Companies are already littered with so-called "knowledge bases" built to capture knowledge, but they sit unused because no one bothered to think through the dynamics of access and reuse of the contents. Thus, knowledge acquisition efforts, whenever possible, should be focused on retaining knowledge that clearly will affect future decision making and actions, instead of just capturing information about the past.

5. *Take into account specific knowledge-related barriers that can disrupt transfer practices.* Gabriel Szulanski, who has done some of the most in-depth research on barriers to knowledge transfer, has identified three specific problems that should be of particular concern when the objective is retention of human capital.[6]
   • *Nature of pre-existing relationships between knowledge source and recipients*: One potential barrier to knowledge transfer efforts is the quality of the social relationships among the experts and their successors. If people

do not know, like, or trust each other, there is less likely to be shared understanding of background theories and context needed to communicate knowledge in ways that will make it useful. If poor quality relationships between knowledge sources and recipients are a barrier to knowledge retention, this argues for early management intervention to improve social relationships needed to support future knowledge transfer efforts. It also suggests that certain knowledge-sharing practices will be a waste of time when pre-existing relationships are inadequate.

- *Inability of recipient to recognize value of new knowledge*: Sometimes it's called a "lack of absorptive capacity," which describes less experienced employees who, because they can't recognize what they don't know, are unable to use the expert knowledge that is available to them. From a practical standpoint, the more inexperienced replacement employees are, the more handholding and contextual knowledge they will need in order to make sense of things their veteran predecessor took for granted. When deciding how to transfer knowledge, a lack of absorptive capacity argues against tactics such as documentation and classroom training, which can't fill in gaps in background knowledge needed to take action.

- *Lack of clarity about how knowledge causes outcomes*: As technology systems, scientific advances, and work processes become more complex, it becomes harder even for experienced individuals to see the relationship between the key components of their knowledge and how they interact. For example, describing to a new programmer how a huge customer database works at American Express is an exceedingly difficult task for even the most knowledgeable and patient systems analyst because of the complex relationships among the multitude of elements that make up the database. Szulanski calls this a problem of "causal ambiguity." He argues that when there are so many things to know and the relationship between the different elements is so complex, then even the expert's depth of understanding is limited. This means there is much more likely to be a gap between the experienced employee's formal explanation and the actual work practice.[7]

A cynic might say, "This really means the expert doesn't know what the hell he (or she) is talking about." But it's not that simple—or funny. In reality, more and more knowledge is harder to communicate today, in an explicit, linear fashion because it relates to increasingly complex systems and operating environments. From a practical standpoint, as a manager, this means paying close attention to the types of knowledge you need transferred. Don't underestimate the causal ambiguity surrounding knowledge the organization must retain. This has important implications for what transfer practices can be successful.

These five principles must be taken into account when choosing and implementing knowledge transfer practices. Accommodating all of them does not guarantee success, but ignoring any of them will greatly increase the chances that your knowledge retention efforts will fail. The three practices described below are designed to address the question: How can we improve our capabilities for retaining explicit and more structured implicit knowledge to sustain performance levels? The decisions your organization faces are which practices to use or how to enhance current transfer activities to better support knowledge retention? Practices supporting the sharing of less-structured implicit, as well as tacit knowledge will be described in chapter 6.

Transferring Explicit Knowledge

The scenario has become commonplace. The time before a veteran employee leaves is short and resources are limited, but management wants to retain that individual's expertise, some of which already is or can easily be made explicit. When this is the case, knowledge is most likely to be transferred in one of three ways.

1. *Documentation*: Explicit knowledge of work practices and project histories can be retained by documenting key activities and facts. These materials are stored in paper files or in some kind of electronic database to be accessed by successors in the future. This approach captures basic local knowledge needed to perform a task, but the successor must be motivated to seek out these materials, and there is little chance for clarification or elaboration on the knowledge retained, unless mechanisms for follow-up questions are established.

2. *Interviews*: Limited direct face-to-face meetings or interviews between the veteran employee and his or her successors. This allows more direct transfer of broader types of intellectual capital—explicit, implicit, and some tacit knowledge. It also gives successors a chance to ask for clarification if something is not immediately clear. Unfortunately, successors often have not yet been identified when veteran employees leave, so there can be no direct handoff of responsibilities. This means most interviews must be conducted and edited by third party facilitators, who may have limited knowledge of the particular work area.

3. *Training*: If the knowledge captured through either documentation or interviews is relevant to many others in the organization, it may be

packaged into formal training materials and offered to a broader set of employees. This not only increases the opportunities to leverage a particular expert's knowledge but it also makes it more likely that the knowledge will be retained by the organization in the long term. The limitation of training for knowledge transfer is that trainees can't question the original expert to test the veracity of the knowledge. Nor can they clarify points of confusion that arise as the expert's approach is being taught. (This, of course, assumes that the expert is not doing the training, which is usually the case.) The three sections that follow will help you make more effective decisions about using documentation, interviews, and training for transferring more structured knowledge.

Role of Documentation

Documentation is a practice that can be used to codify and preserve explicit knowledge when time is of the essence (e.g., a key employee is leaving next month). But, more often, documenting knowledge for future use should be an ongoing process, not a way of catching knowledge just before it walks out the door. Unfortunately, many documentation processes are broken, or nonexistent, and leaders don't realize it until the lost knowledge actually threatens operations.

In one major U.S. city government, for example, a senior industrial hygienist unexpectedly left his job in the Office of Environmental Health and Safety, giving his colleagues only three days to transfer knowledge about his work. He had files and records of all industrial hygiene work done in his unit for the last seven years. But in many cases the paper records had been lost and the electronic files were unorganized, so only the departing employee knew what they were. No one in the office had time to open, read, interpret, and refile the scores of documents, which could protect the city in future litigation over workers' compensation claims. This lack of documentation would only exacerbate the extremely high costs of workers' compensation claims for this urban administration.

One way to check if current documentation practices are effectively preserving knowledge is to ask whether your key employees could pass the "bus test."[8] In other words, if your star scientist, chief engineer, or policy analyst was hit by a bus on the way to work tomorrow would their documentation practices put the organization at risk or greatly degrade capabilities. Of course, the sudden loss of any employee is disruptive, but from a practical standpoint could a successor come in and make some sense of the expert's files?

If documentation practices are poor and disorganized and they could potentially hurt the organization's capacity to operate, then the time to start

fixing them is now. Because, as many organizations have learned, once employees are in the process of leaving, they are not very motivated to go back
and clean up the files they are leaving behind. In fact, some savvy professionals and managers will recognize that by leaving their files in disarray, or even
nonexistent, they can assure themselves lucrative consulting contracts for a
few years, as employees bring them back to supply knowledge that would
otherwise seem lost (more on utilizing retirees in chapter 8).

To make documentation a valuable knowledge retention practice, another challenge to overcome is to make it less distributed and inaccessible to
others once a project team disbands or individuals leave the organization.
Documents frequently end up on floppy discs, shared hard drives, or in file
cabinets. And there are often multiple versions of working drafts. Corning,
Northrop Grumman, and NASA are among the many organizations who
have struggled with this problem. They have all sought to make documentation more useful by standardizing and centralizing document storage and
access. This will be addressed in more detail in chapter 7, since solutions
inevitably involve IT systems.

Finally, in some cases, organizations will need to create new documentation practices from scratch. For example, when trying to bring one Department of Energy (DOE) nuclear weapons lab under configuration control,[9] engineers realized they did not know why certain changes had been made in
the lab's ventilation system. These changes had created a potential safety
problem that could have led to the release of radioactive materials into the
atmosphere. Lost knowledge due to poor documentation about past changes
to the ventilation system made fixing the problem much more difficult. Poor
record keeping about changes to the configuration of nuclear weapons facilities in the United States has been of concern to nuclear safety experts for
years.

Dr. John Mansfield is a member of the Defense Nuclear Facilities Safety
Board (DNFSB), which advises the Secretary of Energy on nuclear safety issues at DOE sites. "The first rule of dealing with an aging workforce," said
Mansfield, "is to make sure you have accurate schematics and isometrics,
which are the 3-D plans showing where pipes actually go. In DOE facilities,
they're always drilling through walls and hitting wires." As part of an effort
to develop up-to-date schematics for all nuclear weapons facilities, DNFSB
recommended that DOE formalize the process of creating a "cognizant engineer" (known as a "cog") for each site.

Cogs control all of the blueprints for a facility. No changes are allowed
without first submitting a work plan to this person who must sign off on the
revised schematic. "So even if the engineer drops dead, you have an up-to-
date plan of the plant in the computer," said Mansfield. "Before that DOE
was relying on people's memory of changes made 30 years ago."

The experience at DOE shows that in the long term, inadequate documentation can be very costly, and even dangerous, in certain situations. Given the expected increase in retirements, however, problems of poor documentation will become increasingly evident as more experienced employees leave behind badly flawed systems for preserving explicit knowledge about operations and the context surrounding important decisions. The implicit or tacit knowledge these veterans used to compensate for idiosyncratic documentation will be gone. What will be left will be a lot of unusable paper and electronic files. If you can't vouch without hesitation that current documentation will be valuable assets for future employees, then there are three steps management should take:

1. *Audit current documentation processes so you know for certain where the gaps and weak spots are.* There is really no excuse for being caught by surprise by inadequate documentation.

2. *Honestly evaluate the quality of the relationships management has with key employees.* Using documentation to retain knowledge is ultimately a human-centered process. And employees in today's organizations who control critical knowledge that needs formal documentation are not powerless drones who jump at any management request. "Rebellious teenager" is a better metaphor for understanding the harried professionals and managers who are likely to be asked to document what their successors need to know. ("You want me to do what? No way!") That's why using documentation to transfer knowledge is heavily dependent on the quality of the relationships between management and employees who have knowledge that the organization needs formalized. If management is viewed as controlling and uninterested in the welfare of its employees, getting more than token support for documentation efforts is unlikely. Thus, if you are in an organization where many veteran employees are alienated by past layoffs, reorganizations, and rancorous labor negotiations, then don't expect much payoff from new documentation initiatives. Until top management begins building quality relationships with its employees, asking them to invest in knowledge retention for the future will be unproductive.

3. *Don't even think of adding documentation on as an additional task for experienced workers.* That is, unless management takes away some other time-consuming activity or finds a way to make the documentation process a seamless part of existing work processes.

There are usually three reasons documentation isn't being created and well organized to support knowledge retention. (1) There is no process for doing so. DOE addressed that by designating cognizant engineers at each site. (2) There is no time to create and organize documents capturing explicit knowledge. Leaders must address the time crunch to experts' satisfaction. And (3) there is no perceived benefit for the departing experts. Management must also find a way to build benefits into the process for veteran employees, if they are to get cooperation. Managing dilemmas like these will be addressed in more detail in chapter 11.

Interviewing/Debriefing

Interviewing potential retirees, or mid-career employees leaving critical positions, is one of the most popular—and most problematic—forms of knowledge retention. Interviews (also referred to as debriefing) should be used when management is faced with the imminent loss of critical knowledge that can be retained in no other way. Interviews are appealing because they can help make both implicit rule-based knowledge and implicit know-how more visible. Interviews also can be scheduled and carried out quickly and at relatively low cost. But there is a trap that almost every organization falls into when they use interviews for knowledge retention. Managers don't anticipate the difficulty of converting raw interview data into knowledge that is accessible and useful for those who could benefit from it. As a result, a growing number of organizations admit they have invested thousands, and even millions, of dollars interviewing employees before they leave—often on videotape—only to find that the veteran's knowledge goes totally unused by their successors. But the news is not all bad. Let's look at two organizations that have had some success using interviews.

To capture knowledge from potential retirees, as well as other experts, the World Bank has used both videotaped and audio taped debriefings. The latter are transcribed into text documents. More than 60 videotaped interviews have been conducted in the Bank's Africa Regional Unit. The Bank has no formal process to identify who will be interviewed. Instead, said Nicolas Gorjestani, senior advisor and chief knowledge and learning officer, the key is being strategic in choosing individuals or teams to interview. One colleague who had been with the Bank for 30 years proved to be a gold mine of observations and reflections before leaving. He had extensive technical and managerial expertise and a multidimensional perspective that produced a very provocative interview, which has turned out to be one of the most watched in the series.

To get the interview into a valuable and accessible format, Gorjestani's team had to edit it down into a series of two- to five-minute video clips that captured the real "nuggets" of what the veteran employee had to say.

Often the knowledge captured in these interviews is more local and specialized. Braz Menezes, an urban planner, who knew more about planning projects in Brazil than anyone in the Bank's Latin America unit, was interviewed just before he retired a few years ago. Sitting down with just a tape recorder, Menezes was asked a series of questions that probed for knowledge gained from his experiences in Brazil. Questions included: How has decentralization affected urban projects in medium-sized Brazilian cities? What is the best way to conduct a slum upgrade project? Which local officials and ministries are most important and which are not? What are the best ways to recover project costs?[10] Interviews with Menezes, whose input was key to many Bank–sponsored projects in South America, were transcribed, edited, and posted on the World Bank's intranet. Hyperlinks were embedded throughout the 30-page interview so users could easily access thousands of pages of other materials related to the specific projects and practices the retiring planner referred to.

TVA has also begun interviewing some employees, such as senior engineers and technicians, who are close to retirement and deemed to have critical operational knowledge about the utility's plants. TVA has evolved an interviewing process to surface and capture knowledge about task performance (e.g., What reports do you use?), general facts (e.g., Which vendors do you use?), and lessons learned (e.g., What are you most worried about the company not knowing when you leave?). This knowledge, which could potentially be lost to TVA, is then dealt with directly, either by building it into training materials, codifying it in procedures or checklists, engineering it out through process improvement or technology upgrades, or by using other resources.

Several important lessons emerge from the experiences of those who have tried using interviews to transfer and retain knowledge.

1. *Focus on packaging and formatting interviews so the content is highly accessible, searchable, and action-oriented.* "Companies need to break out of their document-centric view of the work and think more about how they can effectively organize and package information elicited in interviews," said Larry Wilson, creator of Knowledge Harvesting, a methodology for eliciting implicit knowledge. One way to increase the likelihood of reuse is to make sure you have identified specific customers for the knowledge being captured. Note that early adopters recording interviews on videotape have found existing video search technologies largely inadequate for gaining fast access to key ideas. The technology will no doubt continue to improve, but make the vendor prove that their product is fast enough to suit your users' needs.

2. *Recognize that knowledge captured in interviews will only be reused if the culture is already oriented to knowledge sharing and learning from others.* NASA and Sandia Laboratories learned this lesson when younger engineers and scientists proved to be uninterested in accessing interviews done

with veteran employees. One way to overcome this lack of interest in what "old hands" know is to involve some less experienced employees in the interview process. This is likely to increase the perceived legitimacy of the veteran's knowledge and make it more relevant to their successors. It is also a great way to accelerate the learning of more junior employees.

3. *Use facilitators trained in eliciting expert knowledge because they will know the types of questions that will produce the most useful responses.* Some domain expertise is also important for focusing interviews in critical areas.

4. *Always ask the interviewee to review the content of the interview as edited and packaged before it is released to others.* Not only will this avoid passing on inaccurate knowledge, but it also encourages the expert to be more candid in revealing what works in actual practice without worrying about being misquoted or embarrassed by revealing politically sensitive information.

5. *Finally, choose interview candidates strategically. Don't even think about interviewing everyone who leaves in depth.* Identify employees whose knowledge will be most costly to lose. For example, the World Bank focuses on those who have knowledge that is strategically important but still relatively rare in the organization. When Delta Air Lines had to interview retiring employees on short notice, they had supervisors identify who among the departing employees represented a "critical job loss," and interviewed only those who met four additional criteria: they (1) were outstanding performers; (2) occupied positions in which there were no other incumbents or no one was trained as a back up; (3) were considered a go-to person during crises; and (4) had great contacts inside and outside of Delta.

The technical operations division, which includes Delta's maintenance technicians and engineers, had 120 people nominated for interviews, primarily because employees in this division had the most unique skill sets, took the longest time to train for a job, and were among the longest tenured at Delta. (There were 66 people who had been with the airlines more than 40 years!) Jim Smith, director of performance and learning for technical operations, knew his group needed to interview these people in less than a month, so he established priorities by matching departure dates against the criticality and uniqueness of the individual technician's knowledge. In the end, his team was able to interview 85 of the 120 people targeted before they left the airline, including all of the most critical nominees.

Role of Training in Knowledge Retention

Unlike documentation and interviews, which inherently emphasize knowledge capture activities, training is a knowledge transfer practice that is naturally focused on the delivery of knowledge to potential users. This means its effectiveness in actually transferring useful knowledge is likely to be more closely monitored than when producing documents or interviews. Training, of course, is a massive field, but we are concerned here only with applications of the practice that play an important role in supporting knowledge retention. In this context, training is an effective solution when the goal is to: (1) transfer leadership or management skills more quickly to a new generation of employees to replace those who are retiring; or (2) accelerate or broaden the development of specific technical or professional skills that would otherwise be diminished or lost.

Losing many veteran executives and middle managers to retirement will create increased opportunities for younger, less experienced employees to take on new responsibilities. But because many firms have downsized or limited hiring in the last 20 years, there is often a shortage of mid-career employees who have followed traditional career paths to gain the knowledge needed to fill upper-level management roles. A common refrain is: "We don't have 20 years for them to learn from experience." This means many organizations must accelerate the learning of their younger employees so they can adequately fill the roles of those retiring. Training will play an important part in this type of knowledge transfer, which is critical for sustaining performance. Here is how one organization began to address the problem.

The Federal Highway Administration (FHWA) reduced hiring in the 1990s, as the organization downsized, like most government agencies. Nevertheless, FHWA employees continued to retire and less experienced personnel were promoted more rapidly than usual to fill their slots. Thus, the agency found itself with a new group of mid-level employees in a variety of field office positions who lacked critical knowledge about the intricacies of the federal aid programs they were required to manage. The challenge was how to transfer this knowledge, which had historically taken years for individuals to develop.

To begin addressing the problem, FHWA created a customized training program, dubbed "Federal Aid 101." A highly experienced division administrator, who had recently retired from the agency, was hired back to design and teach the course. This executive had held many positions within the agency over the years, both in field offices and in headquarters, so he brought a broad perspective and tremendous experiential knowledge to the program.

Because most employees in government today are less likely to follow long-term career paths, involving frequent new assignments and relocations, this type of deep knowledge of agency operations, policies, and key personal relationships is more difficult to develop. But the retired administrator was able to pass some of this knowledge on through the training, which was given to field operations engineers, district engineers, and mid-level managers. It covered a wide variety of issues, including budgeting, personnel, environmental regulations, construction projects, relationships with state organizations, and federal aid issues.

This example points to a number of principles that can help your organization's training support knowledge retention needs.

1. *Training should balance current performance and future knowledge needs.* Any training that supports knowledge retention must also support current strategic objectives. The FHWA could not fulfill its mission of continually improving the U.S. highway system unless its staff had the knowledge needed to administer complex federal programs. The "Federal Aid 101" training helped pass on experiential knowledge gained by the retired administrator, but it did so in a way that made this knowledge immediately applicable for participants.

   Training that supports knowledge retention needs must align business objectives with specific intellectual capital that could be lost, as well as the capacity of particular employees to absorb this knowledge. This last factor sometimes can be a big problem. The McLane Company found many of its younger supervisors lacked the problem-solving skills they need to make use of management practices being taught in the firm's leadership program. This would make it impossible for them to use knowledge passed on by more experienced managers. McLane had to redesign the course to make sure its supervisors gained the requisite problem-solving capabilities. In another example, Wasatch Life needs candidates for its management development program to sustain its bench strength and replace managers lost through turnover, but it carefully screens employees first to check their ability to learn from experience. "The last thing we want is a blocked learner," said Wasatch Life's consultant in executive and organizational development. If training is to support both current and future organizational needs, executives must continuously assess the fit between strategic objectives, existing knowledge at risk, and the ability of less experienced employees to absorb and use that knowledge to create value in the future.

2. *Be sure to use the most effective training formats available, given knowledge being transferred.* The FHWA program was expert-led training, but often the most effective approach will be some type of "blended solution" that combines instructor-led sessions, with self-paced e-learning or

computer-based training components, video, on-the-job coaching, action learning projects, and so on. Technology has greatly expanded training options, but this has also increased the likelihood of turf battles between traditional training groups, e-learning advocates, and knowledge management staff. To effectively support knowledge transfer needs, there must be a common understanding that these methods all represent potential solutions that must work together to support learning and knowledge retention.[11]

Ultimately, what matters of course is that the training methods used lead to desired behavioral changes and improved capabilities. Siemens has found this is often best achieved by combining instructor-led workshops, which also provide cross-cultural networking opportunities, along with e-learning modules and active project work. Each training method has particular benefits and drawbacks. From a retention perspective, Siemens is notable for the explicit attention paid to the importance of building social networks through training. Management recognizes that participants sometimes benefit most by knowing how to communicate effectively with key experts to encourage follow-up discussions on topics covered in a training session.[12] Would your organization benefit more by paying special attention to the social capital that can be built through training?

Also notable is Siemens's commitment to action learning, as a critical part of the training process. The firm incorporates "business impact projects" in training wherever possible. This is based on a belief that employees and the company get the most out of training when they apply new knowledge in short, results-oriented projects that produce near-term, measurable benefits for the business.

Experience-based learning, whether in the form of simulations, short-term projects, or special assignments, plays a critical part in accelerating the learning needed to fill knowledge gaps that threaten to undermine performance in technical, managerial, and leadership roles. But action learning is just one technique useful for developing and transferring intellectual capital. When deciding how training can best support knowledge retention, the entire portfolio of methods should be considered, given the types of knowledge that must be transferred.

3. *Target training at employees expected to play an important role in the organization's future.* Resources are much too scarce today to be offering training indiscriminately, letting a thousand flowers bloom, as the saying goes. Training investments that support knowledge retention are offered at the right level of intensity to those employees who are going to make the biggest impact on performance—both in the short and long

term. The changing demographics of the workforce and changing values of younger workers means organizations must make certain their training investments take into account likely career paths.

For example, the Canadian military has historically invested heavily in the upfront technical training for personnel such as communications and electrical engineers. This front-loaded training was designed in an era when young recruits were expected to spend their entire careers with the Canadian Forces (CF). That doesn't happen much anymore. In recent years, technicians in the CF have begun routinely leaving the service just as their training finishes preparing them for more lucrative civilian positions. Thus, the Canadian military has been forced to rethink how it rolls out training to recruits in technical specialties. Poorly timed training can actually encourage employees to leave the organization because their new knowledge is more valuable elsewhere.

While there is a need to invest in employees who will continue to create value for the organization, this also means training should be closely aligned with career opportunities. In an attempt to become more performance oriented, some traditionally paternalistic firms have begun counseling employees on their realistic career opportunities with the firm. This can be beneficial in two ways. It lets high potential employees know they are valued and is likely to increase their interest and commitment to developing their capabilities, often through training programs. On the other hand, employees with more limited career prospects are encouraged to have more realistic expectations. This may create short-term resentment, but it is also likely to reduce frustration over missed promotions. It even increases the chances of holding onto a valuable employee by creating some kind of creative though less ambitious career path. Equally important, it allows management to focus training investments where the knowledge transferred will produce the biggest benefit.

4. *Explicitly recognize the role of your trainers in preserving organizational knowledge.* In one division of Siemens, for example, trainers work with process experts to create training materials that are continually refined based on feedback from participants. Trainers are also responsible for the knowledge contained in the presentations, which are available through the company's intranet, along with contact information for the relevant process experts. Siemens tries to keep two trainers knowledgeable about every topic or process, so there is always a backup. In this sense, trainers become a very important part of the organizational knowledge base, providing some continuity even if local content experts leave the firm. This fact is reinforced by the company's decision to

use trainers who are Siemens employees, instead of hiring vendors or outside facilitators. This way, Siemens's trainers are more motivated to continually develop their company-related expertise and to provide training participants with the most up-to-date knowledge available.[13] When organizations are worried about losing intellectual capital critical for sustaining future performance, training roles can take on new importance as a resource for bridging potential knowledge gaps across generations of employees.

5. *When knowledge retention is a key driver, consider whether training might be more effective if designed and conducted by local business units.* This sounds like heresy to any centralized training group. But the fact is most knowledge essential for operations, or even in key strategic roles, exists primarily on a local level within particular groups or functions. When Wasatch Life couldn't develop and retain managers fast enough to support the growth of its variable annuity business, something had to be done. The loss of experienced managers was hurting the performance of key operational groups. Leaders in the business unit didn't think the corporation's centralized HR function could respond fast enough to their specific training needs. So the unit created its own "renegade" program, which would develop a new generation of supervisors and managers with the skills needed to support their life insurance operations.

   Although the program was eventually taken over by corporate HR, the experience at Wasatch Life shows that when knowledge transfer is a pressing need, the solution may be best initiated at a local level. Local design of a training effort not only assures a faster response to a pressing problem but it also helps ensure that the training will add immediate business value and will have the full support of business unit leadership.

Of course, training is only useful as part of a knowledge retention strategy in certain jobs and for specific types of knowledge. Delta Air Lines, for example, has recognized it can incorporate lessons from veteran mechanics into its training materials and maintenance manuals because this knowledge deals with repetitive tasks where actions can be standardized. Delta's engineers, however, tend to deal with "one-off" problems and their knowledge is seen as more abstract and more specialized than that of the mechanics (e.g., how to do a stress analysis vs. how to replace a part). Thus, the engineers' knowledge is not a good candidate for transfer by training.

When threatened with knowledge loss many organizations are likely to gravitate to documentation, interviews, and training as the most logical—

and familiar—knowledge transfer practices. The danger, however, is that these approaches encourage management to overlook the retention of more implicit and tacit knowledge. Although difficult to transfer, these uncodifiable types of knowledge also represent a much more costly resource to lose. Approaches to this problem will be outlined in the next chapter.

6

Transferring Implicit and Tacit Knowledge

Work activities today are more dependent on specialized scientific and technical knowledge, as well as on work processes integrated across functions. As a result, knowledge critical to the organization's future success is more complex, abstract, and context dependent. This means most knowledge that needs to be retained is going to be implicit or tacit. This chapter will describe four practices that are better suited to transferring these types of intellectual capital (see figure 6.1). Each practice has different strengths and weaknesses and will produce different results. Some practices, such as storytelling and communities of practice, are highly interdependent and they will usually be more effective when used in combination over time.

The indirect practices described in chapter 5 implicitly assume that management can control what knowledge is retained. They focus on managing content. The more direct knowledge transfer practices described below recognize that when it comes to retaining more tacit knowledge, the best leaders can do is to create the right environment and mechanisms for sharing knowledge. These practices focus on creating a positive context for knowledge transfer because, in the end, management cannot actually control what knowledge is transferred.[1] Leaders can only try to influence behaviors that support retention.

Storytelling

Storytelling is a fact of organizational life. It is the way people make meaning out of their experiences. We all share knowledge everyday through the stories we tell. Stories reveal what employees think about their leaders, colleagues, and customers. Stories can be an excellent tool for diagnosing an organization's culture, if executives will only listen to the stories being told by their staff.[2]

Since storytelling is a natural behavior, the only question is whether it is used to support or undermine knowledge retention. From this perspective, it is important to understand that one of the major values of stories is their ability to communicate knowledge that can't be represented as propositions

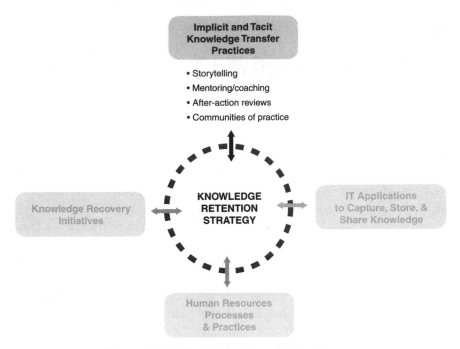

FIGURE 6.1. Implicit and Tacit Knowledge Transfer Practices

or rules. Stories can be effective for transferring both implicit knowledge about how things get done, as well as deeper tacit knowledge that reflects the values shaping behaviors.

For example, the senior hotel designer for a large entertainment company has more than 40 years of experience building hotels. He's seen it all. When less experienced members of the design team seek his advice, he often responds by telling stories describing previous designs that succeeded or failed. When trying to decide what size guest rooms should be in a new hotel, the veteran designer tells stories from his past experiences that show larger rooms produce more satisfied return guests, even though smaller rooms are more cost-effective to build. These stories not only help young designers understand all the factors that go into decisions about room size but they also communicate a value that holds long-term customer satisfaction as more important than short-term cost considerations.[3]

While stories are inherently recognized as valuable by many employees, the idea of intentionally pursuing them as a knowledge transfer tactic is sometimes regarded as "flaky" because stories violate Western business norms that value analysis over narrative. Nevertheless, stories are a critical building block for the transfer—and retention—of the most critical and valuable knowledge in organizations.

Different Uses of Storytelling at NASA

NASA uses storytelling in two very different ways to help support knowledge retention. Since early 1999, the library at NASA's Jet Propulsion Laboratory has sponsored storytelling sessions conducted by veteran JPL scientists, engineers, administrators, and project managers. The monthly program serves several purposes. It helps share the Lab's distinguished history of space exploration with a new generation of employees. Whether it's the experience of driving the Mars Pathfinder Rover or the challenges of architecting a deep space network, these stories are intended to convey what it felt like to be part of a pioneering project.

Storytelling at JPL communicates important aspects of the culture in a comfortable face-to-face setting, but the sessions are also audio taped or videotaped for access by those who can't attend. Teresa Bailey, program coordinator, explained:

> We wanted to get the history and culture of JPL more widely known. We have this unwritten mission that is doing what no one has done before. Feeling connected to that is a lot of what keeps people at the Lab. Storytelling helps socialize newer employees into this culture. Even though technical challenges may be discussed, the stories are more focused on first-hand accounts—what it was like to be there and live the experience. Because the program is completely voluntary, people are engaged or they would walk out the door. They are being entertained by learning about their own organization's culture. Where else can you get that?

NASA's Academy of Program and Project Leadership (APPL), the agency's training and development group, also uses storytelling to help retain other types of knowledge. The space agency's expanding pool of smaller projects, coupled with the looming retirement of its most experienced program and project managers, led APPL to start a knowledge-sharing initiative, which uses storytelling as a primary vehicle for transferring project management expertise. APPL's program encourages the transfer of both implicit and tacit knowledge among project managers (PMs), using a series of story-based knowledge-sharing meetings that are supplemented by *ASK*, a bimonthly online magazine. *ASK* is dedicated to stories about project management in NASA.[4]

For example, one *ASK* story recounted how, as a young project manager, the author had turned down a project to transport the Hubble Telescope from California to Florida. The effort was seriously underfunded and the transportation plans threatened the sensitive hardware. The story contains important lessons about when and how to turn down a project at NASA in a way that can actually enhance a manager's career. Another story related lessons learned about gaining political support at NASA headquarters for an unmanned Pathfinder program whose future was in jeopardy because it didn't appear to be aligned with the agency's mission.[5] Stories in *ASK* frequently provide insight into the informal practices that determine how projects actually succeed at NASA.

APPL's knowledge-sharing initiative in NASA, which started as a grassroots initiative, has become a major program that uses storytelling to facilitate learning in several different types of workshops. A semi-annual forum for master project managers brings together 40–50 of the best project managers in NASA, private industry, and other government agencies for three days of sharing stories and learning from peers. While leading practitioners from the broader project management community are invited to share their experiences, the stories of NASA's project managers are central to the program. Many of these stories are subsequently published in *ASK*. These published stories, which capture project management challenges, solutions, and lessons learned, are then used in one-day workshops held in individual NASA centers for less experienced project management staff. Participants read and discuss the stories. They are also likely to hear firsthand a story of project work from a veteran manager before they begin reflecting on their own project experiences with peers at their site. Finally, workshop participants practice sharing their own project knowledge in the form of oral and written stories. Ultimately, the goal of APPL's integrated, story-driven knowledge transfer initiative is to build both local and national communities of practice that routinely share project management knowledge to sustain this capability across the Agency.[6]

There is a strong belief among APPL leadership in the value of storytelling for transferring and retaining knowledge. "Generating, sharing, and discussing stories is an excellent way of converting tacit knowledge to explicit knowledge, and an effective method for quickly assimilating new learning," said Dr. Edward Hoffman, APPL director.

One example of how storytelling can effectively pass on knowledge that influences decision making was reflected in the experience of Roy Malone, head of logistics services at NASA's Marshall Space Flight Center. Shortly before attending an APPL forum for master project managers, Malone was told his budget had been cut 12 percent. He spent a month trying to find other ways to deal with the $1.1 million budget cut, but in the end Malone knew this meant he would have to lay off people.

During the masters forum, Malone heard a story told by a program director in the U.S. Air Force, Judy Stokley, who described how she had handled a similarly painful downsizing challenge. The logistics manager returned to Marshall inspired by the storyteller's "humanitarian" approach, and he proceeded to adapt a number of the actions she used to his own situation. For example, he began working with his key managers to find money from other sources to reduce the number of layoffs necessary. Malone also told employees about the cuts the department was facing, giving those who would be let go a three-month warning. Finally, he held a series of open meetings with employees to let them vent their anger at the cuts and to educate them as best he could about the center's financial situation. In the end, Malone attributed the lessons he absorbed from the Air Force director's story to helping minimize the impact of the layoffs he had to implement.[7]

But there is also a recognition at NASA that storytelling is limited in terms of what types of knowledge it can transfer and who will benefit from it. Charlotte Linde, an expert on uses of narrative who works for the space agency, has found that storytelling is good for conveying events that require interpretation, such as how a program manager dealt with conflicting organizational priorities. But she has not found stories a useful way to transfer knowledge about how to accomplish a technical task, which involve facts and technical issues but little interpretation. The only exception, she said, is when teaching new members of a technical group. Maybe it is more accurate to say it takes a special kind of creativity to share technical knowledge through stories. This is evident in a new series of training manuals, such as *Head First Java*, which rely on entertaining stories to teach normally dry technical subjects.[8]

The use of stories is likely to gain increased credibility as knowledge retention is recognized as a more compelling problem. Organizations such as the World Bank, IBM, and Corning are already making productive use of storytelling and there is a growing body of research on the valuable role stories can play in transferring knowledge.[9]

Getting Started with Storytelling

Using storytelling to support knowledge retention needs has a lot of benefits, but actually creating value with this practice requires attention to several critical factors.

1. *Be clear about the purpose of using stories.* Narratives intended to pass on knowledge will have a different form than stories designed to motivate action or to communicate cultural values. It's easy to get distracted by the content of stories themselves and lose sight of what you are trying to achieve by using them.
2. *Create regular occasions for telling stories.* Those who have stories must

have a setting where they can comfortably tell them to an audience who wants to listen and is able to make use of the lessons they contain. NASA, for example, created the forums for master project managers and workshops at individual Centers for more junior personnel. Both settings create opportunities for the exchange of stories and signal management's support for this kind of knowledge transfer.

3. *Make sure the audience has enough context to interpret the lessons contained in experts' stories.* Some of the tales told in NASA's masters forums would probably not be very memorable or useful for its most junior project managers. That's because they lack the experience, the sophisticated understanding of organizational context, and the related job responsibilities that would enable them to interpret lessons from a veteran's story. The example of the logistics director told earlier is a good example of a listener whose experience and responsibilities were well matched with the storyteller's narrative, enabling him to quickly adapt the story to his own situation and use it to inform his actions. Be clear about who the audience is for the stories being developed. This is the first step in assessing their capacity for finding lessons in the material.

4. *If stories are not being told face-to-face, pay special attention to packaging and how the narratives will be accessed.* Capturing oral stories on video or as text in a database or hard copy format can be very problematic. The impact of these stories will be greatly diminished unless considerable resources are devoted to editing the narrative into compact, useful segments and making them easily accessible to those who can readily use the knowledge. NASA's project management journal *ASK* is one good example of the editorial effort required to make stories valuable to a larger audience. Another example is a monthly safety bulletin produced by the office of the NASA Aviation Safety Reporting System. *Callback* is distributed to 85,000 pilots, air traffic controllers, and other interested readers. Each issue uses stories drawn from 2,500 safety-related incidents reported monthly by aviation industry personnel and private pilots to pass on experience-related lessons. While not intended explicitly to retain knowledge about safety, *Callback* is an excellent illustration of how stories can be used to transfer critical knowledge across broader communities.[10]

Mentoring and Coaching

The last time Sandia National Laboratories was involved in the development of a nuclear weapon was in 1992. Veterans in the Lab have a tremendous amount of knowledge about the unique technologies that go into these warheads, such as explosively-driven thermal batteries or small high-powered radar systems. These technologies, which are only used in nuclear weapons and may sit for 20–30 years, need to be extremely reliable and safe. Part of the solution for transferring the crucial implicit and tacit knowledge about designing and maintaining these esoteric technologies lay in the Lab's corporate mentoring program, which was launched in the 1990s.

Hundreds of people have participated in the program, which tries to match up experienced weaponeers with younger employees. Managers are required to designate a mentor as part of the new-hire program for weaponeers. But because of Sandia's extensive hiring programs in recent years, middle managers have complained about the tremendous time commitment required to socialize and train new employees. As a result, the Lab started using more retired weaponeers as mentors.

Mentoring and coaching[11] are probably the most effective ways of directly transferring critical implicit and tacit work-related knowledge from one individual to another. Mentoring supports the sharing of the broadest range of knowledge, from detailed technical skills and tacit cultural values to career development advice, in a relationship that ideally allows the expert to monitor the degree to which knowledge is actually being absorbed (see figure 6.2 for a summary of the impact of different practices on knowledge transfer). Mentoring, of course, has many purposes and many benefits. But from the perspective of knowledge retention it can help in three specific areas.[12]

Depending on the context, mentoring (or coaching) can help transfer technical, operational, or managerial skills. That is, how to perform specific aspects of a job. Mentoring also helps a protégé learn "who does what and how" in the organization. Providing introductions to influential decision makers and specialized experts helps less experienced employees develop the relationships they will need to succeed in the organization. One manager explained the value of this social knowledge when he said, "It's one thing to have somebody's Rolodex, but it's another to get people to return your calls." Finally, mentors can also pass on cultural knowledge about organizational values and norms of behavior. Because this knowledge is tacit, it is almost always communicated by observing the mentor as a role model or symbol of effective performance.

Mentoring can be a very valuable practice for stemming the loss of knowledge because it is so effective at transferring the complex types of knowledge previously described. But there are significant barriers to implementing successful mentoring programs today. You need to do four things to use this approach successfully.

1. *Focus efforts in critical areas.* A manager in the engineering organization at chemical giant DuPont showed why focus is important when he said,

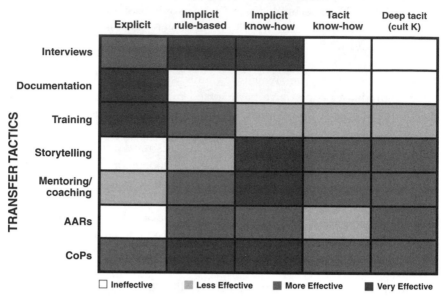

FIGURE 6.2. Impact of Different Practices on Knowledge Transfer

"We're never going back to the protégé/mentor model and the cast of thousands where all less experienced people have mentors. We can't afford that in time or money, and we can't get that many experienced people."

Realistically, mentoring efforts today that support knowledge retention must be focused in critical areas. Sure, mentoring programs may extend beyond the development of strategically important personnel, but priorities should be set so knowledge is being transferred from your most essential personnel first. Concerned about the looming retirement of its top managers, for example, the McLane Company introduced its mentoring program at the senior executive level first where the CEO and executive vice presidents began mentoring division presidents as part of their developmental process. McLane's top managers had spent their entire careers building the international logistics company and they needed to pass on their intimate knowledge of the business.

Top executives initially met with division presidents to identify growth objectives, such as developing strategic selling skills. Then, the mentors talked monthly by phone or in face-to-face meetings to provide coaching and feedback about their protégé's performance on a particular activity, such as giving a high-level sales presentation. Discussions that centered on how a presentation went and what might have been done differently supported experiential learning and provided opportunities for feedback and relevant stories based on the mentor's expertise.

2. *Anticipate time and resource constraints.* Many managers today claim they don't have the resources to support mentoring initiatives. Jeanne Holm, NASA's chief knowledge architect, described how mentoring became more problematic when the space agency implemented its "faster, better, cheaper" project management strategy. As a result, the number of projects at JPL jumped from 4 to 40 in five years. She said:

> We've had to take some really junior folks and put them in relatively senior positions. In these positions they have had to learn their trade on the job, with little help from the most experienced staffers. We had 80-to 90-hour work weeks as the norm on some projects. So the idea of people additionally spending a little time mentoring somebody was ludicrous.[13]

While learning complex jobs on-the-fly has become common in many organizations, this kind of discontinuous transition carries significant risks of increased mistakes, reduced efficiency, and missed opportunities caused by lost knowledge. In order to use mentoring to help retain knowledge, leaders will have to find ways to overcome resource and time constraints. One way NASA has tried to do this is by bringing back recent retirees to participate in its teaching and mentoring program sponsored by APPL. NASA has joined a growing list of organizations that are drawing on its retired experts to mentor younger employees. Effectively using retirees to retain knowledge will be discussed in chapter 8.

Another way to sidestep complaints of limited resources for mentoring is to design this responsibility into the job descriptions of particularly valuable experts. One business unit of Northrop Grumman's Integrated Systems sector has done that with its Engineering "Super Grade" technical fellows program. Currently about 80 key technical experts in the unit's engineering function have been promoted into this role, which is the technical equivalent of a middle management position. As technical lead for a particular area, such as stealth technology or radar cross-section analysis, technical fellows have specific responsibilities for mentoring and other knowledge transfer activities in their domain of expertise.

Finally, another way for leaders to confront the apparent lack of time available for mentoring is to model the behavior themselves. This is what executives at the McLane Company did. McLane is a fast-paced, action-oriented firm and the best way for leaders to demonstrate the importance of developing employees through mentoring was to take up the practice themselves to show its importance to the rest of the organization. The problem of balancing dilemmas created by conflicting objectives such as employee development and cost controls will be addressed directly in chapter 11.

3. *Train mentors specifically on how they can help their protégés.* The objectives of mentoring can vary greatly from teaching specific skills to providing general career development advice. If retaining organizational knowledge is a key objective, then mentors will probably need help in identifying what knowledge most needs to be shared.

At the World Bank, for example, a primary purpose of mentoring is to introduce less experienced employees to a network of people who will be helpful in the future. The bank also places a heavy emphasis on action learning or learning-by-doing, and leaders recognize that protégés are much more likely to absorb tacit knowledge by observing it in the context of daily practice. Thus, the practice of "shadowing" more experienced mentors is frequently encouraged.

NASA, on the other hand, recognizes that one of the most critical things mentors can help the organization retain is the passion its veteran employees have for the challenging work of space exploration. One study of mentoring at NASA concluded, "These visionaries take with them not only their technical knowledge and skill, but also the excitement and interests they hold for their work. It is those interests we want to duplicate in future generations."[14]

Helping mentors clarify the types of knowledge they should try to pass on is only half the battle, however. Perhaps more difficult is working with veteran experts to overcome inherent cognitive barriers that undermine their ability to effectively pass their knowledge to less experienced employees. There is considerable research that shows expert mentors can have a very difficult time transferring their knowledge to less experienced colleagues.[15] This is because, even if they are motivated to share it, experts store and process information about their work in abstract, conceptual forms that are difficult to retrieve and communicate to less experienced protégés. In addition, research shows that the more knowledgeable someone is about their job, the more likely they are to underestimate what novices actually need to know to learn it. There are several things organizations can do to help mentors overcome natural biases that undermine effective knowledge transfer.

First, clarify the knowledge gap that exists between a mentor and his or her protégé. The larger the experience gap is the more likely a protégé will have trouble understanding the mentor's lessons. When the gap is large, try to involve someone with an intermediate level of knowledge to help translate the expert's knowledge into concepts the novice can understand. There has been research that shows someone with an intermediate level of knowledge is actually more effective in sharing expertise with novices because they relate better to the novices' experience base.[16]

Second, be sure to encourage lots of two-way interaction between mentors and protégés. This lets the less experienced employee question the expert and allows the mentor to adapt their teaching based on the protégés questions and performance. It is in these sometimes seemingly "inefficient" conversations that the most important learning takes place.

Third, encourage shadowing or action learning assignments whenever possible. Tacit knowledge is best surfaced and transferred through observation and experiential learning. Shadowing encourages the protégé to ask questions that are unlikely to occur to the more experienced mentor, and experimenting with new knowledge greatly increases the chances it will be absorbed and remembered.

As scientific and technical knowledge becomes increasingly complex and abstract the barriers to transferring it between generations of employees won't get any easier. Nevertheless, there are steps management can take to identify pitfalls in sharing expertise that will increase the chances of successfully retaining vital knowledge.

4. *Create an effective infrastructure to support mentoring.* Informal mentoring has always happened in organizations, but more formal mechanisms are needed to build a sustainable mentoring program that can meet the challenges posed by changing workforce demographics. At the World Bank, the HR department identifies where mentoring could be of value and finds experienced people willing to serve as mentors. Then HR helps launch the program and trains mentors initially, although the programs are ultimately managed by the operating units they support. Among the tasks that must be addressed are: (1) clarifying the purpose and business reasons for introducing a mentoring program; (2) identifying those who most need mentoring; (3) creating a process to identify and train potential mentors; and (4) defining how the program will be managed and coordinated.[17]

After Action Reviews

Mentoring may be the most effective practice for transferring expertise from one person to another, but sometimes the knowledge you are trying to retain is less well understood and more likely to exist in a larger group. For transferring this type of knowledge, a process known as the "after action review" will be a better solution.

In reality, the lessons of experience are constantly being lost in organizations today. Working in complex, high-pressure environments, a great deal of potential learning is wasted because employees have no process to reflect on their actions, capture this new knowledge, and integrate it back into ongoing activities. But a growing number of organizations are using after action reviews (AARs) to generate, retain, and reuse knowledge that is a by-product of ongoing operations. First employed by the U.S. Army more than 20 years ago, an AAR is a brief, focused process that helps groups to crystallize and validate new knowledge or learning from a recent event or project that all members have participated in. The process is built around four questions: (1) What was supposed to happen? (2) What actually happened? (3) Why were there differences? (4) What can we learn from this and do differently next time?[18]

Analog Devices has adopted AARs to generate and retain knowledge that can be used to continually improve its product development process. Each product development team holds weekly meetings to reflect on their recent performance and to see what new lessons can be applied to improve its effectiveness. This new knowledge is captured in brief written summaries, which are consolidated with lessons from other new product teams and used every six weeks in a full review of all product development projects. Knowledge collected from the teams' experiences is then used to improve the overall product development process itself.[19] By using AARs to facilitate experiential learning and knowledge retention within the teams, Analog Devices supports ongoing process improvements in its business that would be impossible if employees' unarticulated experiential knowledge was being allowed to dissipate in the crush of daily activities.

AARs are often thought of simply as a tactic for improving team learning and performance. But they do more than that. By helping teams reflect and learn from their experiences, AARs generate new knowledge that is shared by group members and, thus, is more likely to be retained as the group evolves over time. But global energy giant BP learned that the best way to capture project-based experiential knowledge is by holding regular AARs. When teams wait to hold them until after a lengthy project is completed, then much new knowledge is lost.[20]

BP has learned that using AARs to support short-term learning and knowledge retention can have big payoffs, such as when it engaged in complex negotiations with the Vietnamese government to create a gas and power industry in that developing country. BP began using AARs to help coordinate and accelerate the learning of its teams that were negotiating 10 different contracts simultaneously with Vietnamese officials. Unless lessons gained from the daily negotiations could be shared with other members of the project, the initiative was unlikely to succeed. After each discussion with government officials, BP negotiating teams began using AARs to reflect on their experiences. They found the tactic a very powerful way of thinking collectively about what they had done, what had happened, and what changes they needed to make in the next meeting. The lessons from the AARs were briefly summarized in writing and circulated to other negotiating teams, as well as to BP management. Management reviewed a summary of the key AARs at their weekly meeting and used insights gained from the teams' observations to adjust the overall negotiating strategy going forward.[21]

In this case, AARs helped BP retain critical knowledge in several ways. First, they enabled individual teams to articulate knowledge gained during the negotiating process, immediately using it to improve their performance. Knowledge emerging from these group discussions and then applied in practice was much more likely to be retained by the group itself and by individual team members for future use. In addition, the written AAR summaries provided useful background knowledge for any new personnel joining the negotiating teams. These summaries also provided a historical view of the negotiations overall and helped ensure that lessons from the complex process would be retained by the management team.

AARs are a flexible process that can also be used to help groups identify what they need to learn in order to improve performance. In the process, this approach will improve the dynamics of knowledge transfer between veterans and less experienced employees, in part because it applies expertise directly to current or future problems, instead of simply collecting the war stories of "old timers."

For example, Harley-Davidson Corporation was about to introduce a new product. But before beginning full-scale production, the plant manager wanted to oversee a series of pre-builds to identify quality problems ahead of time. Before starting the production line, the manager asked his team to articulate what they were going to have to do to perform to the initial quality standard he had set. In this meeting, veteran members of the manufacturing team drew from their experience in predicting what it would take to succeed. The line was turned on and the new product was built for one day. The manufacturing team then did a series of AARs to reflect on how the pre-build had gone, given their predictions. This not only allowed the team to validate or rethink their initial assumptions about production, but also the veterans' knowledge was tested in front of the junior staff who were able to decide for themselves how valuable it was. This pre-build process was repeated several times by the plant manager who raised the production standard each time.

The manufacturing team used AARs repeatedly to integrate what they learned from each pre-build into a new set of planning assumptions about what had to be done to meet a higher production standard.[22]

"Using AARs this way doesn't just focus on fixes," said Marilyn Darling, president of Signet Consulting and an expert on using AARs. "Instead, by articulating planning assumptions there is a natural transfer of knowledge going on between group members. This knowledge is then validated or challenged by observing what happens in real time."

Storytelling and mentoring are practices that can transfer existing knowledge that will otherwise be lost. But today's volatile work environment demands that new knowledge be constantly created to respond effectively. This means when teams are not proactively learning from their experiences they are actually losing knowledge that could be valuable to the organization. AARs help create this new knowledge in a team setting that also increases the chances it will be retained.

Communities of Practice

When organizations are worried about losing expertise from specific functions or types of employees, or when there is a need to develop important capabilities in new employees more quickly, then communities of practice (CoPs) can be a vital knowledge transfer solution.

CoPs have generated a lot of interest in recent years, as organizations recognize the value of supporting natural interest groups that share common languages, values, and problems. These natural communities—or networks— can be leveraged to improve knowledge sharing and problem solving across organizational boundaries, and they have proved their value in doing so.[23] But CoPs have an additional benefit when lost knowledge is a concern for management. Supporting the connections and health of communities of key types of experts or managers can go a long way to supporting the retention of both critical individuals and their knowledge in the organization.

Communities can do this in several ways. First, a well-organized CoP can provide professionals who feel isolated with a much needed sense of connectedness to others in the organization who are facing similar challenges and who have similar perspectives on the business. For example, one global chemical company links its maintenance managers around the world, who can seek help on problems related to their unit's maintenance processes. At the same time, CoPs encourage employees to share their expertise more broadly, thus making this knowledge more likely to survive in the organization after a single expert leaves. Communities of practice also provide resources for bringing new members of the community up the learning curve quickly. They do this partly by making available the latest codified knowledge in a particular domain (e.g., FAQs on a Web site) or by speeding up the development of a new person's social capital because they are joining an active network of experts oriented toward sharing and helping each other.

Shell Oil Company is one firm that has benefited significantly from the use of communities of practice, or "networks," as they are called in Shell. Networks serve multiple purposes in this global firm, but in some cases these communities have come to play a role as "knowledge stewards" for a particular area of expertise in the company. For example, to connect professionals who were distributed across project teams, Shell created networks of employees who shared a common discipline. One such network consisted of geologists, reservoir engineers, petrophysicists, and other geoscientists who were all concerned with a particular geological formation known as turbidite structures. This group of about 15 top experts in the field soon took on the name "Turbodudes." They continued to meet weekly for several years, talking informally about the technical problems individual members were confronting in their work and considering alternative solutions. These ongoing interactions have spawned many rich one-on-one relationships that are an important source of daily knowledge transfer.[24]

BP's 3D Mod network is another example from the energy industry of how communities of practice can support knowledge retention. This far flung group includes employees from a variety of disciplines seeking to improve the management of subsurface oil reservoirs through the use of three-dimensional reservoir modeling. Although members of the community rarely meet face-to-face, they help each other improve their modeling capabilities by sharing what they have learned through an electronic collaboration tool such as Microsoft Exchange.

Community members post electronic messages ranging from technical queries, bug fixes, and requests for help, to debates about good practices. A moderator, who is well-respected by network members, facilitates discussions and encourages debate.

The community remained at about 100 members for 6 years. But in that time there has been a significant turnover of members, as interested employees and contractors join the community when it is useful to them and leave when it's not. About half of the members change over a two-year period.

Over time, members of the community have edited and validated the content of many messages appearing in discussions, formatting them into FAQs, so this cumulative knowledge can be easily accessed and reused through the Web site by new members.[25]

Not all knowledge retention needs are the result of retirements, of course. Many firms must deal with very high levels of turnover among younger workers who have accumulated considerable operational knowledge during their tenure. Best Buy, the world's largest consumer electronics specialty retailer, must cope with annual turnover of about 90 percent among its young sales associates who sell a fast changing mix of high-tech products in more than 500 stores throughout North America. Best Buy has discovered that communities of practice can be an essential element for retaining knowledge generated by its mobile workforce.

As a result of its high employee turnover, which is normal for the retail industry, Best Buy must continually bring new staff up to speed quickly to replace departing sales associates and the knowledge they acquired about selling a broad range of home office products, consumer electronics, appliances, and software. To transfer and retain product and sales knowledge across a rapidly changing employee base, Best Buy created a methodology for launching and supporting communities of practice.[26]

One of the first communities the company began supporting was associates responsible for installing car audio equipment. Linking employees performing this job in mobile installation bays throughout the United States, management's goal was to reduce costly installation errors and increase customer satisfaction. The community's technology infrastructure helped employees share their experiential knowledge and tips about installing audio equipment. It also provided an easily accessible version of all technical manuals online. The business impacts of the mobile installation CoP were significant. Employees seemed to benefit by using knowledge of their peers to avoid costly mistakes. This resulted in a decline of both claims per installed units and damage claims, improving profitability for the car audio equipment product lines.

Best Buy has since applied its CoP methodology to support a series of firm-wide retail communities in product areas such as appliances, digital imaging, home theater, and computers. Community members can now share sales ideas and product information tips, continually refreshing and expanding their community's knowledge. The knowledge that associates gain by being part of a CoP increases sales by helping them become productive faster. And when employees do leave, the knowledge they have shared as "tips" and insights about products and sales tactics remains as a resource for the community and the company.

These examples show that CoPs can take on many forms. They may be small groups, like the Turbodudes at Shell, or large networks of audio equipment installers at Best Buy. Members can all be experts in their field, or a community can include a range of skill levels. Communities can also consist of members who know and trust each other completely, making knowledge sharing a natural and easy activity. Or a network may connect employees in diverse locations who will never meet, making knowledge sharing more of a challenge.

In reality, there are many types of communities or networks that can improve organizational knowledge retention if they are supported effectively. Saint-Onge and Wallace identified five characteristics that define successful communities:[27]

1. *Conversations*: Productive questions and discussions are the key to learning. In effective communities, all members are encouraged to express opinions, discuss problems, and promote their successors.
2. *Collaboration*: Learning usually happens through social interaction. Successful CoPs support mutual problem solving and knowledge sharing among colleagues in nonhierarchical exchanges.
3. *Commitment*: Effective communities consist of members who believe it is important to contribute their time to support the group's purpose. They believe in the value of their community. Senior management has also expressed commitment to the importance of communities for knowledge transfer and retention by making resources available to help build and sustain them.
4. *Connectivity*: Communities are only valuable when their members have ways of easily connecting, whether it is face-to-face in periodic forums or conferences, or by using an elaborate technology infrastructure that supports electronic communication and collaboration tools.
5. *Capabilities*: Finally, effective communities continually build, refresh, and sustain the skills, attitudes, values, and knowledge that organizations need to implement their strategic objectives.

Communities of practice hold a lot of potential for supporting long-term knowledge retention needs, but the experiences of companies like BP and Shell Oil also raise important issues. Both firms have extensive experience trying to build distributed global communities to facilitate knowledge transfer, and they have learned that it is much more difficult to build social networks across different organizations that are also geographically distributed. Language barriers, lack of common terminology, and lack of trust all inhibit knowledge sharing and take considerably longer to overcome. Thus, expecting communities of practice to be an important vehicle for facilitating knowledge retention in global organizations requires patience and a long-term commitment to supporting their development.

One particularly innovative CoP that relates directly to the problem of knowledge retention was a cross-company community founded by Siemens and BMW to address the challenges of losing expertise through retirement and attrition. The "Leaving Experts Community of Practice" had six companies as members, including Intel, Infineon Technologies, and Winterthur Insurance Switzerland.[28] All the firms participating in the community have been confronted with high retirement and turnover levels due to mergers, layoffs, and employee dissatisfaction. One of the primary goals of the community is for members to collect and exchange information about the knowledge transfer methods they are using to reduce the costs of losing expertise through turnover.

Other organizations frequently ask to join the Leaving Experts network, but the community moderator said two main criteria are used to evaluate possible new members. First, they must be experienced in dealing with the problem of losing expertise and able to contribute lessons of value to other companies. And, second, they must not be a direct competitor of any existing members of the community.

It is impossible to address all the nuances of CoPs in this book, but the Shell, BP, and Best Buy examples point to the potential that communities hold for retaining critical organizational knowledge. If senior management needs to make decisions about where to invest in resources that support CoPs, the first choice should always be groups that have capabilities most essential to the strategic objectives of the organization. These are the communities that should be supported first. If this criterion provides no obvious candidates, then look for informal groups with important knowledge that have already demonstrated an interest in collaborative problem solving.

Effectively improving the transfer of knowledge to sustain organizational capabilities depends largely on making the right decisions about what knowledge to retain and then changing employee behaviors and business processes to support your objectives. The transfer practices described in the last two chapters provide examples of how these changes can be enacted. But making those new behaviors and processes a reality increasingly depends on fast evolving information technology applications. How computer technologies can be applied to specifically support knowledge retention is the subject of the next chapter.

7
Applying IT to Capture, Store, and Share Intellectual Capital

Most executives concerned about organizational knowledge retention recognize that their major challenges are changing behaviors or work processes. Information technology (IT) plays a secondary role in reducing the costs of knowledge loss. There are two reasons for this. First, most practical knowledge either cannot be captured in a computer system or it won't be accessed in a digital format by those who might benefit. Second, unless the organization's culture encourages knowledge sharing in a specific work context, then applying IT to knowledge transfer problems will have almost no impact. Except in unusual cases, leading with a technology-based solution is a recipe for failure.

Nevertheless, IT has an important role to play in many organizations where technology can enhance four activities needed for knowledge retention:

- *Connecting people* by linking less experienced employees with experts
- *Accelerating learning* through more intense collaborative interaction, e-learning programs, and direct support for problem solving
- *Capturing knowledge* by collecting and organizing critical documentation
- *Mapping human knowledge* for better management of HR assets

Executives will have to identify the specific combination of IT applications that best support their own organization's knowledge retention needs (see figure 7.1). That's because every situation will vary depending on workforce demographics in particular units, the types of knowledge and tasks involved, the organization's culture, and its current installed base of technology. The examples provided in this chapter should be viewed not as answers, but as a source of ideas about what is possible when confronted with the threat of lost knowledge. Your particular situation will dictate which applications are most helpful.

Connecting People

When it comes to knowledge retention, the most frequently mentioned IT application was "expert locator systems," which are also commonly known

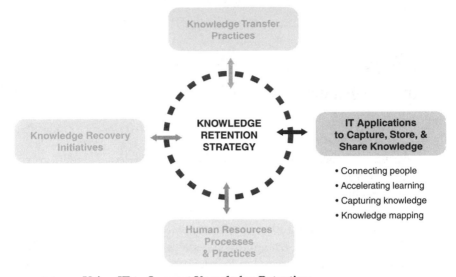

FIGURE 7.1. Using IT to Support Knowledge Retention

as corporate Yellow Pages. Energy giant BP is one firm that has derived significant benefits from an expert locator system. To speed the development of new relationships and social networks after its merger with Amoco, BP management created a knowledge directory, called BP Connect, which allowed employees to search across the expanded global company to find colleagues with relevant knowledge and experience. This searchable intranet repository helps BP employees quickly locate expertise on a particular subject.[1]

Expert locators like BP Connect can be good for knowledge sharing in general, but they are particularly valuable for organizations trying to retain knowledge lost when employees leave or take another assignment. That's because one of the first casualties when organizations lose high-performing, experienced employees is the loss of individual social capital, that is knowing who has specific knowledge or who can get things done. Many personal links are lost through turnover, but expert locator applications increase the chances that some connections can be reestablished when successors use the system to identify who knows what. At BP, for example, new employees are encouraged to use Connect to build their personal networks more quickly, which accelerates their productivity.

Expert locators also increase the chances of recovering critical knowledge that has drifted away from a unit or department over time. CNA, the Chicago-based insurance company, has gone through major reorganizations to support its changing business strategy. Restructuring is one way organizations frequently lose valuable knowledge.

This appeared to have happened when a Canadian policyholder filed a potentially very expensive claim involving old lawsuits. The claim was based on a policy written by a company that had merged with CNA. Fortunately, colleagues of the CNA consultant handling the claim seemed to recall that all Canadian policies had been sold off to another insurance company right after the merger. Was CNA still responsible for this policy? If not, who was it sold to? This knowledge would have been lost to the claims consultant if CNA had not implemented an expert locator system. The consultant posted his question about the Canadian claim on the expert network. And the next day an executive in another part of the company confirmed the sale of the policy and identified the Canadian insurance company now responsible for the claim. Locating the executive who had this knowledge not only saved the claims consultant many hours of research, but also spared CNA from settling a potentially costly claim.[2]

Expert locator systems can also increase the chances of drawing on the knowledge of employees who have left the organization. Of course, some people don't want to have anything to do with their former employer, but many are glad to answer brief queries that could save their successors tremendous time and money. When employees leave BP, they are able to delegate control of their personal profile in Connect to a colleague who is remaining with the company. The profile not only provides a fragment of organizational memory, but it also offers a way for those leaving to provide contact information for future queries. Of course, employees who have left cannot be counted on to supply much important information for free, but an expert locator system at least increases the chances that some valuable knowledge can be recovered.

Like all IT software supporting knowledge management needs, the technology used for expert locator systems is evolving. Older homegrown applications like BP Connect simply act as databases to identify people who might have certain knowledge. But a new group of vendors, such as AskMe Corp., Autonomy, and Tacit Knowledge Systems, have begun selling advanced expert locator systems with features that, in some cases, create expert profiles automatically, or rate the quality of experts' responses from the user's perspective and store responses to frequently asked questions for future use.

Expert locator applications hold great promise for organizations concerned about knowledge retention but don't underestimate the difficulty of implementing these systems. One manufacturing firm that was worried about turnover in R&D learned this lesson the hard way. Management tried to implement a database of expert profiles for locating scientists and engineers with key knowledge. The system was expected to speed up the integration of new employees, reduce the unnecessary hiring of external experts, and identify gaps in the firm's knowledge base.

One problem the company discovered immediately was the difficulty of keeping individual profiles up to date. The personal information requested by the system was too extensive and employees saw no benefit in participating. As a result, the little-used system was shut down in a year. Those who have implemented successful expert locator applications point to several lessons learned.

1. *The system must fit the culture.* At BP, individual profiles are highly personal with informal photos and family details. The goal is to help people connect at a personal level so they will be more motivated to share knowledge. This works at BP, while CNA has a much more impersonal system relying on software from AskMe Corporation.

2. *Build both bottom-up and top-down support.* Ultimately, expert locators cannot work unless a critical mass of employees believes in their value. This requires a lot of evangelizing and education upfront. On the other hand, employees are unlikely to be interested unless they know that knowledge sharing is a priority for senior management. CEO Sir John Browne helped build the credibility of BP Connect by putting his own profile up on the system. CNA also had highly visible executive support for its expertise network.

3. *Keep your purpose clear and narrowly focused.* The objective of BP Connect is to give employees enough information to generate brief exchanges with experts who can save them tremendous time and money. Meaningful knowledge transfer is largely about creating relationships between people. The more ambitious your objectives become, the more competing agendas you will have to negotiate. For example, will your application compete with existing HR systems?

Accelerating Learning

Connecting people who have knowledge with those who need it is an essential step in retaining intellectual capital. But it may not be enough. IT applications that enhance the ability of employees to learn from each other can also improve knowledge transfer and retention. There are at least three types of IT applications that can accelerate learning.

1. *Technologies that intensify collaboration*: Intuition says that groups who are communicating and interacting frequently and efficiently are much more likely to be sharing knowledge effectively. Thus, using IT to intensify collaboration opportunities between experts and less experienced employees can improve knowledge retention. But be forewarned. So-called "collaborative technologies" are designed to produce many dif-

ferent outcomes, such as improved communication, file sharing, and document management. These capabilities may not support your immediate knowledge transfer needs. If your primary concern is knowledge retention, you should be very clear about the results you are looking for through improved interactions before venturing into the jungle of products being marketed as collaborative "solutions."

2. *E-learning applications*: The need to transfer knowledge to less experienced employees quickly and cost-effectively also makes e-learning applications an attractive option in some situations. So far, however, the hype around electronically-supported learning has far exceeded the actual benefits in most cases. It turns out there are many barriers to effectively using Web-based technologies to accelerate learning. Nevertheless, there are some early examples of e-learning applications that have demonstrated significant benefits that contribute to knowledge retention.

3. *Support for problem solving*: There are some IT applications that can actually help experts be more explicit about their thinking processes and the knowledge they bring to bear on a particular situation. These systems can also capture that knowledge for future use. Here are examples of how these three types of IT systems can improve knowledge retention.

Technologies That Improve Collaboration

There is a vast universe of software products today that claim to help people collaborate more effectively. One analyst group estimates that more than 1,000 vendors are now selling so-called "collaborative technologies," including the "Big 3"—Microsoft, IBM, and Oracle. Unfortunately, IT marketers have used the concept of "collaboration" so broadly that it has become meaningless as a way of identifying a specific set of technology-supported activities.

Thus, your organization will have to define specifically what improved collaboration would look like if transferring knowledge is the primary concern, as opposed to increasing innovation, for example. (Of course, almost every executive wants to increase the rate of innovation, but if you are bleeding critical knowledge in certain areas, it's necessary to set more realistic expectations for the moment just to maintain performance levels.) One way to identify the particular collaboration behaviors needed is to ask: If this group was collaborating ideally effectively so knowledge was being transferred to less experienced employees, what would be happening? How would we know that critical knowledge was being retained by the organization?

One answer to these questions might be that more and less experienced members of specific communities would be able to find each other and communicate easily to share essential knowledge. And the knowledge exchanged would also be captured for future use. It is likely that members of these communities would be distributed geographically, so they need an IT infrastructure that makes this intense collaboration possible.

This was the challenge faced by leaders in the U.S. Navy who wanted to accelerate knowledge transfer from senior program managers to less experienced colleagues in the acquisitions community. Veteran program managers in the U.S. Department of Defense acquisition workforce spend billions of dollars annually on everything from stationary to the next generation of weapons systems. Not only do these acquisition experts recommend what systems or equipment to buy, but they also define specific characteristics in terms of cost, delivery timing, and choice of vendors. Most of this knowledge is acquired through years of experience in the procurement business. Unfortunately, with more than 50 percent of the Department of Defense civilian workforce eligible to retire by 2005, most of these veteran program managers will start leaving soon, taking with them decades of experiential knowledge in a field where the wrong decision can cost the military millions of dollars. And, remember, when lost knowledge costs your government money, those are also your tax dollars going down the drain.

To speed up the transfer of this valuable knowledge to younger program managers, the U.S. Navy created an online community of practice (CoP) for its program managers and their acquisition teams. The community relies on a simple technology platform that serves as the online "home" for a network that has grown to more than 3,000 active members. The Navy chose an application called Tomoye Simplify as the Web-based platform that acquisition personnel would use to participate in the program management CoP. Using a Web-browser, the technology lets community members find experts, share and access knowledge using simple fill-in forms, and have conversations with peers on topics ranging from contract and risk management to systems engineering and budgeting. The Navy's initial CoP effort proved so successful that it has been moved into the Defense Acquisition University where it has been renamed and expanded to serve a broader community of acquisition program managers in the U.S. Department of Defense. Additional communities have also been created to support knowledge transfer among other parts of DOD's 150,000-member acquisitions and logistics workforce.[3]

There are, of course, dozens of IT-driven applications that can enhance communications between employees—e-mail, instant messaging, electronic whiteboards, Web conferencing, to name a few. But increased communication does not necessarily mean that critical knowledge is being shared in ways that improve knowledge retention and organizational effectiveness. In fact, communication overload can actually create tremendous distractions for employees making it more difficult to accelerate the acquisition of critical knowledge. Collaborative technologies can certainly add value in organizations, and they will no doubt play an important role in transferring knowledge across generations of workers. But where knowledge retention is a primary concern be cautious that this broad array of new communication and content management options doesn't overwhelm your IT budget. Nor should these technologies be allowed to distract senior management from its focus on strategic objectives and its role in leading the behavioral changes that are truly essential for meaningful knowledge sharing and collaboration.

E-Learning Applications

When it comes to management development and technical training, many organizations today find themselves with executive development programs that still rely on offsite classroom sessions and intermittent meetings with mentors, which make it difficult for managers to tie learning to their daily activities. In addition, the growing number of lower-level technical training programs in many firms are costly to develop and administer, and employees are reluctant to take time out to attend. And, in some cases, critical knowledge about certain relatively routine technical tasks has become concentrated among a few veteran employees.

While these conditions may not have been so troubling in the past, they are becoming very problematic with the expected turnover among experienced managers and technical experts in the years ahead. That's because current technical training and management development programs cannot transfer knowledge fast enough to the next generation of employees. This is one reason why e-learning applications, which use Internet-based technologies to support either synchronous or asynchronous learning, have exploded in recent years. Despite the implementation challenges, e-learning offers many advantages over traditional forms of work-centered training and education. Here are three ways organizations are applying e-learning applications to reduce the impacts of lost knowledge due to employee turnover.

Executive Education: U.S. Navy's FLAG University

Every year the U.S. Navy promotes 50 to 70 men and women into its executive ranks, in both military and civilian roles. These new senior officers suddenly find themselves with a set of complex responsibilities for strategy, budgets, and resource allocation. To help its 600 top leaders acquire the skills and knowledge needed to handle each new assignment, the Navy has created a specialized executive development program known as FLAG University.[4]

But instead of just providing a series of classroom experiences, the Navy is using a Web-based IT system to help provide a structured continuum of learning experiences and events that are offered to each executive given their current career path. Every Navy senior officer has their own secure Web page where they maintain a personalized senior leader learning plan. Ultimately, the system will allow executives to conduct confidential self-assessments to identify improvement needs for their current and future positions. The customized self-assessments are scored against a database of knowledge, skills, and abilities developed for every executive position in the Navy.

For example, a rear admiral who has assumed command of an organization responsible for managing a major procurement initiative can go to his or her secure personal Web page and take a self-assessment for the new position. In conducting this exercise, the officer might discover he or she needs increased knowledge about how defense contractors determine pricing structures. The system then helps the officer search for an appropriate learning experience, which may be an online course offered by a vendor, a residential program at a university, or a connection to a recognized expert on the subject.

At the executive level, the Navy recognizes that the technology is not effectively used as a training vehicle itself. Instead, the power of e-learning technologies is in self-assessment, connecting people, and providing access to specialized educational resources to help create a "customized" development program for each senior officer and civilian executive. A Navy learning officer explained that the goal of the program is to surround the Navy's leaders with learning opportunities that are relevant, current, and consistent, throughout their FLAG career.[5] Where executive talent needs to be developed quickly in an increasingly complex environment, e-learning applications can support more efficient, targeted diagnoses that knowledge leaders most need and help manage an evolving inventory of learning experiences.

Speeding Time-to-Competency in Vulnerable Technical Areas

Employee turnover as well as organizational growth are creating an increased need to rapidly develop technical skills in a new generation of employees. But organizations are also looking for ways to contain training costs, even as they are forced to speed up learning processes. This scenario makes e-learning applications an attractive solution.

NASA has seen a serious problem developing in its workforce for several years. Leaders at the U.S. space agency know that many of their most experienced engineers and scientists will be retirement eligible in the next few years. To complicate matters, enrollment in aerospace engineering graduate programs dropped off more than 15 percent in the 1990s. This has put serious pressure on the need to transfer knowledge to younger employees, as well as on recruiting new workers from a shrinking pool of recent graduates.

One part of NASA's response to the problem is an e-learning initiative designed to help develop the skills of current aerospace workers and to encourage others to enter the field. NASA is using an e-learning program created by the Florida Space Research Institute, which offers about 50 self-paced lessons on subjects such as logic circuits, instrument calibration procedures, propulsion systems, hydrogen cryogenics, and the history of rocketry.

About 1,400 people participated in the Advanced Learning Environment program when it was first offered in 2002 with a mission to educate a large number of current and future aerospace workers, while keeping costs low. No one is pretending that an e-learning system can solve all of NASA's knowledge retention problems, but it can help. "The whole purpose of this system was to make sure there is a transfer of knowledge," said one executive involved with design of the e-learning system.[6]

The utilities industry in the United States is facing similar shortages of experienced technicians in the years ahead. To address this issue, a group of power companies, associations, and unions formed a partnership to develop education programs to train the industry's current and future workforce. But because of rotating shifts and travel schedules, it is difficult for utility workers to attend traditional classes. Thus, the Energy Providers Coalition for Education (EPCE) in collaboration with Bismarck State College, created an online associates degree in electronic power technology, as well as two certificate programs. EPCE has created similar online programs for the nuclear power industry. Coalition members contributed their content expertise to ensure that courses in the e-learning programs are comprehensive and relevant in the current work environment. Students can access their course materials online 24 hours a day, 7 days a week. They submit assignments to an instructor by e-mail and exams are conducted online. Courses cover the basics of electrical systems, safety, industrial communications, applied math, and computers.

Learning from Expert Systems

For at least two decades a dauntless group of IT experts have been touting the potential for embedding human expertise into computer systems to improve productivity. Not surprisingly, this has proved incredibly difficult to do for most skilled work, and there are plenty of examples of failed expert systems. For example, Nynex, the regional telephone company that later became part of Verizon, spent tens of millions of dollars building a system that would store the knowledge of the company's most valuable experts. Unfortunately, the system was a bust because it could not replicate the problem-solving processes used by the experts, which is what made them such valuable employees in the first place.[7]

With retirements looming, however, a fear of losing critical technical expertise could create a new impetus for applying IT to make it unnecessary for successors to acquire the same level of knowledge. Instead, most of the knowledge will be embedded in the technology.

One example of where this has worked comes from DebTech, the R&D technology division of the De Beers Group, the largest diamond mining company in the world. DebTech incorporated the expertise of its most experienced machine technicians into an expert system database. The system uses ClickFix, a Web-based diagnostic and predictive maintenance tool, to help less experienced mining machinery technicians diagnose problems, conduct recommended tests, and determine appropriate actions. By retaining expert maintenance knowledge, the database, whose instructions are changed continually based on lessons from the field, reduces downtime due to faulty diagnoses of machinery problems or inadequate repair procedures.

As with any initiative that attempts to systematize what has historically been human expertise, there were implementation issues. The DebTech team found that the maintenance experts sometimes had contradictory opinions on the best diagnostic processes to use, and these conflicts had to be resolved. Diagnostic procedures also had to be modified when they proved unfeasible in practice. And, of course, younger technicians had to be convinced that there was value in using the codified knowledge of more experienced technicians.[8]

E-learning technologies and the methodologies for implementing them are evolving rapidly. Still, there are limitations to the types and complexity of knowledge that can be effectively transferred through an online medium. And many barriers remain to designing and managing effective online learning experiences. But e-learning also provides important advantages for knowledge retention, not the least of which is the ability of the technology to validate that knowledge has actually been transferred. E-learning systems can measure what learning has occurred and where gaps remain in certain types of employees' knowledge. These measures can be valuable in a budget conscious era, if they are evaluating knowledge transfer that really matters to the organization. Ultimately, when management must increase the amount of training and its accessibility in order to educate a new generation of skilled workers, while also containing costs, a compelling case can be made for exploring e-learning options.

IT Support for Problem Solving

One other type of IT application that can accelerate learning is software that provides direct support for thinking and problem solving in teams. One refinery for a large global metals producer used a production process that relied on highly lethal chemicals. The plant's general manager realized he faced a major knowledge retention problem when it became apparent that his senior operating superintendent, who had begun working at the refinery when it was being built 27 years ago, was due to retire. In addition, 60 percent of the refinery's staff had 25 to 30 years of experience in the plant, while many of the remaining employees had worked there two years or less. Thus, there was an urgent need to transfer the knowledge of veterans to less experienced employees. The risk of losing critical operations knowledge in a production process using lethal chemicals posed a huge safety concern for plant management. Even if an accident resulted in no injuries, there were significant implications for the environment and the community.

Initially, the general manager planned to hire a journalism student to engage the retiring superintendent in discussions around problems with specific pieces of equipment and processes where he had unique experiential knowledge. But in conversations with several consultants, the manager realized that, even if the veteran superintendent remembered how he had solved a specific problem years ago, the chances of all the necessary variables lining up again in such a complex production process were very slim. Thus, the general manager became convinced that he needed some other way to capture the more tacit problem-solving processes used by his veteran employees.

The problem became even more pressing when the refinery experienced major quality problems after a recently rebuilt processing tank came back on stream. As a result, the company lost millions of dollars in revenues when it was unable to fill orders for long-standing customers and temporarily had to sell some of its product at a lower cost. Management was very concerned because the refinery's other tank had to be rebuilt within a year. A similar quality upset had occurred 15 years previously, the last time the tanks had been rebuilt. Operators needed to determine the root cause of the problem quickly and retain that knowledge for future overhauls.

Refinery Uses Question-Based Reasoning Software

To find a solution, the plant manager brought together everyone involved with maintaining and operating the equipment. The group used a new type of question-based reasoning software from PHRED Solutions, a Colorado software company. The intranet-based application is designed to help make explicit the reasoning of team members when solving problems. In the process, the system also helps share and retain the tacit knowledge developed during these problem-solving sessions.

By working through PHRED's guided problem-solving model, the refinery staff was able to analyze what they had done and what had happened when the first tank was rebuilt. They discovered the root cause of the tank malfunction was that the glue used in certain seams in the tank liner was creating quality problems that could not be identified during sampling tests. "You don't want to trust people's memory on a huge problem like this, and you need to be confident you got to the base cause," said the refinery's general manager when explaining his decision to use the software. The resulting solution proved itself when the plant's other tank was rebuilt and returned to service without incident.

The refinery subsequently used the PHRED application to make explicit the reasoning skills of its most experienced operators in solving more routine problems on the plant floor. Working with the question-based reasoning software, shift teams met and began thinking through the types of operating problems they ran into regularly. Problems included:

"A pump won't transfer the slurry."
"We're getting a high level in the tank and can't control it."
"Why is reactor filter life reduced?"

The software guided the shift teams through these problems, asking them to state the problem, analyze its impact, design a temporary fix or determine the root cause, and define a more permanent solution.

The most significant benefit of the process was the new dynamics that became evident in the way team members interacted when responding to the questions while one team member typed answers into the system. One of the group leaders in the plant noted, "It turned out the experienced people were very willing to share and the younger employees were amazed at what they didn't know. So information was being passed on through a dialogue process that doesn't occur on a daily basis. But we also wanted to document it so people who are not around can benefit from the knowledge."

The refinery's general manager was even more surprised by the impact of the technology-supported sessions. He said:

I had always assumed people were withholding knowledge, but in reality they just didn't have a forum to share it. The senior operators never had a way of sitting down with the younger guys and transferring what they know. But the software gives them a reason to sit down as a group, and it's not a finger-pointing exercise. It's a pure learning experience. They can say, "Here's what came up, and here's why we dealt with it like that." We're just starting on this, but I'm hugely encouraged. I think we've found the mother lode in terms of how to transfer knowledge.

NASA's Technical Questions Database

While the refinery used question-based reasoning software to facilitate knowledge transfer between older and younger workers, the U.S. space agency has taken a different approach to leverage the knowledge of its shrinking pool of technical experts. With NASA veterans retiring and other experienced employees leaving for Internet companies in the 1990s, management at the Jet Propulsion Laboratory found it increasingly difficult to locate experienced engineers who could conduct the performance reviews that had to occur during each project's lifecycle. The proliferation of projects combined with the loss of expertise meant senior people were stretched very thin. As a result, both design and operations suffered.

For example, when reviewing one of several space programs that failed in 1999, JPL's director of flight safety blamed a lack of expertise in design oversight for the loss of the space probe. He said, "My investigation found a very simple, straightforward fault. It was a fragile design, one that clearly violated an obvious [design] principle. If we had had some of our more experienced individuals on the job—individuals who had done this kind of work before—I guarantee the flawed design would not have gotten through; they would not have approved it."[9]

To address this shortage of expertise, JPL implemented a "Technical Questions Database" to leverage the knowledge of the lab's best engineers and managers. To build the database, the lab's technical experts, which included electronics, test, and optical engineers and software designers, were asked to provide the key technical questions that they might ask during project development or in a formal review meeting. These questions, which are organized by technical discipline areas, are intended to identify problems that could occur on NASA flight projects. With the database, even if JPL doesn't have people with enough experience to know what questions to ask during reviews, at least the questions are brought up by the team itself. The database, which is continually updated with new expert input, is intended to act as a "mind tickler," raising issues that designers, program managers, and review board members should be considering. NASA's Jeanne Holm explained, "The worst thing is getting into reviews and getting torn apart. With this database, a new project engineer now can say, 'In order to get ready for this review, I need to be able to answer these questions.' So teams are better prepared and at least they have thought through the things our most senior people would have asked."

Capturing Knowledge

Managers realize that most critical knowledge resides in the heads of individual employees. But the fact is that with the incredible complexity of business, government, and nonprofit operations today a great deal of essential knowledge is now being captured in documents or other physical and electronic artifacts. For example, documents may provide details of new product development efforts, where hazardous chemicals are stored, the history of an aircraft maintenance problem, or plant drawings for a nuclear facility. Academics may argue about what's in these documents. Is it really knowledge, or just information? But from management's perspective, who cares? As they say in Boston, this stuff is "wicked important," and you damn well better not lose it.

The problem is that this growing collection of mission-critical documents is often spread throughout the organization, and frequently stored in individual or departmental file drawers or on electronic hard drives. Not only is access to this knowledge limited by its location but the number of people who actually know the location is also likely to be restricted. And a lot of the people with the most knowledge about the content and location of these critical documents are probably leaving their organizations in the next few years.

There are three types of IT applications that can be particularly valuable in helping to retain access to these burgeoning types of structured knowledge, or critical intellectual capital that can be realistically stored that way: (1) Web-based searchable repositories; (2) databases of compelling lessons learned; (3) electronic documentation of high end knowledge work tasks. The major difference between these applications is the degree of behavioral changes required of employees in order for the organization to get value from the system. Here are examples of each of these types of systems that were implemented to support knowledge retention.

Web-based Repositories

Technologies supporting enterprise-wide content management systems have exploded in recent years with many firms, such as Autonomy, OpenText, Documentum, and Xerox, offering a broad range of integrated document and information management and retrieval capabilities. The systems now available provide many functions, one of which is knowledge retention. A global chemical company offers one example of how these systems can help.

At Dow Chemical, research scientists used to have to wait five to seven days for the firm's Business Intelligence Center to manually locate lab reports, product tests, and other proprietary research documents stored in offsite warehouses. In addition, time was taking a toll on certain mission-critical documents that had words and images literally fading off the page. In some cases, only one hard copy of these key research documents existed, creating a serious risk of knowledge loss. In addition, several mergers and acquisitions had generated huge new volumes of research documents describing technology breakthroughs and product development that Dow scientists were eager to study. If these materials were inaccessible, scientists were likely to undertake research to create knowledge that already existed in the company. So the problem was how to create a single global knowledge base that would allow scientists to locate and retrieve key documents quickly.

Dow called on Xerox to help it create a Web-based searchable repository for research dating back to the 1930s. Xerox specialists scanned and enhanced the image quality of deteriorating documents, transforming them into searchable PDF files. Today, 5.5 million pages of critical documents, including early patented research, are stored in a secure structured database accessible to more than 3,200 Dow scientists and research partners around the world. Since implementing the enterprise-wide content management system, access to Dow's research documentation has quadrupled, and the chances of duplicating existing research are all but eliminated. In addition, the firm has derived significant cost and time savings, since it no longer maintains 30 different paper collections, with their inherent duplication, at three different sites. Nor does it suffer the costs of manual document retrieval, filing, and copying tasks. But, most important, the system preserves knowledge and intellectual assets that are essential in supporting Dow's future business.[10]

In another example, Kellogg Brown & Root (KBR) designs, builds, and maintains offshore oil and gas production platforms. These complex projects produce scores of technical and engineering design documents that must remain instantly accessible to employees on the platform to enable proper maintenance and repairs. But once a platform was built, it could take 10 people up to two years to locate, assemble, and translate all design documents into operating manuals for the offshore crews. And if documents were not immediately available when problems arose, platform operations could be jeopardized until the necessary manual was located.

KBR now deploys a system provided by Documentum with most new projects the company undertakes. The sophisticated document database captures all technical documents in a standardized electronic format. Even more important, it maintains records of changes and an accurate history that meets design, regulatory, and insurance requirements. The system allows platform operators to quickly access just the current technical documents they need in response to questions or problems, and it ensures management that they are always working with the most timely and up-to-date information. Like the system at Dow, the Documentum database has produced tremendous cost savings for KBR, virtually eliminating the costs of retrieval, transfer, and the communication of critical documents from design to operations. But, equally important, the knowledge embedded in the latest design documents remains accurate and accessible for future platform operations.

It's one thing to save knowledge to support future business research and operations, but IT can also preserve documents that could impact public safety for decades. The Office of Civilian Radioactive Waste Management (OCRWM) in the U.S. Department of Energy has faced this problem. The office was created in the early 1980s to implement federal policies for permanent disposal of high-level radioactive waste and spent nuclear fuel in order to protect public health and the environment.

Over time, OCRWM developed vast legacy databases, including archived geographical records and information collected over time from various agencies. As a result, too much time was being spent by employees manually cataloging and searching for critical information. With staff in this DOE office inevitably retiring or leaving for other jobs, the human knowledge about the content of these databases was also being lost. To address these problems, OCRWM has deployed Autonomy's easy-to-use infrastructure technology, which improves access to information from the legacy databases. The Office of Civilian Radioactive Waste Management is also using Autonomy's profiling technology to help more than 2,000 users across the United States identify and connect with colleagues who have relevant expertise. The example of OCRWM shows how technologies supporting knowledge retention will almost always be used in combination to support different activities related to finding, preserving, and accessing intellectual capital. Web-based repositories hold a lot of promise for helping to retain explicit document-based knowledge, but remember this is still a relatively small part of your organization's overall knowledge base.

Lessons Learned Databases

Lessons learned repositories have come under a lot of criticism in recent years, much of it justified because these collections of text-based knowledge often go unused. In some cases, however, where historical knowledge is critical to diagnosing current-day problems, these databases can really pay off. For example, a business unit of Northrop Grumman's Integrated Systems sector has created central repositories to collect and share lessons learned around the implementation of particular aircraft technologies. This way engineers who were not involved in the original project can access highly relevant historical knowledge about specific aircraft parts. For example, the company's F/A-18 attack/fighter jet program (which Northrop Grumman works on as Boeing's principal subcontractor) has a Web-based system that captures years of technical knowledge about structural problems with the aircraft. Thus, if an issue surfaces with a cracked part, for example, an engineer first checks the system for knowledge gained from previous incidents that could be relevant. Engineers can also add information to the system using a Power Point template that can include pictures, drawing, and notes to explain actions they took to address a problem.

It is important to note that the F/A-18 problem tracking system is kept up to date because it has been integrated into daily work activities. Engineers meet weekly to discuss unresolved problems. But before discussing a new issue, an engineer must input information about the problem into the database. Once resolved, the outcome of the problem is recorded and the experience is captured as a lesson learned.[11]

There is a major difference between the F/A-18 database and the document management systems described in the previous section. The systems at Dow Chemical and KBR did not require significant behavioral changes to capture the documents. But the F/A-18 lessons learned database requires ongoing active participation for engineers who must input their experiential knowledge into the system. This can represent considerable behavioral changes for employees, who may resist at first.

Lessons learned repositories have been a popular knowledge management "solution" for years. But, like expert systems they have proved very difficult to maintain over time. Current employees often do not see any benefit for themselves in contributing what they have learned. And their successors don't feel compelled to access the system, either because it is too difficult to use, or the knowledge available is viewed as obsolete.

From a knowledge retention perspective, however, there is a subset of these lessons learned databases that are likely to be worth the effort. These are systems that capture compelling knowledge that future employees will definitely view as essential to their effectiveness. This would include databases providing maintenance records about complex or high-risk technologies, such as the F/A-18, or systems that capture lessons learned from performing dangerous or expensive tasks done infrequently, such as disarming nuclear weapons. In these contexts, employees are more likely to appreciate the value of maintaining lessons learned systems over time. And it is worth top management's extra effort to make certain the behaviors necessary to capture critical knowledge are sustained.

Electronic Documentation of Knowledge-Intensive Tasks

There is one other IT application that can help retain access to intellectual capital that can be stored electronically. In some organizations, management knows exactly where its most critical knowledge assets are located, but they are often inaccessible and subject to the whims of individual experts. This knowledge might be in the heads of a handful of top salespeople, or in a special group of engineers, or in the lab notebooks of leading R&D scientists. Historically, this knowledge has resided with individual employees and left when they did. But as leaders increasingly recognize the value of these intellectual assets, finding ways to retain them becomes more compelling. Sometimes part of the answer will include IT applications that can capture knowledge as it is developed in practice.

For example, Berlex Laboratories is a biopharmaceutical company that recognized its most important intellectual assets resided with its research scientists. And, as in most life sciences firms, much of this knowledge was kept in handwritten laboratory notebooks, which were very difficult to search and share. If a Berlex scientist or patent lawyer needed to access someone else's research, first the notebook had to be located and then often illegible handwriting had to be decoded. Finding research results that were several years old or stored in another country was even more difficult. Berlex management knew that the loss or inaccessibility of this research knowledge was hurting the company's performance.

To address the problem, the company worked with Documentum to create a system that enabled Berlex scientists in R&D facilities around the world to record their research using familiar Microsoft Word and Microsoft Excel interfaces. The research notes from scientists in each lab are replicated on a central server in Berlin every night, so they are available to other Berlex employees searching for related materials. Today the system has completely replaced paper laboratory notebooks in the company's major R&D sites. Some 800 scientists in the United States, Germany, and Japan use the electronic notebook system, which makes it easier for them to capture their own research results, access research of colleagues, and collaborate on current projects.

Of course, the system also provides longer term protection against lost knowledge. "Knowledge contained in paper notebooks becomes less valuable after it goes into storage because few know what information resides where, and too often the only one who can read it is the one who wrote it," said one Berlex information manager. "Knowledge that can be easily accessed and understood, however, retains its value much, much longer."[12]

Capturing knowledge developed in practice by specialized professionals and experts has always been very difficult. As the value of retaining this knowledge becomes increasingly evident, however, management's appetite for IT systems supporting applications such as electronic notebooks will grow. But the behavioral changes required to work with this type of system are substantial. Managers often underestimate the difficulties involved in changing the behaviors of high end knowledge workers to share their knowledge. Any attempt to capture what your most valuable employees are learning requires a budget for change management that is almost never big enough. Success stories like Berlex will become more common, but they won't happen easily.

Mapping Human Knowledge

Knowledge retention, as defined in chapter 1, includes the acquisition, storage, and access to intellectual assets. The IT applications described in this chapter so far all support activities related to these tasks. But managers often can't invest in improving the retention of knowledge unless they know where it is actually located in their organization. That's why IT can play an important role in mapping human knowledge. There is a danger, however, that knowledge mapping can become an overly technical exercise, obsessed with taxonomies, classifications, and local details.[13] One example can be when knowledge mapping is used to locate and categorize documents that contain only explicit knowledge or information. There can be value in this exercise, but when the problem is identifying critical knowledge to retain there are other forms of mapping that may be more useful. Ironically, the two examples described here are not generally thought of as knowledge mapping, but that is a major benefit they provide.

Mapping Skills and Competencies

Shell Chemical's global technical skills resource management process was described in chapter 4 as an example of a human resources initiative that gives the company an overview of its skills inventory. This global process enables Shell to proactively manage its skill base so that employees are adequately trained to fill new positions. It also makes sure the company is not caught short in specialized skill areas, such as manufacturing control engineers or senior process engineers, when more experienced employees retire. To support its new process Shell had to build a database that could track technical skills across its international sites. The database is a key tool that enables skills resource managers to continually analyze the overall health of their skill families, such as process or project engineers.

In essence, the database gives Shell Chemical executives a map of the company's current distribution of technical competencies so they can make more effective strategic human resource decisions and, in the process, identify any emerging gaps in critical knowledge areas.

Building a global database like this proved to be much more challenging than building a database to serve a more centralized employee population. Developers, for example, discovered that job titles were different in different countries or had different meanings. For example, in Shell's U.S. operations, "engineer" is a professional title. But in some parts of Europe, it is more of a para-professional title, not implying a four-year degree. What U.S. managers call an "engineer" tends more to be called a "technologist" in The Nether-lands. The emotional and cultural barriers to finding common job titles, which reflect similar knowledge, can be huge. And dealing with these prob-lems in a database can require significant compromises, so the actual knowl-edge reflected in the local terminology is not lost.

Northrop Grumman's Integrated Systems sector relies on an IT system to provide a similar map of skills in the organization. Ironically, the original purpose of this IT application was quite different. X-Ref started as an expert locator system created in 1997 when Northrop Grumman's B-2 bomber pro-gram was scaling back. It provides detailed employee profiles listing experi-ences and skills. Initially, the system was intended to provide cross-references between people and parts used in the bomber. For example, if there was a problem with an environmental control valve in a few years, Northrop Grumman employees could use the system to find out who the original engineers were who worked on the part. Individuals' profiles re-main on the system even after they leave the company.

Today, X-Ref has 100 percent penetration within the engineering and production functions across Northrop Grumman's Integrated Systems. The 14,000 profiles in the system detail the specific experience and skills of em-ployees ranging from vice presidents to mechanics. As a result, the system has also become an essential staffing tool for program managers who are trying to find the most qualified people for new projects. Discipline manag-ers, who are responsible for all hiring, firing, and movement within their specific engineering discipline, use X-Ref to track talent within their disci-pline and to help develop talent and plan career paths for Northrop Grum-man's engineers. Thus, this homegrown system is an example of an IT appli-cation that provides multiple benefits that support knowledge retention. First, it enables one-on-one social connections needed to keep critical knowl-edge about Northrop Grumman programs accessible to less experienced em-ployees. Second, it gives management a competency map of the organization so they can identify employees who are best qualified to staff new programs. Finally, it helps discipline managers work with key employees to make better career development decisions, increasing the chances of retaining skilled en-gineers.

Who Talks to Whom? Mapping Collaborative Relationships

Improving knowledge retention also means identifying strategically important informal networks in an organization, which reflect its social capital.
This is the tacit knowledge embedded in relationships that is evident in high
levels of trust and the ability to collaborate effectively. It is these networks of
relationships that are essential for the communication and collaboration
needed to transfer knowledge from experts to less experienced colleagues.
(Often these informal networks are also described as communities of practice
when they consist of people performing similar tasks or dealing with similar
problems in their work.) Even if executives recognize intuitively that critical
knowledge could be at risk, they often do not know which employees have
the expertise that others depend on. But it's impossible to implement an effective retention strategy without first identifying and diagnosing the characteristics of these strategically important informal networks.

A new class of software that produces social network diagrams has
made the task of social network analysis (SNA) much more practical.[14] Tools
such as InFlow and UCI NET now make it possible to make visible the normally invisible patterns of social interaction that underlie most significant
knowledge transfer (see figure 10.2).[15] Here are some examples.

One large international pharmaceutical company had gone through a series of mergers and its R&D scientists were not collaborating effectively. The
researchers worked in five labs spread across three countries. In the reorga-
nized company, executives wanted to know who the key scientists were and
who they were working with. Leaders engaged a consulting firm to conduct
a diagnosis using the social network analysis software InFlow, which was
used to collect data from the scientists about who they went to for ideas or
help with work-related problems. In the immunology area, the diagnostic
revealed ten scientists who together held most of the organization's critical
knowledge related to future drug development. Not surprisingly, all of these
key scientists that others in the organization relied on, according to the analysis, were older and had lots of inventions to their credit. Losing them would
be a disaster for the company.

The biggest concern revealed by the SNA analysis was that the veteran
immunologists were not collaborating with each other. Instead, they were
talking most frequently with academic colleagues outside the firm at nearby
universities. Using the InFlow tool to diagnose patterns of interaction among
the company's most valued R&D employees focused management attention
on doing everything they could to retain those researchers identified as invaluable experts. And, equally important, an initiative was launched to help
build an internal community of practice among the company's immunologists to improve collaboration. The network analysis created a clear picture

of who the key players were that needed to be encouraged to participate in the new community.

The central Information Technology and Telecommunications Services group for the Canadian government, which has about 1,600 full-time staff, provides another example of using an SNA tool where knowledge retention and succession planning are major concerns. This unit, which includes hardware, software, and telecommunications experts, provides technology services for government agencies. Like most federal agencies in Canada, the IT group has an aging workforce and is going to lose considerable leadership and technical expertise in the next few years. For example, they expect to lose 40 percent of their senior managers within five years. HR planners wanted to identify what technical skills the organization would need to retain or develop in order to achieve its five-year strategic objectives.

As a first step in developing a succession plan, they used a software tool called Knetmap to identify who were the "go to" subject matter experts for specific skills and which of those people were likely to be leaving. Knetmap uses a series of e-mail queries sent simultaneously to hundreds of the unit's employees to generate a set of relational maps showing who individuals rely on when they need help with particular types of problems. This knowledge mapping exercise put the organization in a good position to begin developing succession plans and knowledge transfer activities for key leadership and technical roles. However, the process of making knowledge networks visible also revealed some barriers to diagnosing threats of lost knowledge. It turns out that organizations have very different degrees of tolerance for making their networks of practical expertise visible. Some groups welcome the explicit mapping of social relationships to diagnose levels of trust and power, and the distribution of knowledge. But others are highly reluctant to reveal these relationships and require all names to be disguised or left off social network diagrams. In bureaucracies an overriding concern can be fear of embarrassment or the revelation that an individual who is supposed to be knowledgeable is actually ignored or marginalized by colleagues. There can also be concern for the privacy rights of the individual, which is now an embedded ethic in many government institutions.

As organizations become more concerned about the threat of lost knowledge due to turnover, using software to map social networks will be an increasingly attractive diagnostic step. To be sure, developing diagrams of social networks will remain unacceptable in certain organizations. But for those able to deal with the emotional and political fallout of making visible the individuals who are most valued because of their practical knowledge, there can be significant benefits. Mapping social networks helps focus executive attention on the informal networks critical to organizational success. Thus, management can create appropriate interventions to improve knowledge sharing and retention. Initiatives can also improve the quality of informal networks, which contain personal relationships that are a major source of employee job satisfaction. This is likely to increase employee loyalty and retention of key talent.[16]

Conclusion

One environmental, health, and safety director visited his organization's IT department just before the building they were in was demolished to make way for new offices. In the department he found rows and rows of old 18-inch IBM computer tapes. But the organization no longer had technology capable of accessing this data. The director grabbed an old tape as a reminder of this irony. "Now anytime I go to an IT meeting to talk about document capture or content management, I just bring that IBM tape with me and put it on the table," he said. "My message is clear. Focus on the process and the people, not the technology. And keep the technology simple and scalable, so we can always move the documents to a new platform if necessary."

Information technology clearly can help organizations transfer and retain knowledge. But, in practice, few IT applications will be implemented primarily to retain knowledge. Performance objectives are likely to be stated in more creative terms, such as to improve overall knowledge sharing, collaboration, or innovation. Nevertheless, if your organization needs to be concerned about knowledge retention, then management should begin to evaluate existing and planned IT systems to see if they support or undermine your retention needs.

When assessing whether any particular software is going to meet your specific needs for retaining knowledge, as described in this chapter, there are two questions you should ask every vendor. The first, or course, is "Who's buying lunch?" The second one is "Who do I contact at your reference accounts to learn more about how they are getting value from this IT application?" Whether it's expert locators, e-learning, or document management systems, there is a tremendous amount of change occurring in the underlying technologies that can support knowledge retention. But the cost of continuing to lose critical knowledge while some vendor works out the bugs in their software is too great. You don't have time to be somebody else's beta test site.

Look for opportunities to apply IT, but always be skeptical. You can count on the fact that it will be harder than it looks to get the results you hope for. This is especially true if you are asking employees to change their behaviors in order to use the technology. The more behavioral change required, the riskier the investment. Problems of managing these changes will be addressed in chapter 11, but first there is the problem of dealing with critical knowledge that has left your organization. That is the subject of the next chapter.

8

After the Knowledge Is Gone

There's a story that has circulated on the Internet that tells about an engineer who had an exceptional gift for fixing things mechanical. After serving his company loyally for over 30 years, he happily retired. Several years later, the company contacted him regarding a seemingly impossible problem they were having with one of their million-dollar machines. They had tried everything but no one could get the machine to work. Finally, in desperation, they called on the retired engineer who had solved so many of their problems in the past. The engineer reluctantly took the challenge and spent a day studying the huge machine. At the end of the day, he marked a small "x" in chalk on a particular component of the machine and stated, "This is where your problem is." The part was replaced and the machine worked perfectly again.

Soon afterward the company received a bill for $50,000 from the engineer for his services. When they demanded an itemized accounting of his charges, the engineer responded briefly:

One chalk mark $1.
Knowing where to put it $49,999.

If this story made you laugh, that's probably because you recognize the truth in it. Of course, a tremendous amount of practical knowledge is always leaving organizations. Fortunately, losing a lot of that knowledge does not matter, either because it's relatively obsolete or it's easily replaced. Some knowledge, however, like knowing where to put the chalk mark, is critical to future organizational performance. And it can be worth a lot of money! As we have seen, given current demographic trends, there is going to be a much greater loss of this vital knowledge in organizations that have grown more technologically and structurally complex in the last decade. This chapter describes three strategies managers can use when employees leave the organization with critical intellectual capital (see figure 8.1). Recognizing these alternatives ahead of time and when it is best to use them gives leaders a chance to plan and set up the infrastructure needed to make these solutions effective.

Management has two objectives when employees depart with hard-to-replace knowledge essential to future effectiveness. First, leaders may want

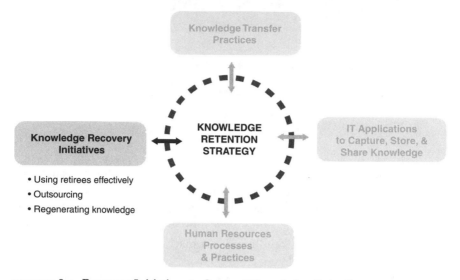

FIGURE 8.1. Recovery Initiatives to Support Knowledge Retention

to keep the experiential knowledge of former employees (e.g., know-how, know-who, know-where) accessible to the organization for use in ongoing operations or special projects, to solve unexpected problems, or to pass on to successors. The solution here means keeping former employees connected to the organization by rehiring them as contractors or consultants.

But when rehiring ex-employees is not a viable solution, then management must decide between outsourcing as a way of replacing diminished competencies or regenerating these capabilities inside the organization. Let's examine these three options and the management considerations involved.

Effectively Utilizing Retirees

One of the most notable HR trends in the workplace today is the increased reliance of organizations on rehiring retired employees as contractors or consultants.[1] An AARP/Society for Human Resource Management study found that 62 percent of the organizations surveyed were currently hiring retired employees as consultants or temporary workers.[2]

Organizations take four different approaches to utilizing retirees: (1) some have strict policies against rehiring them; (2) many more bring retirees back as contractors or consultants only by informal arrangement with individual managers; (3) some have tried to limit the practice of rehiring by implementing policies that dictate in what situations retirees can be brought back into their organizations; and (4) a few, such as Monsanto, MITRE, and Cigna Insurance, have created formal programs to actually encourage the reemployment of retirees. Given the looming shortage of experienced professional and managerial talent in certain areas, it is only a matter of time until more organizations will have to shift to the latter approach. Monsanto's Retirement Resource Corps offers a useful model.

After downsizing extensively in the 1980s, Monsanto's management recognized that too much good talent was leaving the company prematurely. Thus, the company launched its Retirement Resource Corps (RRC), a worker reentry program designed to keep Monsanto lean while also retaining the intellectual resources of many of its veteran employees. Since the early 1990s, the company has used the program to systematically reemploy recent retirees on a per diem basis either to train the next generation of employees or to work on projects especially suited to their talents. "Just because someone is retiring doesn't mean their manager can't keep drawing on their knowledge," said Liz Thien-Reich, the sourcing manager who oversees the program. "The Retirement Resources Corps is a way to have retirees keep coming back in the door."

The RRC is run out of the company's procurement department. Three months after Monsanto employees retire they automatically receive a letter asking if they are interested in returning to work at the company part-time. Six months after formally retiring, former employees can begin working up to 1,000 hours per year. The company currently has a database of 1,000 retirees who have expressed interest in returning part-time. At any given time, 300 of these retirees are back in the company as per diem employees, working on a project basis in R&D, information technology, engineering, or administrative roles. Compensation typically is negotiated between the hiring manager and the retiree.

Some retirees return every year, such as one international tax expert who, in her late 70s, still works several months a year. Another former research lab director, who had taken a retirement package at age 58 but returned soon after, said, "I knew I was coming back part-time. I wasn't ready to retire."

Monsanto benefits financially because these former employees are no longer in the company bonus program, nor do they qualify for company health insurance benefits. But more important, the company retains knowledge. "When retirees come back in the door, there's no training needed. They know the way Monsanto works," said the former lab director. "But when a college grad or a Ph.D. walks into a new job here, you're looking at six months before they become productive."

The experience retirees bring to their new roles can add value in a variety of ways. They know where knowledge is located in the organization. For example, what databases already capture the information needed for a new project? In another case, they might have a good idea of what pitfalls to avoid when designing a new safety program for environment, safety, and health. "Business moves so fast these days that experts returning part-time can tell people what *not* to do, which is really important," said Thien-Reich.

Monsanto's management does not try to measure the business value provided by its reemployed retirees, recognizing any number would be too subjective. Instead, Thien-Reich and her colleagues ensure the Retirement Resource Corps is a "cost neutral" program by calculating a running cost avoidance figure that reflects the difference between the program's administrative and per diem salary costs and fees that would otherwise have to be paid to outside employment agencies. The RRC saves the company more than $600,000 annually, and that is without taking into account the business value of the retirees' knowledge being retained in the process and the motivational benefits for aging workers.

MITRE Corp. offers another example of proactive efforts to retain knowledge by rehiring retirees. MITRE does technical research and development for the U.S. government, including the Department of Defense, the Federal Aviation Administration, and the Internal Revenue Service. The average age of the company's 5,000 employees is about 45, and because of the unique knowledge they acquire management wanted to find ways to encourage MITRE's older workers to stay with the company beyond normal retirement age. One program the firm initiated to help retain access to its experienced workforce is called "Reserves at the Ready." Under the program, workers who have been with MITRE at least 10 years can become part-time, on-call employees who are available to work on projects throughout the company. Keeping veteran employees working part-time for the company allows them to mentor younger staff members and to pass on technical expertise as well as detailed knowledge about the ins and outs of working with MITRE's government clients.[3] When a former employee joins the Reserve program his or her resume is posted on MITRE's internal Web site. Division managers frequently search the site for veterans who can provide specialized skills on new projects. One 68-year-old mechanical engineer, for example, has been asked back three times to work temporarily on military contracts because of his special expertise in analyzing and pricing military equipment.

A growing number of organizations are rehiring retirees part-time, but some also recognize the value of bringing veterans back explicitly as mentors because remaining full-time employees are too busy to mentor their junior colleagues. Sandia Labs and NASA both have formal programs that use retirees as mentors. APPL's program at NASA, which is called Leaders as Teachers and Mentors (LT&M), has tried to build a community of interest among retirees who want to return to teach program management or leadership courses, and pass on their knowledge in other ways, such as mentoring particular project teams. LT&M is attempting to build a core of 100–200 retired managers who can teach and mentor emerging program managers in key competencies such as risk management, safety, and project reviews.

Programs to reengage employees after they retire can be challenging to set up and create new administrative costs, but in an increasingly tight labor market the opportunity to leverage years of experience and expertise, even on a limited basis, is crucial.

Of course, there are a variety of ways to keep retirees, or other "alumni" connected to the organization, and new communication technologies certainly make the task easier. The World Bank, Sandia Labs, and NASA, for example, have built databases to track retirees, what special knowledge they have, and their willingness to work on temporary assignments or to return as mentors in the organization. For example, NASA's Leaders as Teachers and Mentors program has a database that captures a variety of information about retirees who want to stay involved with the Agency. The system includes information about the individual's work experiences at NASA, their specific competencies, their current teaching and mentoring activities, as well as details about their availability and interest in participating in future APPL-sponsored programs.

Using a simpler tactic, Siemens, the German-based multinational electronics and industrial firm, sometimes gives out cell phones to highly valued experts who have recently retired. It seems some retirees like getting calls from former colleagues who have questions only they can answer. The ego gratification of feeling they are missed offsets the inconvenience of the occasional phone call. "Besides when their phone rings during a bowling match with their buddies, it makes them look important because somebody at their old company has a question only they can answer," one manager noted wryly.

Web-based portal technologies have made it much more practical to set up and manage networks of company alumni. In addition to the personal networking benefits provided to former employees, these virtual communities can help keep people connected to their previous employer. There are several potential benefits for the organization of keeping alumni networked. An alumni community can keep ex-employees available for brief questions or temporary assignments, enlist their help with recruiting efforts, or even provide a pool of potential candidates for rehiring.

That's what happened at one national hospital system that has struggled, like most in the industry, with a chronic shortage of experienced nurses. This hospital group used technology from SelectMinds to develop a customized alumni relationship management system. The Web-based application provides easy access to valuable resources for former nurses, including information on credentialing, alumni events, and opportunities for continuing education. In three months the community had more than 3,500 registered users. The hospital system used information collected in the alumni database to launch a targeted recruiting campaign. This led to filling more than 40 critical nursing vacancies with former staffers. Not only were traditional recruiting costs avoided, but also the rehire campaign was directed only at nurses who had been excellent employees in the past, which reduced the hidden costs of poor hires. Most important, however, the organization's VP of human resources noted that nurses rehired with the help of the alumni network were already trained and could confidently take on their new roles, which had an immediate impact on patient care.

When it comes to utilizing ex-employees, whether they are retired or at mid-career, every organization's situation will be somewhat different. But effectively leveraging the critical knowledge and skills of former employees means knowing your options, and the pros and cons of each. Organizations can:

1. *Create a formal program to manage a pool of skilled retirees available for temporary assignments.* These programs, like Monsanto's Retirement Resource Corps, involve more overhead to manage and require formal policies for bringing back retirees, which individual hiring managers may try to skirt.

2. *Proactively track the expertise and availability of former employees for consulting assignments.* With this approach, which is used at the World Bank, the organization does not get involved in matching retirees with managers' needs. The program just provides information about what experts might be available. The rest is up to the hiring manager. This type of program only works if managers are actively oriented to using the database.

3. *Encourage managers to routinely seek ways to stay connected with former employees.* This approach is used at Siemens, but its success depends primarily on the relational skills of individual managers and their recognition of the value that a specific retiree's knowledge has for the organization.

4. *Create the infrastructure to support an alumni community.* In some cases, there will be a large enough group of former employees who have positive feelings for the organization that they would like to be part of an organized alumni community. This is particularly true where employees feel a strong identification with the organization's mission and culture. Alumni networks are a more indirect way of leveraging the knowledge of ex-employees, but they are worth considering as part of a larger set of initiatives to build a retention culture.

5. *Let contracting and consulting agreements with ex-employees remain an informal process handled by individual managers.* This is the way most organizations deal with retirees today. Contracting agreements are based primarily on personal relationships between managers and retirees. This may seem like the most practical approach, but it can also undermine knowledge transfer practices among older employees who know their expertise is their ticket to a comfortable consulting relationship after they retire. When older workers are routinely hired back as contractors they have much less incentive to share their knowledge with others before retiring. "Your knowledge is your security here," said a retired research scientist who had returned as a consultant. "If you didn't still have the knowledge, they wouldn't want you back."

Using retirees as contractors or consultants because they have precious experiential knowledge not available elsewhere is now common practice in many organizations. And this solution will inevitably become more popular as retirement rates increase, in part, because it is the easiest way to avoid the immediate costs of lost knowledge. But rehiring retirees introduces a new set of management challenges that need to be explored as the practice grows. One concern, for example, is how to avoid becoming dependent on the knowledge of part-time contractors. One chemical company executive illustrated the problem when he said, "If an edict went out tomorrow that said, 'No retirees can be used as contractors' that would be quite a challenge for us. It's dangerous to let your business become dependent on people who can just go play golf."

Outsourcing Intellectual Activities

Most outsourcing decisions have historically been a matter of management choice. Leaders outsource single tasks, functions, or entire processes to cut costs or because they believe there is strategic advantage in reallocating their in-house resources. But what if there appears to be no choice? The experts whose knowledge underlies a specific capability may be retiring, and it is impossible or unrealistic to replace them to maintain the same level of performance. Maybe the retirees cannot work enough hours as contractors, or they can't fill the same roles they left, or management can't risk critical operations on part-timers. In this case, outsourcing intellectual activities may no longer be optional.

Of course, companies regularly outsource special capabilities. Oil and mining firms use real estate firms to manage their surface land resources. Some pharmaceutical companies successfully outsource parts of their R&D work. Ford has used ABB to develop new assembly plants at 70 percent less than it would cost in-house. And Royal Dutch Shell is famous for the use of scenarios in its strategic planning process, but they outsource scenario-building activities to outside experts.[4] Executives have begun to recognize that the strategic benefits of outsourcing go beyond short-term cost savings. This is because specialized service firms often can develop greater knowledge, invest more in capability development, learn from a broader set of customer interactions, and hire better trained professionals than organizations who only use the capability on a limited basis.

But just as the siren call of rehiring retirees can seem like an easy and obvious solution, outsourcing has its own set of pitfalls. When knowledge retention is a primary concern, there are five principles to keep in mind before signing an outsourcing contract as a way of sidestepping the organization's need to retain vital knowledge.

1. *Organizational strategy should drive consideration of outsourcing decisions.* Historically the primary driver behind outsourcing has been cost-cutting, particularly in support functions such as IT, HR, finance, and logistics. But, as management has grown more comfortable with giving up control of particular functions or entire business processes, outsourcing has increasingly been seen as a way to create strategic value.[5] The organization's strategy should determine vital knowledge needed to support future goals. When these different capabilities are matched with the list of specific knowledge at risk, a set of possible candidates for outsourcing emerges. For example, one global chemical company believed that designing and building its own chemical plants to the highest industry standards was a core competency. Its current growth strategy required more plants. But an increase in retirements among its most experienced design engineers and the difficulties of finding replacements made this competency a candidate for outsourcing, even though management had always considered it something that had to be done in-house.

   In practice, of course, strategic outsourcing decisions will almost always be made in a context where the threat of lost knowledge is only one factor. Other factors in the decision are likely to be: (1) management's previous experience and orientation to outsourcing; (2) status of the function or process as a core competency or support activity; (3) the political context—that is, the willingness of managers to give up control over the tasks; (4) interdependence of the tasks with other functions; (5) awareness of the costs of maintaining the status quo; and (6) the availability of alternative outsourcing suppliers. Outsourcing decisions are often complicated, but with threats of lost knowledge added to the mix, they can become increasingly complex.

2. *Recognize that turnover puts very different types of knowledge at risk.* In some cases, outsourcing will be the logical way to manage this risk. Managing legacy IT systems maintenance is a good example of this scenario. The loss of your few remaining employees with extensive experience working on older core technology systems can be mitigated by outsourcing these tasks to large organizations that specialize in this type of work. In other situations, outsourcing may be a necessary solution, but it also introduces some serious new management challenges. The chemical company that had traditionally designed and built its own plants found the need to outsource these core tasks to specialized engineering firms created a different set of management issues. The firm had continually built improvements into each new facility based on the lessons learned from its previous projects. But outsourcing would break this internal learning cycle. It also meant the chemical company would have to compromise slightly on plant design and construction, since it was being done by others. Most important, however, was the new management mindset required to support the outsourcing of what had traditionally been viewed by the culture as core competencies. This was a significant barrier to overcome. Nevertheless, engineering service firms existed who could handle the work if the relationship was well-managed.

In other situations, however, the nature of knowledge used may be impossible for outsourcing suppliers to replicate. Managers at Pratt & Whitney recognized this problem in their Liquid Space Propulsion group, which developed new rocket engines for space flight. One particularly difficult area was in engineering analysis work, where the unit could not keep engineers long term without burning them out. Pratt management wanted to reengineer the analysis work because they needed more of it done and done faster. Outsourcing seemed to be one possible solution until they looked closely at how the work was actually done.

A blown rocket engine or fuel pump test is very costly. Equipment test failures require an immediate explanation and alternatives for the demanding government customer. A new engineering analysis is needed overnight and also before the new design is completed. Meanwhile, new software and analysis technology seems to keep coming out faster than engineers can learn to use it. One engineer explained:

> This kind of analysis is so tricky and so unique that if you're not in our business you don't have the necessary experience to be good at it. There are not enough "qualified" resources anywhere, so it is unlikely we'll find them in a non-competitive outsource

company. The engineering process is iterative and requires a daily face-to-face working relationship between the engineers and the analysis people.[6]

It is possible these and other barriers to outsourcing engineering analysis work could be overcome. But this example illustrates a situation that managers in science or technology-intensive business will increasingly face. A growing number of mission-critical tasks will demand fast decision making in areas that require technical knowledge that is continually evolving, as well as strong interpersonal relationships with key stakeholders and experts in mutually dependent domains. Activities such as these are questionable candidates for outsourcing.

The point is managers will inevitably be faced with many scenarios where the risk of losing knowledge makes outsourcing an attractive response. But the challenge is to accurately differentiate these situations, to recognize the types of knowledge required, the degree to which tasks are standardized or ad hoc, the types of interdependencies that exist with other stakeholders, and the need to understand local context and culture to perform effectively. All of these variables should be considered when evaluating an outsourcing option. In the end, certain tasks or processes will lend themselves relatively easily to outsourcing, others will create serious challenges for management, and still others will be virtually impossible to outsource, if current performance levels are to be maintained. Given the organization's overall strategy, management's first task is to make these distinctions.

3. *Evaluate the risks of outsourcing specific knowledge.* At first glance, some capabilities or functions will appear to be good candidates for outsourcing, but sometimes the easy way to avoid knowledge retention problems can turn out to be very costly later on. Outsourcing, for example, has been a very popular strategy for IT functions in many large organizations. And the development of new software applications is one capability that is likely to be delegated to an outside supplier, both because outsourcing development is cheaper and it can be increasingly difficult to hire and retain experienced programmers. But delegating software development to an outside vendor, in part to avoid the hassles of retaining knowledgeable programmers, can overlook other risks for the organization.[7] Effective software development is highly dependent on successful deployment of the new technology. The interactions between people writing code and those implementing the application are usually critical in determining the value ultimately derived from the software. But outsourcing development divorces the two interdependent

activities and potentially wipes out whatever social knowledge exists between the programmers and those deploying the new application. As a result, implementation costs can soar and the overall effectiveness of practical IT innovation can decline.

Management must recognize the nature of knowledge that might be outsourced, as well as the vital knowledge that is created as a result of constant interactions between those doing the outsourced work and others in the organization. In other words, understanding the interdependencies between groups—those being outsourced and those staying—is critical to evaluating the risks of delegating certain tasks or processes to outside suppliers.

Another consideration when evaluating the risks of outsourcing specific intellectual activities is the difficulty of ever bringing that knowledge back into the organization if it becomes necessary. One consideration to make it easier to rebuild your organization's knowledge base is to keep some capability on staff to maintain daily involvement in the outsourced activities. This way the organization doesn't lose all of its knowledge in this area, which would make it much easier to regenerate, if necessary.

4. *Examine the stability of your outsourcing supplier's knowledge base.* When retaining experienced staff is a major factor in pursuing an outsourcing option, make sure your potential supplier has a human knowledge base that is more stable than yours. While outsourcing suppliers usually can retain more specialized experts supporting the capabilities they provide, don't blindly assume their critical knowledge base is stable enough to continually meet your performance requirements.

For example, when an aerospace company outsourced certain product design work, they found the supplier's engineering resources were spread so thin that it was very difficult to get the attention of key engineers for follow-up work once the initial design was delivered. And, if one or two of these veteran engineers ever left, the aerospace company could have been seriously set back. Outsourcing vital expertise does not reduce your organization's dependence on this knowledge. It just makes the dependence a little less evident.

Service firms often don't like to talk about the high utilization rates of their best experts. Applying this intellectual capital to more and more clients, of course, is how they make money. But if these experts are overextended or being burned out, your supplier's capabilities may be seriously hurt, which may affect their performance for your organization. The key is to keep tabs on your supplier's knowledge base.

5. *Needed: top management champion.* If lost knowledge threatens strategic objectives, senior executive sponsorship is necessary because recom-

mendations to outsource intellectual activities are not likely to come from lower levels of the organization. In fact, even when human resources are depleted, unit managers may actively resist outsourcing, fearing loss of jobs, prestige, or power. One of the challenges for senior executives is that functional or department managers usually have the best understanding of what knowledge is most critical for sustaining current performance. At the same time, no matter how difficult it becomes to retain or hire experienced staff, unit managers are unlikely to recommend outsourcing as part of the solution to address threats of lost knowledge. To complicate matters, there will be times when local managers accurately recognize the dangers of outsourcing certain intellectual activities, such as engineering analysis on new rocket engines, because of the nature of the knowledge involved. This may not be as evident to senior management. Thus, one dilemma for top executives is to determine when resistance to outsourcing is legitimate, given task interdependencies and the nature of the knowledge involved, and when it is just political, driven more by local interests. Making these distinctions will be key in making the right choices about what to outsource when essential knowledge is becoming very difficult to retain.

Of course, not all capabilities can or should be outsourced, even when the knowledge underlying them is at risk. In some cases, the intellectual capital is too context-dependent to be delegated to an outside supplier. In other situations, knowledge will be deemed too sensitive for competitive or even national security reasons to rely on outsiders. One of the great challenges for leaders in the years ahead will be finding ways to preserve knowledge critical for future performance that is threatened by employee turnover, very difficult to transfer, and too sensitive to outsource. In some cases, the only choice will be to re-create the knowledge in a new generation of employees.

Regenerating Lost Knowledge

Critical knowledge can disappear from your organization overnight. It's a common scenario. You can't maintain existing performance levels simply by hiring a new expert because none exists or no one is available. The work cannot be outsourced, and the former source of the knowledge is not available for consulting. Sometimes really valuable knowledge just disappears. This happened a few years ago to a leading medical practice in Boston that specializes in diseases of the cornea and other unusual eye conditions. A member of the group's medical staff, Dr. Eleanor Mobilia, who was in her seventies, was considered one of the world's experts in fitting specialty contact lenses. This isn't about contact lenses that make you look sexier or change the color of your eyes. For people with some cornea diseases, whose eyes aren't correctable with glasses, well fitting contact lenses can be the difference between a lifetime of normal eyesight and near blindness.

Dr. Mobilia had seen thousands of patients from around the world in her 50-year career and had conducted research on contact lenses for decades. She was training a protégé to someday take over her practice when she suddenly fell ill and died.

Her young colleague Dr. Janet Rand was now unable to call on Mobilia's expertise when confronted with a difficult fitting after a corneal transplant. Rand recalled:

> There are a lot of different scenarios for the shape of the cornea due to how the eye heals. They're like snow flakes. Everyone heals differently, so it's a very inexact science. Dr. Mobilia had fit thousands of eyes of each shape and she knew the type of lenses that would best be tolerated. I'm sure she had a plan for how to fit patients with really irregular corneal transplants. But most of her knowledge there was lost.
>
> After she passed away, I had a transplant patient with an eye that was so flat the lenses would just fall off. Nothing I tried worked. I wish I could have called her in on that patient and I would have learned what she would have done in that situation. I'm sure she knew by looking at some patients, this is impossible and not to even try fitting them until they had further surgery. Without that knowledge you just put people through months of trying to fit them and get their hopes up unnecessarily.

In this case, Rand had no choice. With the venerable pioneer in contact lenses technologies gone, the young doctor had to regenerate knowledge that her group once had ready access to.

This scenario of having to re-create complex technical and scientific knowledge that was previously available to an organization is happening regularly today. "There are definitely cases where we've got big problems," said one aerospace industry executive. "And big costs are associated with losing knowledge. We've become good at fire fighting and fixing those breaks in knowledge continuity, but there's a price to pay for that approach." The fact is organizations throughout the industrialized world will increasingly have to scramble to re-create knowledge they once had use of, but are unable to retain.[8]

Regenerating knowledge that is costly and time-consuming to create is the last thing managers want to do. Not only is it a frustrating waste of resources, but it is, frankly, embarrassing. What executive wants to admit to stockholders or taxpayers that an important knowledge asset their organization once controlled, or at least had access to, is now unavailable? It is particularly painful when the implications for performance are obvious. As a result, few companies will talk publicly about the vital knowledge they have lost or may lose in the years ahead.

But this is a scenario your organization is likely to face soon. A core group of experts has left without transferring enough critical knowledge to their successors. They aren't available for consulting and you can't outsource the work. Like it or not, the knowledge is gone. Executives rarely think about strategies and tactics for re-creating lost knowledge and there is no straightforward methodology for solving this problem, but there are at least five things you can do when it happens.

1. *In the area where departing experts have left a gap, figure out what knowledge their successors do actually have.* Of course, every situation will be somewhat different, but this may mean making sure those left behind articulate their own current model of the problem domain where the expert excelled. For example, Dr. Rand, who was already well trained in optometry, knew the fundamental problem in fitting contact lenses was always balancing the quality of a patient's vision, the comfort of the lenses, and the health of their cornea. What she did not know was what her late mentor had learned about designing lenses for particularly difficult cases where it was hard to find a satisfactory compromise between these three variables. The first step in regenerating intellectual capital is discovering the current state of intellectual capital in the area where valuable knowledge has been lost.

2. *Use existing artifacts and documentation to spark ideas and questions.* Product design firms are particularly good at keeping knowledge alive, partly because they consciously embed ideas in an inventory of objects that their designers can examine and experiment with.[9] For Rand there were several types of artifacts that yielded knowledge her mentor had not passed on. Rand inherited all of Dr. Mobilia's diagnostic contact lense sets, which doctors use when trying different lenses on patients to find the right fit. Although they had never discussed how Dr. Mobilia used the lense sets, through trial and error Rand "figured out" which lense type her mentor would use in different situations.

   Another artifact that helped regenerate knowledge was the contact lenses actually being worn by returning patients. "I didn't understand that Dr. Mobilia fit lenses flat on the eye until after she passed away," said Rand. "Patients would come in and I'd notice their lenses fit flat. I realized I had to figure out if she did it that way because she had learned that was the best way to go, even though a different way of fitting lenses is taught in school now."

Patients' charts were also a helpful artifact in reconstructing some of Dr. Mobilia's knowledge. Whenever Rand saw one of her mentor's patients, she would, of course, review the patient's chart for any notations about the shape of the cornea. She could then match that information with the actual lenses Dr. Mobilia had fitted on the patient's eyes. This way Rand slowly rediscovered what lenses her mentor had deemed most effective in different circumstances.

Although, her predecessor's writing was clear, Rand was frustrated by the brief notations on the charts. "I wish there was more of her thought processes in the notes," Rand said. "For example, she never noted which lenses *didn't* work before the final lense was chosen. That's important so you don't make the same mistake again." Rand's observation about the value of knowing what does not work was a common theme in this research. One of the frustrations at NASA, for example, is having lost so much knowledge about what engineering designs have been rejected over the years, and why. Sometimes passing down knowledge about which alternatives were not chosen and why is as important as knowing what worked.

In the end, Rand used her observations of the work her mentor had left behind in dozens of patients with specially fitted lenses. She combined these observations with insights gained from the charts, as well as from using the diagnostic lenses. Along with an up-to-date knowledge of the external literature, these inputs helped her clarify some of the gaps between what she knew and what her mentor had apparently known. Rand was sometimes still left wondering what Dr. Mobilia had done to figure out a solution to specific problems. But she used the artifacts left behind in her mentor's work to fill in some of the gaps in her own knowledge and to accelerate her learning.

3. *Reconstruct the relevant social network of veteran employees who have left.* Even when an expert departs, important fragments of their knowledge may still be available from other people who interacted with them regularly. Thus, to regenerate critical expertise it can be very helpful to contact key people who ex-employees worked with, both inside and outside the firm. This can be done several ways. Ideally, you want a departing expert to identify key members of their network before they leave. In an example of this, NASA's Jet Propulsion Laboratory has tried to map mentoring relationships as part of an experts' directory. That way, even if a veteran employee retires, NASA staff can contact some of the people with whom the retiree worked most closely. These protégés will most likely have absorbed some of their mentor's knowledge. Participation in this system is strictly voluntary in that it is up to employees whether or not they reveal mentoring relationships.

Another valuable technique for mining an old social network is to create an adapted version of a "peer assist." This technique has been used most successfully by energy giant BP. Peer assists are usually designed as meetings where people from other groups or organizations are invited to share their knowledge with a team that is requesting help on a specific problem.[10] But a modified version of one of these meetings can be designed to brainstorm about how to regenerate knowledge that appears to have left the organization.

A peer assist helped reconstitute a social network at the Communications-Electronics Command (CECOM), which is responsible for the procurement of all the U.S. Army's communications and electronics equipment. CECOM is working to retain the knowledge of its veteran civilian contracting officers, many of whom are retiring in the next few years. The military procurement process is exceedingly complex. So when one person had to unexpectedly take over a procurement project in midstream, she decided to conduct a peer assist at the urging of a consulting team from SAIC that was engaged with CECOM on a larger knowledge retention initiative. She pulled in a group of contracting officers who had experience in procurement projects of similar size and scope. Speed was essential on this project because procurement funding could disappear if not spent within the current fiscal year. When the group met, it turned out that one of the people invited had been the original contracting officer on the project, a fact unknown to the new project leader. This unexpected connection made with someone working just down the hall instantly gave the new contracting officer access to the project's history, which she assumed had been lost. Other knowledge gained in the meeting helped save about a month's time in completing the project.

Sometimes valuable knowledge can be re-created by connecting with other colleagues or external suppliers, who have worked with departed experts. When trying to understand her mentor's approach to fitting contact lenses, Janet Rand has relied on a consultant who works at the laboratory that makes the lenses she prescribes for her patients. Rand recalled, "At the lab, I discovered they could tell me how Dr. Mobilia did things because they worked with her on the lense designs. I've told the lab consultant, 'I've found a patient who needs a Mobilia-style fit.' Sometimes I'll say, 'Here's what Dr. Mobilia did. Do you know why she did that?' And the consultant will say, 'Yes, I remember talking with her about that kind of cornea. Here's what she was thinking, and here's the advice I gave her.' "

When employees with unique expertise leave your organization, you can never re-create all of their essential knowledge. But reconnecting with fragments of an expert's social network about a specific problem is a good tactic for regenerating at least some of what they knew.

4. *Hire an outside consultant who is an expert in the area where knowledge has been lost.* This will be a viable short-term option in situations where external expertise exists that is both affordable and accessible. Of course, the consultant will not have contextual knowledge about working effectively in the organization, and this will probably limit the value of his or her contribution. But being able to accelerate the transfer of content knowledge about the field to less experienced employees may be worth the investment. If you can find an outside consultant to help regenerate lost knowledge, be clear about their role when contracting with them. Consultants often prefer to keep their new client dependent on them for their content expertise, instead of helping to fully develop new capabilities inside the client organization. Be clear about what capabilities you expect a consultant to help regenerate in your employees within a particular time frame. Otherwise, this becomes just another outsourcing relationship, and knowledge once viewed as essential to the organization becomes increasingly distant.

5. *Re-create knowledge by working on specific problems.* In reality, much of the valuable knowledge that is lost can only be regenerated through experience. Dr. Rand had regenerated specialized knowledge about fitting contact lenses by working with scores of patients since Dr. Mobilia passed away. In the process, Dr. Rand reflects on what she learned from her mentor, what she has learned by observing Dr. Mobilia's former patients and by talking to her mentor's former colleagues. Finally, her knowledge base is continually expanding as she sees how patients respond to different contact lenses, given their individual conditions. This form of ongoing hypothesis testing is the key to rebuilding experiential knowledge, and unfortunately it takes time.

Conclusion

There is no way to avoid the fact that many organizations in the industrialized world are going to lose more and more critical intellectual capital in the decades ahead. In some cases, this is going to have serious impacts on performance. Leaders who want to minimize the damage caused by lost knowledge must begin thinking about the strategies their organizations will use to deal with essential intellectual capital once it is gone. In some cases, executives will retain access to knowledge by rehiring retirees. In other instances, outsourcing will make the most sense. But sometimes there will be no choice but to look for ways to regenerate certain knowledge the unit once had. Understanding these options is a prerequisite to making the best decisions in each situation. But recognizing what will minimize the risk of knowledge loss is only the first step. The final section of this book addresses the challenges of implementing knowledge retention solutions and how they will change the look of your organization in the future.

PART III
Implementing Retention Strategies

The previous section described many ways that leaders can influence knowledge retention in their organization. But how do you get started? The final four chapters focus on the realities of implementing these initiatives. First, it is helpful to take a brief look at some of the pioneers who have begun addressing threats of lost knowledge. There are useful lessons to be taken from their experiences.

The threat of lost knowledge can be overwhelming, but the journey must begin somewhere, and chapter 10 will help you identify where and how to take those first steps. Knowledge retention initiatives, however, will always be threatened by an array of barriers that strive to preserve the status quo. There are some good reasons why organizations continually lose knowledge, and chapter 11 will explore four dynamics that you must anticipate to successfully create change in this area. Finally, since the importance of retaining intellectual capital is only going to increase in the years ahead, executives need to view the problem from a strategic perspective, an approach that is outlined in the final chapter.

9

Stemming the Flow of Lost Knowledge

Stories of Early Adopters

Union Pacific Railroad is the oldest company on the New York Stock Exchange, having been first listed more than 140 years ago. None of its roughly 47,000 current employees were around then, but to Union Pacific's HR planners it must feel like they were. The largest railroad in North America has a workforce whose average age is 46. And with federal law now allowing full-benefit retirement at age 60, in this heavily unionized industry, Union Pacific has a lot of engineers, master mechanics, and crew dispatchers getting ready to retire. "The people retiring have a lot of informal knowledge about how things work at the railroad," said Marques Wilson, the company's director of workforce planning. "The key issue for us is how do we retain their knowledge so the railroad continues to run efficiently and effectively."

As Union Pacific's leaders develop a strategy for building their workforce of the future in the face of major demographic changes, top management is confronting a series of challenges that your organization may also need to address.

This chapter will describe how several organizations have proactively responded to the threat of lost knowledge. These stories may give you some ideas that relate directly to your situation. But don't worry if, like Union Pacific, you're just getting started. No one has figured out all the answers to knowledge retention. Some organizations may have a head start, but there's still time—if you get started now. Chapter 10 will provide principles for action to get traction on these initiatives.

Sandia Labs' Knowledge Preservation Program

Sandia National Laboratories is responsible for designing, developing, and maintaining all of the 5,500-plus nonexplosive components that go into U.S. nuclear weapons. But when the United States stopped building new nuclear warheads in the early 1990s, the Department of Energy (DOE), which oversees the nation's nuclear weapons complex, became concerned about retaining knowledge needed to design and test these weapons.

In response to these concerns, Sandia created a knowledge preservation program, which involved videotaping interviews with lab veterans, who were specialists in particular areas, such as gas transfer systems or radar design. These Q&A sessions were intended to capture experts explaining what they had done and why on particular projects. And also what had gone right and what had gone wrong. John Shaw of Sandia's weapons knowledge management group explained:

> In the nuclear weapons complex we document every weapon in a final development report. In fact, every part has its own characteristics and development report. These reports define the configuration of each weapon when its development is completed. But they don't do a very good job of saying what paths weaponeers tried to develop—where they tried and failed. The Lab is developing and designing things that have never been done before, so there are lots of fits and starts. But we don't document these. And because a lot of the technologies we use are unique, I would say knowledge in the nuclear weapons world is 90 to 95 percent tacit.

The knowledge preservation program produced 1,600 hours of video-tape of hundreds of Sandia employees. It cost millions of dollars, but in the end it had limited impact for several reasons. Shaw pointed out that six hours of videotape might produce only five minutes of critical lessons learned, which made it impractical for less experienced employees to access. In addition, for security reasons, information is shared in the nuclear weapons community only on a need to know basis so the videotapes had to be carefully organized by subject. Even more important, because the technologies used in nuclear weapons changed over time, Sandia's engineers often did not see much benefit in reviewing discussions of older technologies. "When we started at the Lab, there was an assumption that if we created a program to preserve knowledge then employees would use it, but they didn't," said Shaw.

Meanwhile, Sandia's workforce had been getting older and leadership was concerned about developing a new generation of scientists and engineers experienced in nuclear weapons development. HR managers did an analysis of critical skills in the weapons program to identify the most critical skill areas that needed to be sustained. In a review with Sandia's leaders, they answered questions such as: What is the average age in our critical skill areas? What is the average time to retirement for those employees? Which of the Lab's critical skills are most vulnerable today? For example, if the nuclear weapons complex quickly had to resume underground testing, what skills would Sandia need to be able to do that?

Based on their occupation by occupation review of Sandia's nuclear weapons knowledge base, HR identified systems engineering, radar, and microelectronics roles as among the most vulnerable to critical knowledge loss. "Across the board, we found that retirement eligibility of these critical skills was very high," said Julian Sanchez, former HR manager for the nuclear weapons program. Recognizing they had only a three-to seven-year window to transfer essential knowledge, Sandia's leadership now had the analysis it needed to go to the U.S. Congress for additional funding to hire and quickly develop a new generation of weaponeers. This would lead to a series of new initiatives.

Northrop Grumman Reacts to Immediate Knowledge Loss

In 1997 thousands of veteran Northrop employees who had worked on the B-2 bomber program were leaving the company as it went through a major downsizing. Employees with extensive knowledge about the thousands of different materials and processes used to build and maintain the B-2 were leaving that business unit, now part of Northrop Grumman's Integrated Systems sector. Key talent in software engineering, systems engineering, materials and processes, and manufacturing was headed out the door, and management needed to retain their knowledge to support the division's long-term B-2 maintenance strategy.[1]

Initially, Northrop Grumman created a 10-person knowledge management (KM) team, which identified 200 subject matter experts in key areas, such as armaments, software engineering, and manufacturing. Once the experts were identified, the team turned to technology solutions to try to capture their knowledge. Initially, they videotaped about 30 individual interviews or panel discussions with experts who were leaving the company. The videos were put on CD-ROMs because in 1997 Northrop Grumman lacked the bandwidth to distribute the videos online. Management also created a central repository for project documents, so when employees left the information wouldn't languish on old floppy discs and in file cabinets. In addition, an expert locator system was developed that allowed employees to search for knowledge resources by skill, program affiliation, or individual name.

Although management had started to track people and documents, the content in the systems was not having adequate impact on the business unit's knowledge retention needs. When the KM initiative was expanded beyond the B-2 program to the entire business unit in 1999, KM project managers knew they needed to quickly identify the knowledge challenges across the enterprise. So they hired a consulting firm to conduct a knowledge audit to determine where employees actually looked for knowledge they needed in their jobs and how hard or easy it was to access. The audit was conducted by the Delphi Group across the entire business unit in about two months. It was based on 3,400 individual survey responses and a sample of 125 follow-up face-to-face interviews, which revealed there were significant negative employee perceptions stemming, in part, from recent layoffs that inhibited knowledge sharing and retention.

One surprising finding was how much employees valued their colleagues' know-how and willingness to share it. At the same time, the audit showed that about half of the business area's employees spent at least eight hours a week trying to find information they needed to do their jobs. This lack of ready access to critical information cost the company an estimated $150 million annually. This number gave management the economic justification needed to pursue a new, more performance-oriented set of initiatives. These programs would improve both knowledge management, in general, as well as serving knowledge retention objectives, in the face of looming baby boomer retirements. With an average age in the division of 49, and early retirement eligibility beginning at 55, at least 25 percent of the unit's current employees will be retirement eligible by 2008. Further, in 2003, a company-wide team was created to evaluate the potential impacts and provide recommendations to reduce the risk of future waves of baby boomer retirements.

BP Trinidad & Tobago Lack of Experienced Staff Challenges Growth Strategy

Not all knowledge retention challenges are retirement-driven. Increasingly, in some sectors, business growth objectives are going to be threatened by a shortage of skilled personnel, forcing companies to focus on the retention of employees and their knowledge, and on developing experienced workers more quickly. Consultants and HR managers have a slick phrase for this. They like to call it "shortening time-to-competence."

BP Trinidad & Tobago (bpTT), an oil and gas exploration unit of energy giant BP, has already confronted this problem. The industry is faced with a worldwide shortage of geoscientists. And with very aggressive production goals, bpTT has had to devise a strategy to attract, develop, and retain the best talent in the Caribbean nation's rapidly expanding oil and gas production industry. But there were special challenges confronting bpTT in developing a highly skilled workforce to support its growth plans. Because there are significant economic costs and regulatory challenges associated with using expatriate staff to fill specialized geoscientist roles, bpTT has had to become more effective in developing and retaining highly skilled local workers if it was going to meet its aggressive goals.

While participating in a multi-company Workforce Internationalization study sponsored by Accenture, the unit's exploration group used the opportunity to diagnose the effectiveness of current recruiting, training, and retention practices. Accenture's consultants interviewed a large cross-section of employees in the bpTT exploration team to gain a firsthand understanding of existing people practices and processes. They compared their findings to industry best practices, which Accenture had identified in previous studies. The gaps identified led to a proposed action plan based on a model of how a high-performing organization would design the sustainable recruiting, retention, and employee development processes needed to achieve its business goals. "We didn't want short-term band aid solutions," said Azim Ali, learning and development coordinator for the exploration unit.

The consultants, working in collaboration with bpTT exploration staff, suggested initiatives in six key areas. These included setting up a formal coaching program, especially in areas where there were specialized skills gaps, such as seismic imaging and seismic quality control. Initiatives to help develop a globally competitive workforce also addressed the need for mentoring, skill development metrics, and resourcing new employees through a proactive and targeted recruiting process, as well as helping to ensure there is a pool of qualified candidates to meet future geoscience staffing needs.

Initial workforce development initiatives focused primarily on expert coaching, mentoring, and international assignments to other BP locations. Transferring expertise more quickly to junior staff is expected to reduce the "experience cycle time" by 30–50 percent. In some cases, for example, it takes 10–15 years to develop an experienced geoscientist with specialized skills, but bpTT is trying to cut that cycle time to five to seven years. Speeding up the development of local employees is also expected to lead to a proportionate reduction in the number of more costly expatriate staff working in bpTT.

TVA's Knowledge Retention Process

As the largest public power company in the United States, the Tennessee Valley Authority's 13,000 employees operate and maintain 3 nuclear power plants, 4 combustion-turbine plants, 11 fossil fuel plants, and 29 hydroelectric dams. TVA has one of the most comprehensive knowledge retention processes in the utilities industry.[2]

When TVA's management realized that up to 40 percent of its workforce could retire in the next five years, an HR team began to develop tools and a process to help line managers retain critical knowledge that could otherwise be lost to attrition. Team member Jerry Landon said the first step was to decide which positions posed the greatest threat of critical knowledge loss.

In 1999 TVA began surveying employees in nuclear operations to find out if and when they were planning to retire. The survey was strictly voluntary, but initially only about 50 percent of employees responded, uncomfortable, no doubt, with how the information was going to be used. Over time, however, TVA employees have increasingly recognized that their personal responses about retirement plans were only being used to drive workforce planning and not to make individual personnel decisions. As a result, response to the annual e-mail survey has increased to 80 percent, and management uses historical data to provide estimated retirement dates for the balance of the workforce.

To complement retirement data, managers and supervisors provide an estimate of the indispensability of their individual employees on a scale of one to five (most valuable). This is called a "position risk factor" which, when multiplied against the retirement factor, produces a "knowledge risk factor" that identifies areas where immediate knowledge retention action is required. TVA then creates a report for each of its work sites listing the site's personnel and their knowledge risk factors. This is the first step in TVA's knowledge retention process.

Since beginning the process, TVA has identified more than 50 people close to retirement who had knowledge that was judged critical to sustaining organizational performance. These employees included turbine specialists, systems design engineers, transmission technicians, and radiological control supervisors, who manage computer systems that monitor human and environmental radiation exposure.

The second step in TVA's process is to interview employees identified as having critical knowledge to learn the job's specific "knowledge content." These interviews are intended to develop an inventory of each employee's skill sets and know-how. For example, a technician might have extensive expertise for working with three pieces of unique equipment, know how to perform eight testing procedures for troubleshooting, and know the fastest route to six rural substations. (Every second counts during a power outage.) These content interviews, supplemented by conversations with supervisors and other colleagues, almost always reveal more redundancy in knowledge and skills, and more resources and backups than management realized initially. Landon explained, "Even when we identify an expert, all his knowledge is not critical. Maybe in only two of ten areas is he the *only* expert in the company."

As a result of the content interviews, TVA develops a list of potential "knowledge loss items" for each job and then analyzes their importance to decide the most appropriate action to be taken. This phase uses four questions to triage potential lost knowledge:

- What is the relative *importance* of this knowledge?
- What is the relative *immediacy* of knowledge loss?
- What is the cost and *feasibility* of recovering this knowledge, if lost?
- How difficult is it to *transfer* the knowledge?

This analysis helps TVA's management identify which critical knowledge it can retain with relatively minor effort and which will require extensive resources or immediate action. The next step in the process is choosing the most effective tactics for preserving the knowledge, or reengineering operations so retaining this know-how becomes unnecessary. Landon explained:

> In some cases, that might mean assigning a new employee to shadow the employee who's going to retire, or cross-training someone who's currently in a different job. Sometimes, it means documenting a procedure or process that's never been written down. Or perhaps it requires setting up a brown bag lunch twice a week where systems engineers can get together to discuss their work and problem solve together. Some pieces of knowledge can even be eliminated by engineering them out. If 'Lee' is the only one left who knows how to fix some ancient piece of equipment, it may make more sense to replace that equipment than to try to replace Lee's arcane know-how.

TVA developed a knowledge retention process that includes four common responses that can be used to develop specific plans to retain capabilities or to reduce the impact of losing them. These solutions are:

- Codification and documentation (e.g., procedures, checklists, inventories)
- Education and training (including one-to-one coaching and mentoring, classroom, simulator, and on-the-job training)
- Engineer knowledge out (e.g., change processes, update equipment, use "smart" tools and technology, eliminate task)
- Establish alternative resources (e.g., hire outside contractors, use retirees as consultants, "find and buy" hires, share expertise with other plant or divisions, draw from communities of practice or other professional networks)

Identifying critical knowledge, prioritizing what needs to be retained, and deciding on solutions is only half the battle. As we will see in chapters 10 and 11, implementing solutions can be equally challenging. There are several lessons suggested by the initial experiences of the organizations described here.

Like TVA, the sooner an organization starts to develop a knowledge retention process, the more time it will have to improve its knowledge transfer capabilities. Organizations that wait are more likely to feel compelled to fall back on interviewing and other short-term knowledge capture techniques that are not necessarily effective ways to get existing knowledge used in the future. Sandia Labs and Northrop Grumman are just two examples of many organizations that have been disappointed with the value derived from interviews with departing employees. Experience shows that the knowledge captured needs to be very accessible and younger employees need to be highly motivated to seek it out, or this knowledge will go unused.

Another lesson from these early adopters is that there is a lot more support for knowledge retention initiatives when top management sees a direct link between retention and strategic objectives, as was the case of bpTT. If the link to strategy isn't obvious, you can help your case tremendously by developing data that clearly outlines the threat lost knowledge poses to organizational performance. This is what managers at Sandia Labs and Northrop Grumman did to help their initiatives evolve.

Organizations with a recent history of downsizing will find retention initiatives are met with considerable employee skepticism that is likely to undermine the knowledge sharing management is trying to promote. Northrop Grumman's knowledge audit revealed significant employee distrust of management's motives for the retention effort and identified several cultural issues that had to be addressed before leaders could expect widespread support for their objectives. TVA's Jerry Landon learned a related lesson when he went to do his first set of knowledge content interviews with employees who had been identified as having critical knowledge. A pre-interview explanation sheet didn't exactly set the right tone when it started out, "Imagine that you were only going to be here another week, what knowledge . . . " For an organization with a history of downsizing, it's not hard to imagine what conclusion these technicians jumped to and how defensive they were at first about sharing their knowledge.

Finally, implementing a diagnostic process to collect information on what knowledge is really at risk has an important short-term benefit. It can greatly reduce organizational uncertainty about what intellectual capital could be lost. Although their knowledge transfer problems are not yet solved, TVA, Sandia Labs, and Northrop Grumman all felt noticeable relief from having diagnosed and defined their knowledge retention needs.

10

Launching Knowledge Retention Initiatives

Principles for Action

How to Get Started

Leaders in every organization must contend with different contextual factors that shape the types of knowledge they will try to retain and the way they will go about it. Among the variables that define each organization's situation are: (1) employee tenure in different units in the workforce; (2) current attrition rates by length of service (e.g., Is there a lot of turnover among new mid-career hires? Do workers in certain roles always retire as soon as they are eligible?); and (3) projected future growth of the workforce.[1] But no matter what an organization's unique situation is, when it comes to implementation those trying to improve knowledge retention need to do three things:

1. Determine what knowledge is most at risk.
2. Build sustained organizational support for retention initiatives.
3. Decide which initiatives to pursue first.

Determine Knowledge at Risk

This chapter provides an outline for how to start implementing knowledge retention programs. It draws on the cases described in chapter 9, as well as the experiences of other organizations trying to stem the flow of lost knowledge. Determining the knowledge at risk is an obvious first step. What is not so obvious is how to do it. Here are the three things you need to do.

Identify What Knowledge Is Critical

Chapter 2 outlined ways that lost knowledge can undermine the achievement of strategic objectives. Now it's time to put that framework to use. As emphasized in chapter 2, identifying critical knowledge and skills should always be done in the context of the organization's strategy. For example, bpTT recognized that it wouldn't be able to meet its growth objectives unless it developed and retained enough skilled geoscientists in a labor market plagued by talent shortages.

It's one thing when an organization can predict that its current skills and knowledge base are what will be needed in the future. But one of the biggest challenges facing leaders today is clarifying how their strategic objectives are changing the knowledge needs of their organization. Knowledge retention efforts are greatly complicated when knowledge and skills required in the future are changing.

For example, the central technology group supporting the IT needs of Canadian government agencies includes 1,200 full-time professionals, who are experts in a variety of hardware, software, and telecommunications technologies. Current strategic objectives include making all government services available online by 2005 and providing these virtual services to all citizens, even those in remote villages with no telecommunications infrastructure. These objectives require considerable expertise in internet development, internet security, and wireless technologies. Meanwhile, with about 40 percent of the senior members of the entire technology group eligible to retire in the next few years, management must also determine which more traditional IT skills, such as database management and Cobol programming, are most essential for sustaining operations. This is where knowledge retention efforts will be focused.

Figure 10.1 shows the various scenarios organizations—and even individual departments—face that help differentiate the context of their knowledge retention decisions. Functions or units in quadrant II with relatively stable skill needs and an increased attrition rate, due to retirements and midcareer turnover, have the most clear-cut concerns about the costs of lost knowledge. Utilities like TVA will fall into this category in the years ahead, even though historically utilities have experienced low turnover. Meanwhile, units such as the Canadian IT group (quadrant IV), where knowledge and skills needed are changing significantly and where attrition could be high, present much more complex knowledge retention challenges, particularly when management recognizes that some legacy knowledge is essential for future success.

Units with low attrition but rapidly changing knowledge needs (quadrant III) present yet another type of knowledge retention challenge. A mature biotech firm that changed its strategic focus is one such example. Organizations like this will probably have to go through significant culture change and involuntary layoffs, making it hard to sustain the trust needed to support knowledge-sharing behaviors that are integral to retaining old knowledge that is still valuable. The trick is not overlooking this knowledge during the strategic transition. Finally, one global chemical company that had already encouraged most of its older workers to take early retirement, found itself with relatively low expected turnover in the next five years and a stable skill base. Organizations in this situation (quadrant I) appear to have few knowl-

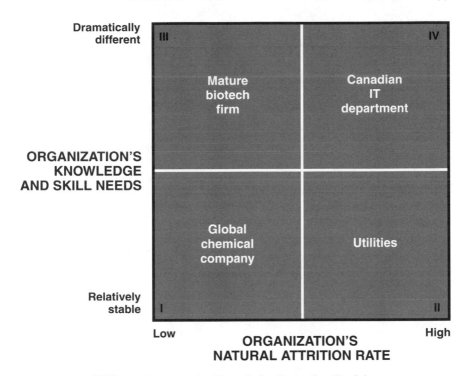

Dramatically different

| III | IV |

Mature biotech firm

Canadian IT department

ORGANIZATION'S KNOWLEDGE AND SKILL NEEDS

Global chemical company

Utilities

Relatively stable

| I | II |

Low   High

ORGANIZATION'S NATURAL ATTRITION RATE

FIGURE 10.1. Different Contexts for Knowledge Retention Decisions
Organizations face different knowledge retention scenarios depending on the stability of their knowledge base, given strategic objectives, and their expected attrition rate. Retention needs may change dramatically when turnover rates climb in sectors such as utilities and government.

edge retention concerns. But it would be a mistake to ignore the potential costs of lost knowledge in this situation. Extensive downsizing can leave a company dangerously thin in areas of expertise critical to business performance. Identifying these "irreplaceable experts" is important to develop transition strategies early. In addition, low turnover among veterans is likely to mean more frustrated high potential mid-career employees who leave for better opportunities. This will lead to future gaps in succession plans for key professional and leadership roles.

Regardless of the scenario facing your organization, when identifying critical knowledge be careful not to settle for generalizations (e.g., "R&D knowledge" or "program management knowledge"). The trick is specifying types of knowledge needed at the level of detail necessary to make management decisions about designing retention solutions. Sandia Labs, for example, did an occupation-by-occupation assessment of critical skills in its weapons program to identify knowledge bases that needed to be sustained.

NASA's Jet Propulsion Laboratory (JPL), on the other hand, did a more open-ended knowledge and information requirements study, which involved talking with about 1,000 NASA project managers, engineers, and scientists. This study identified several types of knowledge that needed to be retained more effectively.

When trying to identify essential knowledge be cautious about reacting to only a few anecdotes. Stories are very important for surfacing areas that need further study, but a more systematic approach will help make sure you don't invest retention resources in areas that may be more visible but have limited impact on the organization's performance. You will be better off with a combination of more quantitative demographic and attrition data, bolstered by stories to illustrate the types of knowledge that need to be retained.

Finally, be sensitive to the subtleties of what defines the "critical" knowledge needed to support organizational productivity. Knowledge managers at NASA's Jet Propulsion Laboratory learned this when they did a detailed needs analysis for the Lab's project managers. They found experienced flight project managers wanted to retain knowledge about what decisions had been made and the consequences of those decisions. For example, did they decide to launch the spacecraft from the space shuttle directly or did they use an expendable space vehicle? And what were the implications of that decision for the program? But project managers in training needed access to knowledge that explained the trade-offs considered by their predecessors on previous missions. For example, why did previous projects choose to use a space shuttle instead of an expendable launch vehicle?

Jeanne Holm, NASA's chief knowledge architect, said, "We found one person's critical knowledge was not necessarily usable by the next person. So we had to find a way to get current project managers to capture knowledge that was critical to the next project manager, but not necessarily to him." The lesson here is that knowledge deemed essential by current experts may be incomprehensible and, therefore, useless to less experienced successors who lack a contextual understanding of how to apply it. On the other hand, knowledge discounted as unimportant by experts in an area may be viewed as essential by those new to the field.

Identify Who Has Critical Knowledge or Where It Is

Deciding what knowledge is essential to sustain future performance is important, but it's not enough. Management also needs to find out who actually has this knowledge currently or specifically where it is stored. Sometimes the answers to these questions will be obvious. But just as often management can make faulty assumptions about where essential knowledge resides. There are several ways to address this problem.

The Tennessee Valley Authority created a process for asking its supervisors to rate employees on a one-to-five scale to identify those whose loss would have the biggest impact on the organization. Finding out who is rated a "five" gives management an initial idea of which employees have unique knowledge valuable to the organization. Unfortunately, TVA has learned that supervisors tend to overrate the difficulty of replacing their subordinate's expertise. "In the initial assessment, they always identify more people as having unique knowledge. We have a lot of "fives," said Jerry Landon, who helped develop the process at TVA.

TVA checks their supervisors' initial high rating with a series of content interviews to develop an inventory of each employee's skill sets and knowhow. Landon explained:

When we look at those folks more carefully we often find there is more redundancy in their knowledge and skills, and more alternative resources and backups than management realized initially. Yes, a guy may have great knowledge about turbines, but we have other technicians who have a history of working with them, too. It turns out that it is the history of that expert's particular turbine that we have to worry about.

As mentioned in chapter 7, another way of identifying who has knowledge critical to organizational performance is by drawing on the growing set of social network analysis tools that can identify individuals who are viewed by their colleagues as "go-to" people when dealing with specific business issues. As the theory and technology underlying social network analysis (SNA) matures, management will increasingly be able to develop graphic displays of the informal relationships that people in their organizations rely on to access specific types of expertise. For example, the Canadian government's central IT group used an SNA tool called Knetmap when management wanted to identify who had the most critical technical skills needed to meet the group's future objectives. An advantage of the network mapping tool is that it shows which employees are actually relied on for their knowledge, regardless of their formal position in the organization. For example, management of the IT unit found there was just one person that everyone relied on for her database expertise (see figure 10.2).

Knowledge audits are another method that management can use in this diagnostic step. Knowledge audits can provide detailed information about the dynamics of knowledge use, identifying things such as cultural barriers to improving knowledge sharing and reuse in an organization, as well as potentially uncovering critical knowledge sources. They can identify what types of knowledge employees see as valuable and where they go to get it. When the Delphi Group conducted a knowledge audit for a business unit of Northrop Grumman's Integrated Systems sector, management was surprised

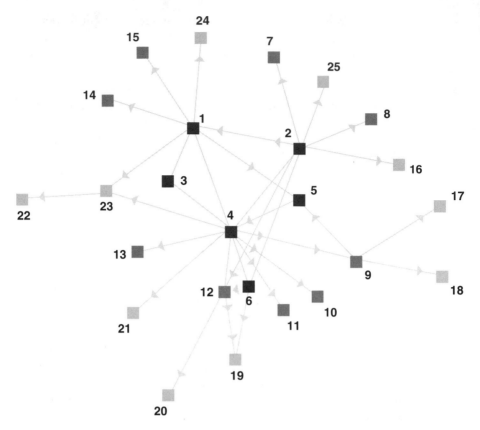

FIGURE 10.2. Social Network Map Reflects Individuals with Most Critical
Knowledge
Social network analysis tools like Inflow allow managers to develop graphic displays of knowledge flows in their organization around specific issues. This helps management see where the loss of particular individuals would
make the organization's knowledge base most vulnerable. *Source*: Valdis Krebs,
www.orgnet.com.

to learn how much more employees valued the knowledge of their coworkers
compared to the knowledge captured in the division's formal systems and
processes.

Regardless of the approach used, identifying critical knowledge and
who has it is an iterative process. Querying employees will almost always
reveal the existence and location of more essential knowledge that senior
management was unaware of. Thus, the process itself adds value by making
actual organizational practices more visible to senior executives, which helps
them make informed decisions about retaining the knowledge needed to improve performance.

Develop an Attrition Profile

This is the last step in identifying knowledge at risk. A 2003 Conference Board survey of 150 HR executives revealed that 66 percent of those organizations responding did not have an age profile of their workforce. This makes it impossible to accurately predict where and when retirements are likely to occur, and hence, when knowledge retention problems could arise.[2]

Sandia Laboratories has been monitoring its aging workforce closely, so it knows where it is most likely to be losing talent in the short term. Knowing the age of your employees is one thing, but knowing when they are likely to retire is equally important. TVA has taken the most direct approach by asking its employees directly in an annual e-mail survey when they plan to retire. Of course, in some organizations this approach might not be possible because of a lack of trust between management and its workforce, but don't assume it's impossible, even if your initial request meets resistance. The key is building trust in how the data is used.

Relying on historical retirement patterns to predict future retirement rates may be misleading today, given the increased dependence on self-funded retirement plans, which have taken a beating in recent years. In addition, changes in how organizations calculate retirement benefits can suddenly make it more compelling for employees to stay on the job longer. Despite the challenges of predicting actual retirements among those eligible, every organization needs the best projections possible to see where an aging workforce could make it vulnerable to lost knowledge.

Retirements, of course, are not the only source of attrition. Turnover among mid-career employees, internal transfers, and the rapid departure of contractors or consultants can also unexpectedly reduce capabilities in short order. Patterns of attrition in all forms should be monitored to identify areas of latent vulnerability. For example, Canada's Department of National Defence/Canadian Forces has recognized that it is regularly losing many of its highly trained technicians to the private sector soon after investing years in training them. This pattern of early departures is forcing the military to rethink its training investments and how it develops and retains its technical competencies over time.

Build Sustained Organizational Support for Knowledge Retention

It is relatively easy to get limited knowledge retention initiatives up and running. NASA, Northrop Grumman, and Sandia Labs had early projects designed to stem the loss of critical knowledge. But these efforts all produced disappointing results and limited impacts. Successful long-term knowledge retention initiatives demand sustained organizational support and there are at least three things that must be done to generate this.

Build a Business Case for Investing in Knowledge Retention

Linking retention efforts to organizational strategy is an essential first step in overcoming a lack of top management support for knowledge retention initiatives. But articulating how lost knowledge will affect strategy implementation means identifying the goals that really matter to potential executive sponsors.[3] This requires a careful assessment of what executives say publicly—in speeches, for example—and what they say privately. A chemical company executive may publicly espouse a strategic focus on growth and innovation to please Wall Street, while private meetings reveal more interest in cutting costs and improving employee productivity. When probing for what your potential sponsor really cares about, be sure the answer is expressed in terms of the ultimate business results. If the initial response is "We need to know how to run our chemical plants more efficiently," keep asking "So what?" until you identify the clear business implication of that goal. The ultimate answer might be, "We need to run plants more efficiently to reduce costs, so we can increase our market share in Eastern Europe." Developing a knowledge retention business case requires an excellent understanding of the company's business model to identify links connecting:

Critical Knowledge → Operations Effectiveness → Performance Objectives → Business Strategy

It's one thing to link lost knowledge conceptually to the organization's strategy, but it is also important to identify in quantitative terms, if possible, where the loss of knowledge can affect group and organizational performance. Here are five areas to look:[4]

- *What will the loss of particular technical or scientific expertise mean for the organization's rate of innovation or, more specifically, new product development?* The departure of a single technical product specialist, for example, can delay the introduction of a new product for months or even longer. The potential lost revenues should be estimated and taken into account when evaluating programs that could reduce the delays by transferring or replacing the specialist's knowledge or by introducing new policies that motivate the individual to stay.
- *How will projected retirement rates or the attrition rate of mid-career employees affect the organization's ability to adequately resource its growth strategy?* Expansion into developing markets actually requires more experienced engineering and technical staff. But if these veterans are leaving the

company in significant numbers, will the organization have the human capital needed to meet its growth objectives? What will be the business impact of missing expected growth targets?

- *What other time-sensitive business processes could be affected where knowledge lost through retirement or turnover increases costs or reduces revenues?* For example, one chemicals company was concerned about lost revenues as members of its aging sales force began to retire. Estimating those lost sales would help justify investments in capturing sales representatives' knowledge and bringing replacements up to speed sooner.

- *What would be the cost of a plant explosion or major quality upset in production?* The loss of experienced production engineers and senior operators can significantly increase the vulnerability of plant operations to costly disruptions. One refinery manager began investing in knowledge retention initiatives just before several senior operators retired. He recognized that a safety violation in his unit would affect the company far beyond the short-term profit and loss statements of his plant.

- *What is the cost of "reinventing" capabilities and processes that the organization once had but has lost or forgotten because of inadequate documentation and turnover?* Identifying the costs of reinvesting in capabilities the company once had can be a powerful way of justifying knowledge-transfer initiatives. One high-technology company recognized the cost of lost knowledge when they figured the fully loaded charges of a research scientist who spent nine months re-creating work another scientist in the company had done several years ago.

Building a business case for knowledge retention initiatives may not be necessary in every organization, but many companies face so many demands on their existing resources that senior management needs to see a strong economic justification for these investments. And the discipline of creating a business case helps ensure that more key stakeholders are onboard because the costs of failure become more explicit. The economic case will also help sustain support for the initiative when resource conflicts inevitably arise. Skipping this step only means that when progress becomes more difficult the retention initiative becomes easier to cut.

Confront Resource Constraints Head On

Savvy advocates of retention initiatives recognize that it is very difficult to sell management on expensive, long-term programs. So they continually seek ways to side step resource constraints.

One common tactic is to invest in projects incrementally. In a small government agency, the HR planner knew he could not convince management to invest up front. He explained, "If I was to say to our managers, 'This process of trying to figure out knowledge loss, continuity management, and succession planning will cost us $500,000 over two years.' I wouldn't get very far." So, instead, he built support for knowledge retention in small ways. For example, he got quick buy in on an eight-week $40,000 pilot project using a social network analysis tool to identify the unit's true subject matter experts. The planner knew the outputs of this project would provide valuable insights and generate excitement among top managers to take the initiative to the next stage. In general, "lack of resources" for knowledge retention is code for "we have other priorities"—such as short-term deliverables. Your strategy should be to use diagnostic tools that will surface data making the threat of lost knowledge so explicit and compelling that leadership can no longer refuse to take action on the problem.

Resource availability for long-term knowledge retention efforts is inevitably tied to the ongoing support of leadership, so it is also important to continually broaden your base of sponsorship. The knowledge management team at NASA learned this lesson when they realized that initial efforts were too narrowly focused on IT solutions, since their lone sponsor was the CIO. Jeanne Holm, NASA's chief knowledge architect, explained that in addition to the CIO, her team now has the support of the agency's chief engineer, who oversees all project management processes, as well as the head of HR and training. "We have initiatives going in all three areas," she said. Broadening executive support for knowledge retention not only provides more access to funding but it also lets you hedge your bets, so when one sponsor leaves the overall initiative doesn't die.

Another threat to knowledge retention programs is their ongoing vulnerability to funding cuts, particularly when they are just another line item in the annual budget. The best defense in this ongoing battle for financial support is to strive from the outset to embed knowledge retention, like quality management, into daily work practices. Knowledge managers at Northrop Grumman learned this lesson the hard way when they encountered stiff competition for discretionary funding to support their retention initiatives. They knew this meant top management wasn't seeing enough value in the programs. This led the knowledge management team to rethink its approach and to focus on three things. First, they had to convince leadership that knowledge retention was not a one-time initiative that would go away after awhile. Second, they began striving to convince line managers to own the problem of preventing negative effects from lost knowledge. As long as retention efforts are viewed as staff programs, they will always be vulnerable. And, third, the Northrop Grumman team's mantra became "find ways to embed knowledge retention in daily work practices." A by-product of line ownership of the problem—and its solution—is keeping knowledge retention overhead as small as possible. "We're trying to embed these practices in everything the Agency does," said NASA's Jeanne Holm. "And we're not going to build a big organization to do it."

Overcome Employees' Lack of Time and Motivation

To develop sustained organizational support for retaining intellectual capital, the behaviors of those who have critical knowledge must be aligned with the organization's needs. In other words, retention initiatives must either be supported by existing cultural norms around knowledge capture, sharing, and reuse or the culture should be changed to support the retention behaviors needed. Evidence that the organization's existing culture doesn't support behaviors needed is usually described as a lack of motivation or time to perform the necessary activities. There are three steps in dealing with the obstacles of time and motivation.

First, recognize that culture will often be a barrier to knowledge retention. Unfortunately, a majority of organizations ignore this admonition when initially confronted with threats of lost knowledge. Sandia Labs, Delta Air Lines, and Northrop Grumman are among the many organizations that have invested in knowledge capture projects by interviewing employees who were leaving. Unfortunately, in reacting to the fear of knowledge loss, they did not think through the motivations of remaining employees to use the materials captured. One member of the nuclear weapons knowledge management group at Sandia National Laboratories explained, "When we started, there was an assumption that if we created a program to preserve knowledge that people would use it. But they didn't. Unlike the Field of Dreams, we learned that if you build it, they won't come." So from the outset it is important to assume that your organization's culture will present obstacles to knowledge capture, access, and reuse. In other words, don't let the immediate threat of losing intellectual capital blind you to the essential elements of a useful solution to the problem, which should include getting the existing knowledge reapplied.

To deal with specific behavioral obstacles to knowledge retention, you need a clear understanding of your culture's norms (i.e., unspoken rules of behavior) around attrition and knowledge use. This may mean drawing on some kind of diagnostic tool to get a clearer picture of the specific cultural issues that need to be attended to. A few years ago Applied Materials, a major supplier of equipment and services to the semiconductor industry, recognized that turnover was having an impact on performance and threatened the company's growth. Before designing a new retention strategy, management asked DBM, a strategic human resource consulting firm, to create an attrition demographic profile, so leadership at Applied Materials could understand cultural norms that were encouraging turnover.[5] And, as described earlier, Northrop Grumman conducted a knowledge audit, which gave its management team a much richer picture of the cultural dynamics surrounding knowledge use. For example, the Northrop Grumman audit revealed considerable stress upon the culture as a result of significant downsizing (in the 1990s). The audit also showed employees were much less willing to share knowledge before their departure if management was involved. They found that if knowledge capture events were presented as something that would help their colleagues, departing employees were much more likely to participate. These findings pointed the way to new management strategies that needed to be pursued to change cultural norms related to knowledge retention.

The KM team at NASA's Jet Propulsion Laboratory conducted its own study of barriers related to knowledge reuse in the culture when its initial retention programs met with resistance. One insight was how reluctant JPL's scientists and engineers were to the idea of "reusing" knowledge. "NASA is very much a cowboy culture," said Jeanne Holm. "People want to say they figured things out themselves. That's one of our culture's strengths—and its problems. So when we talked to folks about reusing knowledge we started calling it 'adaptation' or 'adoption' of existing processes or technologies."

To retain knowledge so it is effectively reused you need to understand the subtleties of how the organization's culture influences knowledge use. When the threat of lost knowledge first becomes a real concern, it will be very tempting to overlook this diagnostic step. But, as the saying goes, you can pay now or you can pay later. The problem is, when you delay taking culture into account, you will probably have wasted precious resources and political support on unsatisfactory short-term solutions.

The third step in dealing with cultural barriers to knowledge retention is an either/or choice. Once you understand the obstacles, such as lack of time or motivation, that undermine behaviors needed to transfer knowledge, you can try to enlist senior management's support in changing the culture to support retention. Or you can adapt your initiatives so that they realistically take cultural constraints into account and complement existing behaviors.

In a growing number of organizations, leaders are already advocating the more effective use of knowledge to create value, even without recognizing the threat an aging workforce can pose to this strategic objective. Leaders in a diverse set of organizations, such as the World Bank, NASA, Sandia Labs, the U.S. Army, and BP have taken up the mantle of culture change in support of building organizations that better apply knowledge to improve performance. Many of the behaviors they are advocating support knowledge retention, of course. But culture change is a long-term proposition, and it requires sustained executive attention, which not all leaders can provide.

So, often, a more practical solution will be to acknowledge and accept your culture as it is and design initiatives that minimally disrupt existing behaviors. For example, the knowledge management team at JPL recognized that it needed to get current project managers to capture knowledge about trade-offs that were considered when making major decisions (e.g. What are the pros and cons of launching off the space shuttle versus off an expendable launch vehicle?) This knowledge would be essential for future projects. But the team also realized that veteran managers "wouldn't spend a minute on this because they were totally under the gun." So JPL designed a document management system that provided other important benefits for current project leaders, while also capturing relevant documents that would retain valuable knowledge for future managers. This system took into account the behaviors and priorities of current project managers, while also meeting NASA's long-term retention needs.

Sustaining organizational performance in a technology-intensive world requires new ways of thinking about process and systems-related knowledge. Given the coming demographic changes, many organizations will have to undertake sustained knowledge retention initiatives. Building a business case for these investments, anticipating resource constraints, and accommodating or changing cultural idiosyncrasies are all essential building blocks of any such effort. The last section in this chapter addresses the decision about where to start.

Which Initiatives to Pursue First?

It's one thing to know what knowledge is at risk in your organization and to know what you have to do to build support for a long-term approach. But a more immediate management decision is where to put a stake in the ground to get started? There are no easy rules to answer this question. Every organization—indeed, every business unit—must consider different contextual factors when deciding where and how to begin. There are, however, four principles derived from the experiences of others that will help you make a better decision.

- Triage knowledge at risk.
- Be clear about the purpose of knowledge retention efforts.
- Be realistic about what the organization can afford.
- Think long-term because retention is an ongoing challenge.

Triage Knowledge at Risk

Getting started means making judgments about which threats of knowledge loss are most critical, demanding immediate attention, and which threats are less serious. Many organizations in the years ahead are going to be losing knowledge much faster than they can possibly capture it, so the only practical strategy—other than denial—is going to be a triage system. To do this right an organization needs to do the following:

- *Develop an effective process for determining knowledge at risk.* This was outlined in the previous section. If you cannot accurately identify most lost knowledge threats, you can't prioritize them. Of course, like any situation filled with uncertainty, mistakes will be made. Real threats will be overlooked and apparent disasters will turn out to be benign. But a comprehensive, generally accurate diagnostic process is essential for prioritizing threats. TVA, for example, had analyzed the criticality of knowledge held by about one-third of its 13,000 employees in mid-2003, as it continued to roll out its knowledge retention process to the entire organization.
- *Seek objectivity when judging how critical particular knowledge is to creating value for the organization.* Experience at TVA and other companies has shown that managers closest to specific practical knowledge can overestimate its contribution to productivity. On the other hand, in technically complex fields, like nuclear weapons development or computer networks, leaders without adequate technical backgrounds can seriously undervalue critical knowledge. A good knowledge triage system is able to evaluate relatively objectively how the failure to retain knowledge in a particular role or function affects organizational performance. Does it stop the production line for days or threaten public safety? Or is it merely an inconvenience for some department whose employees must work overtime? Being aware of the bias many managers and supervisors have about the importance of their subordinates' knowledge is an important step toward being more objective in making decisions about where to focus resources. But so is encouraging leaders to be more open about their own vulnerabilities to misunderstanding the importance of certain technical or scientific knowledge.
- *Recognize realistic time factors for transferring knowledge.* When knowledge loss threatens organizational performance, making decisions about when to address it requires a practical understanding of the time involved in implementing various solutions. For example, when a sales executive retires after handling a complex set of client relationships for 10 years, that account knowledge can't be transferred in a couple of

days. Management is likely to face at least four different types of situations (see figure 10.3) when it comes to the time needed to transfer knowledge versus the time available. When triaging knowledge at risk, you must take this time equation into account.

• *Continually recheck the status of lost knowledge threats.* Triage is a dynamic process. What seems like a relatively benign threat one month may turn out to be very serious problem several months later. For example, the "indispensable expert" who has critical undocumented knowledge about the structure of a key database may be a content mid-career employee one month, but a bored new job seeker six months later. It's essential to continually monitor employees like this, whose loss would create a real problem. The status of specific lost knowledge threats changes frequently and those changes must be caught early to mini-

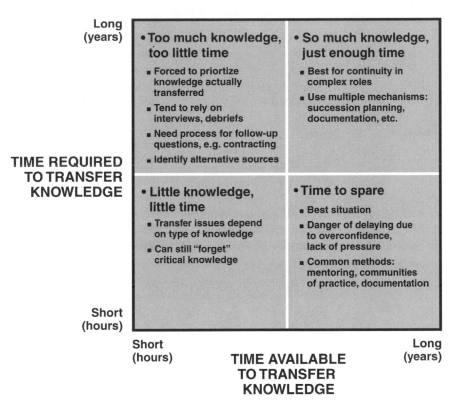

FIGURE 10.3. Matching Timelines and Knowledge Transfer Tactics
The relationship between the time available to transfer knowledge and time actually needed will often vary. This creates different scenarios that require different responses from management and influence which tactics can be used.

mize the damage, and to make sure you are attending to what is most critical at the moment.

Be Clear about the Purpose of Knowledge Retention Efforts

Deciding where and how to launch a retention initiative will be heavily influenced by your explicit and implicit objectives. Often these objectives are vague, for example, "We have to keep knowledge from walking out the door." And they can often become mixed up with broader—and equally abstract—knowledge management objectives, such as "We need to use knowledge to sustain competitive advantage." The lack of clarity in these goals inevitably clouds the real business purpose, which is to acquire, store, and make knowledge accessible so it actually adds value to the business in the future. Access and reuse are the ultimate measure of success—not simply capturing knowledge.

Another decision to be made consciously is whether you are striving to create an ongoing knowledge retention process or simply trying to implement a single retention program. A process, such as that developed by TVA, continually assesses the risk of losing intellectual capital in key parts of the organization and prescribes solutions for knowledge transfer when threats are identified. A program, or a set of programs, on the other hand, addresses specific lost knowledge threats, but do not provide scanning mechanisms to identify new and different retention-related problems. The expert locator system implemented at Northrop Grumman is an example of a retention program that serves an important purpose, but does not identify new lost knowledge threats. Whether you focus on creating a process or implementing a single program will depend on your situation and your resources.

Be Practical about What Leaders Will Support and What the Organization Can Afford

When NASA's knowledge management team at JPL completed their needs assessment, it was clear that program managers were anxious to get a new IT-based system that would capture all design choices for every part on every space craft they built. Capturing this knowledge explicitly would make it much easier to re-create anything JPL had ever built. Unfortunately, this IT-based system would cost $11 million, which was triple the KM group's entire budget.

The JPL team had to make decisions based not only on what was economically feasible but also on what would meet both short- and long-term needs. For example, more mentoring was viewed as important, but it was seen only as providing long-term benefits. Another consideration was what knowledge retention project would provide some results relatively quickly to help prove its value to the organization? Finally, the JPL team also considered which of JPL's internal customers would make a real difference in the Lab's core flight projects if they had better knowledge management support. In the end, JPL invested in a new document management system, which captured and archived critical documents from every space project for future use. This system has become a central part of JPL's work processes. Making decisions about where to invest in knowledge retention will always involve practical considerations, such as the budget available, the trade-offs between long-term and short-term benefits, and which groups, if supported better, would have a greater impact on achieving the organization's overall objectives.

Think Ahead—Retention Is an Ongoing Challenge

Providing some short-term benefits is an important consideration when deciding which projects to start. But, to be successful, knowledge retention, like quality management, must be a long-term initiative. This means when choosing projects you should think carefully about funding mechanisms that will protect the initiative from the budget chopping block. In other words, if your funding source is tenuous and likely to go away, even if the program provides value, think twice about starting it.

Jeanne Holm, NASA's chief knowledge architect, said that at JPL knowledge management and retention programs are almost always sold on a full cost recovery basis. While the KM group received some overhead funds to explore new pilot programs, the long-term ROI measure was: would internal customers pay enough to sustain the service? If this was judged to be an unrealistic expectation, then the KM group had to show a plan for other long-term operational funding. For example, the group knew it could not expect JPL staff to adequately maintain their individual profiles in an expert locator database. Nor could individuals or groups be expected to pay to support the system, despite its overall value for the organization. Thus, Holm's team had to get creative about finding other permanent funding sources. They found they could use some of the IT infrastructure budget to manage the ongoing technology costs for the database server. And, most important, JPL's librarian service agreed to take on the additional task of managing individual employee profiles within their existing budget. Thinking ahead about how your projects could be funded in the long term is sometimes impossible, but it's an important discipline to follow. Working out funding sources up front will increase the likelihood that a retention program will survive to provide long-term benefits. It also decreases your chances of undertaking an initiative that has no chance of survival when the budget-cutting season returns—as it always does.

Deciding where and how to get started on a knowledge retention initiative will sometimes be self-evident. One particularly squeaky part of the organization will have painted a doomsday scenario. And maybe their management is right. Maybe that is where you should invest your retention resources. But, in the next decade, many organizations are going to be faced with a wave of lost knowledge threats. And leaders are going to have to make very difficult choices. What knowledge do you let go? What knowledge do you struggle to keep? The principles outlined here will help you make those decisions more effectively.

11

Overcoming Organizational Barriers
to Knowledge Retention

No one can predict what lost knowledge will cost the industrialized world in the next generation. Will the retirement of the post–World War II generation and the growth of the technology-driven knowledge economy produce only minor disruptions when critical intellectual capital is unavailable? Will the changes turn out to be another overblown Y2K event? Or will the impacts be much more severe? Electricity blackouts, plant explosions, cutbacks in government and health care services, reduced effectiveness in military operations, major quality upsets in manufacturing operations, declining productivity in oil and gas exploration—all of these are possible, even likely to occur in the years ahead.

That's because we have entered a new era. We are now retiring the first generation of managers and professionals who have deep knowledge of complex technical and political systems, multidisciplinary scientific domains, and integrated work processes. These people have lots of hard-to-replace knowledge that didn't exist 30 years ago. Certainly, some older workers are ready to retire and wish to do so. Others have not developed the skills and knowledge needed to keep pace with the changing demands of the workplace, or they don't have the motivation to work as hard as they used to. But for all those experienced employees whose knowledge can be easily replaced if they depart from your organization, there are plenty of others leaving with a treasure chest of expertise (formal or informal) that will be incredibly costly to replace. The challenge for leaders in the decade ahead is to create performance management systems that can identify who has critical knowledge and to develop processes to retain as much of this expertise as possible.

But it won't be easy—even if you know what knowledge needs to be transferred, who has it, and who needs to acquire it. You will recognize this challenge if you have already tried to implement knowledge transfer and succession initiatives, such as a mentoring or coaching program, a lessons learned database, or some direct training. The chances are the results have been less successful than you hoped. So what can you do to improve the payoff of your knowledge retention efforts? To take effective action you must recognize and overcome four types of problems that actually promote knowledge loss in organizations:

- No one gets rewarded for investing in knowledge retention
- Poor interpersonal dynamics between experts and novices
- Organizational dilemmas undermine knowledge sharing
- The psychological trap of "competing commitments"

Chapters 4 through 8 showed lots of ways to improve knowledge retention. But implementing any of these initiatives effectively means confronting these dynamics that actually discourage knowledge transfer (see figure 11.1). These phenomena are not unique to the problem of managing intellectual capital. They are, however, particularly challenging when dealing with the costs of employee turnover because of the abstract, context-dependent, personal nature of the knowledge that needs to be retained. Thus, sophisticated change management practices are needed to respond to these challenges.

Nobody Gets Promoted for Investing in Knowledge Retention

Like convincing taxpayers to replace deteriorating water and sewer systems, selling managers on knowledge retention investments can be hard work, even if you have a good business case. Sometimes it appears that you are asking the organization to expend resources to maintain existing performance levels or to avoid problems that might never happen. It's human nature to think, "Why should we have to spend more to keep things as they are?" (The irony, of course, is that knowledge retention does considerably more than maintain the status quo, as will be shown again in chapter 12.) And many managers will think that, even if a retention initiative is success-

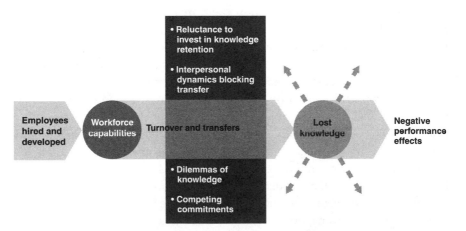

FIGURE 11.1. **Organizational Dynamics That Block Knowledge Retention**

ful, there is no obvious payback for the investment, compared to other opportunities. Aside from this obvious drawback there are other reasons why
it's hard to see the value of investing to minimize knowledge loss.

First, most organizations have historically not rewarded individuals for
retaining knowledge because those actions are not valued in the culture. For
example, one veteran systems analyst was leaving his team where he had
been overseeing credit card databases. He illustrated the problem with this
comment:

> I transferred the whole database update process to a new analyst to
> minimize the impact on the marketing department and that has hap-
> pened. They haven't missed a deadline. That's probably my biggest ac-
> complishment. But nobody has recognized that. If you document and
> teach well, nobody notices, and your value goes unrecognized. If you
> don't your value is missed.[1]

Reward systems must be aligned with your organization's need to keep
knowledge in the unit. That is because cultures that don't reward behaviors
to prevent critical knowledge loss are much less likely to see the value of
investing in programs that encourage such activities. If management believes
in the importance of knowledge retention, then the organization should provide incentives for employees to behave accordingly.

Second, like "knowledge management," the concept of "knowledge retention" is an abstract, ill-structured idea ripe for projecting a variety of management expectations and biases. As a result, there is bound to be lots of
confusion and conflict about the real purpose of any investment in this area.[2]
This problem was evident at the World Bank after its president, James Wolfensohn, began selling a new knowledge management strategy. One case
study reported:

> Initially, there was a lot of argument about what knowledge manage-
> ment—and the Knowledge Bank—was. According to one manager,
> "Only a few got what Wolfensohn was talking about." Many perceived
> it as some kind of IT initiative and some ridiculed it as "star wars." Oth-
> ers saw it as "another flavor of the month program," and still others
> saw it as "no major change from the way we currently work."[3]

Selling investments in knowledge retention is very hard without first developing a shared understanding among key stakeholders about what it is
you are really trying to achieve. Kent Greenes, CKO at the research and engineering services firm SAIC, said that when his group works with clients
the first phase is always devoted to high-level project definition. SAIC consultants engage senior stakeholders and the likely executive champion in a
two-day process to figure out where knowledge transfer can help with main-

stream business issues. In other words, where can knowledge retention make a big difference? "It's much more valuable to go to a project already under-way where potential retirees are involved and acquire their knowledge while on the job," said Greenes. "Because you want the knowledge you're going after to capture the imagination of the organization."[4]

The age and experience of your managers can also undermine the per-ceived value of investing in knowledge retention. One government agency found that it could not get its less experienced directors interested in succes-sion planning to replace many retirement eligible managers. The project's sponsor speculated that the younger directors didn't yet appreciate the knowledge the organization was going to be losing. On the other hand, older managers who themselves are close to retirement may also be reluctant to take up the difficult challenge of knowledge preservation, preferring to leave the problem to their successors.

Finding and sustaining committed sponsorship for retention programs will always be a challenge. The place to start is to find a champion who feels a sense of urgency and emotional commitment to the problem. Then you will need to build a team with the right skills and social contacts to combine op-erational, HR, IT, and knowledge management perspectives needed to ad-dress the problem. Work sessions and stories that help executives feel more urgency about addressing knowledge transfer problems will be an important part of many implementation efforts.

Steve Denning, former head of knowledge management at the World Bank, knows firsthand the power of stories to communicate complex ideas and to motivate senior executive groups. Confronted by a skeptical leader-ship team, which doubted the value of investing in knowledge-sharing initia-tives, Denning told them a story that showed how effective knowledge shar-ing could really improve the Bank's performance. He could just as easily have been talking about knowledge retention. But in reflecting on the value of sto-rytelling in implementing his change initiative, Denning said:

> That story enabled me to connect with the World Bank senior manage-ment and communicate the idea. . . . And they started to think: "Well, that's remarkable how quickly we could respond to that kind of situa-tion in that out-of-the-way part of the world. Imagine if we had that kind of capability . . . all across the organization. Imagine if the whole World Bank functioned like this." And in effect, they said, "Let's do it! Let's become an agile knowledge sharing organization." And so the out-come of the meeting was not, as some had expected a court martial looking into why there were so many flaws and blemishes in the imple-mentation of this massive effort at transformation. Instead, the meeting led to a whole new surge of momentum behind knowledge sharing to

make that something that was uniform across the whole organization. And so I found that storytelling was not ephemeral and nebulous and worthless. Instead I found that it was an extremely powerful tool to get major change in this large change-resistant organization.[5]

Storytelling can be a good way to emotionally engage senior executives in addressing threats posed by lost knowledge. Stories can be told not only to create a sense of urgency by demonstrating explicitly how attrition is hurting organizational performance. But they can also be used to describe solutions that other units or other companies have successfully tried in order to retain knowledge. Examples of success can fire the imagination and energize managers to see retention investments in a more hopeful light.

"Storytelling . . . can help the instigator of change at any level deal with the paradox facing the large organizations of our age—that major change is essential, but the organizations themselves often seem almost immovable," notes Denning. "It can assist in mobilizing large numbers of managers and employees, in support of changes that will initially seem difficult, upsetting, and strange."[6] Altering processes and behaviors to support knowledge retention are just this type of difficult change, and stories can help get it started.

Understanding the Dynamics of Interpersonal Knowledge Sharing

Management's reluctance to invest in knowledge preservation can be overcome, but the interpersonal dynamics between experts and novices (or less experienced employees) can still undermine effective action on the problem. To counter this dynamic you must look for five factors that are likely to impede the effectiveness of direct knowledge sharing between experts and novices (see figure 11.2).[7]

Lack of Motivation to Share or Reuse Knowledge

A young research scientist described a common situation when he recounted his relationship with a venerable expert:

> When I first met him he said he was never going to retire. He loved his work, and he told me his father had worked until the day he died. He wanted to make sure I knew that. And I wanted to make sure he knew I wasn't going to push him out. I had such respect for this man, but when I observed him I would just stand in the corner of the room. He wouldn't let me look through the microscope, so I couldn't learn about

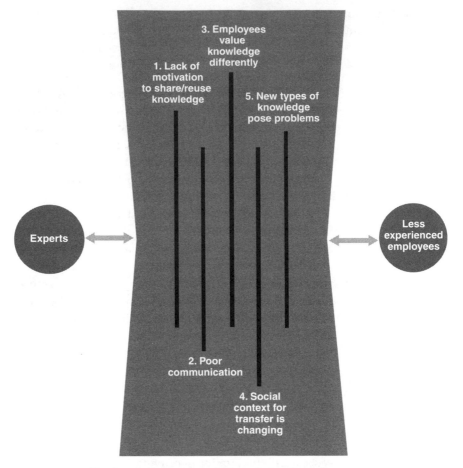

FIGURE 11.2. Barriers to Interpersonal Knowledge Transfer

his experimentation philosophy and what he had learned over the years, what had worked and what hadn't.

When implementing knowledge-sharing initiatives, one of the first things to acknowledge is the most likely motivational state of both the experts and novices who need to share or absorb knowledge. In practice, experts who are leaving can experience a range of emotions. While many feel a natural desire to mentor and give back to the organization, older workers may also feel pushed out, alienated, angry, or anxious to move on to other things. The point is veterans are likely to experience mixed feeling about leaving and these emotions directly affect their motivation to share knowledge.

At the same time, less experienced employees can also have a range of feelings about departing experts (e.g., highly respectful, annoyed, impatient). This not only affects their motivation to absorb and adapt the knowledge of their predecessors, but the feelings can also seriously impact a veteran's interest in sharing. One well-known scientist reflected his frustration at what he felt was a lack of respect for his knowledge: "I refuse to mentor people now because an adversarial dynamic gets set up. It's very subtle, but it's around the need of our younger people to discover new things for themselves. They just want me to dump what I know, so they can get beyond it. But I can't do that."

Unfortunately, research findings about the differences between baby boomers and Gen-Xers predict plenty of discord that will undermine motivations for knowledge sharing and learning across the generations.[8] Researchers generally characterize boomers as more competitive and, thus, likely to hold on to information as a source of political advantage. They are also anxious to be respected for their experiences and achievements, which were gained by "paying their dues," something they implicitly expect others to do. Finally, boomers generally place more value on the development of face-to-face relationships than their younger colleagues.

Gen-Xers, on the other hand, are more conditioned to learning through alternative formats, such as interactive video or computer simulations, and they have less patience for the face-to-face interaction needed to acquire tacit knowledge. They generally want to learn by doing and getting feedback on their efforts, rather than by listening or reading. And they have less inherent respect for authority or seniority than the preceding generation, believing that this respect must be earned and not simply granted because someone holds an important title. These generalizations are not universally applicable because every situation will vary and have extenuating circumstances, but recognizing these tendencies can sensitize managers to patterns that are likely to emerge, so they can react more quickly.

Two themes that come up repeatedly when talking about knowledge sharing are trust and a sense of appreciation for the expert's knowledge. When these are missing on either side of the relationship, knowledge transfer will be much more difficult. If your initial attempts to encourage knowledge sharing have been less than successful, reevaluate the levels of trust and the expert's perception of how his or her knowledge is perceived. Trust and mutual respect almost always take time to develop, which is why you need to start creating the right environment today if you want to be transferring knowledge several years from now.

But, if you are in need of a short-term solution, try combining experts and novices on the same project team. Put less experienced employees in joint problem-solving sessions where they can observe veteran colleagues. That's because the best way to increase the perceived value of an expert's knowledge is to show it in action. And working together on any kind of intense project is your best shot at building mutual trust.

Poor Communication

If you're a baby boomer you knew you were getting old a decade ago when you overheard some young person tell a friend, "Hey, did you know Paul McCartney had another band before Wings?" If you have forgotten the Beatles, you can substitute other names into that story. The point is every generation has its own icons, symbols, and metaphors, which are inevitably used as shorthand to transmit tacit knowledge.[9] Often veteran employees will find it difficult to communicate with junior colleagues because they lack shared symbols and metaphors to explain abstract ideas. For example, one veteran scientist noted: "The 35-year-olds in our group have no clue what I'm talking about when I use a certain symbol that us older researchers take for granted. Here we are in the same field, but we have different training that keeps us from communicating with each other."

Recognizing the absence of shared symbols and jargon early on at least provides the chance to slow down the discussion long enough to fill in the gaps and to build bridges of meaning that will support more effective knowledge transfer. Veterans are likely to become annoyed at their protégés' lack of background or training in certain areas, while less experienced employees may not see the value of certain background knowledge, which they discount as irrelevant. Finding ways to stifle these feelings or to express them respectfully is important for both the teacher and the student, if they are to remain committed to the learning process. Because, if either side feels disrespected, motivation will plummet.

The lack of time for knowledge transfer also adds tension that can hurt the communication process. Veterans who are expected to continue performing their job while training others are likely to feel torn between conflicting objectives, particularly if they are not being rewarded for developing others. And less experienced employees who are trying to learn from experts while doing another job don't have as much attention to give the new material. Making these time conflicts discussable is the first step to working out reasonable solutions for passing on expertise. Leaders who act as if knowledge transfer will occur without providing reasonable time for effective communication are living in a fantasy world.

Finally, everyone who has ever been to college knows there are plenty of smart people who can't teach. Most of us, unfortunately, had a few professors who hadn't figured that out. Given the law of averages, some veteran employees are going to be much better than others at passing on knowledge to their successors. Some of the best experts in your organization will be lousy teachers. There is no easy solution to this problem, but identifying those with poor communication skills early on gives management more time to design alternative ways of transferring this knowledge. For example, you might hook up a tongue-tied expert with an assistant earlier than normal for someone approaching retirement, or identify one of the veteran's trusted colleagues who can act as an intermediary in interpreting and passing on knowledge, or provide coaching in communication skills. These are just three ideas of how to approach experts who have trouble sharing what they know. None of them is ideal, but they are all better than denying that communication problems exist.

Experts and Novices Value Knowledge Differently

People value knowledge differently based on their life experience. When Janet Rand finished her training in optometry, she had been taught not to fit contact lenses flat on the cornea because recent research showed this led to scarring on the eye surface. Her new mentor, however, had been fitting lenses on the most difficult patients for decades, and she still fit lenses flat. "When I started here I thought she was wrong for not using the new method," said the younger doctor. Rand initially discounted her older colleague's approach as outdated. That is until Rand gained more experience and realized that her mentor's actions reflected more sophisticated knowledge that could only be acquired over time by working in the field.

A retiring coordinator for environment, health, and safety in an aerospace plant offered a related story. He said:

> A lot of people can't recognize problems because they haven't lived through them. As I was mentoring a recent Ph.D. from MIT, I walked him through the plant showing him high-tech processes like laser drilling and electron beam welding. This guy was brilliant, but he couldn't find the factory floor from the rest room. Younger people can have plenty of theory but they lack experiential knowledge.

These two anecdotes reflect the different perspectives that experts and novices bring to a knowledge transfer situation. Less experienced employees, often relying primarily on knowledge acquired in training, will sometimes discount a veteran's practical knowledge because it is at odds with their more formal training. On the other hand, experienced employees are just as likely to bemoan the qualifications of their successors, as reflected by this comment from a retiring salesperson for a major chemical firm:

> When I joined the company, many of the salespeople had strong technical backgrounds because they came out of the laboratory. Today, the

tendency is to replace them with people who aren't as expert. They're just basically salespeople. Now there's too much turnover because they often take people out of marketing and just use sales as a training area.

When designing knowledge transfer programs, it is important to recognize that both experts and novices can have dysfunctional perspectives on each other's current knowledge. If veterans judge their successors as inadequately trained and impatient, they are more likely either to refuse to help them or to talk down to them, lecturing in a way that frustrates the junior person. If the less experienced employee misjudges the expert's knowledge base and dismisses it as outdated, he or she may tune out and ignore valuable advice, leading to costly mistakes and unnecessary reinvention of knowledge later on. To avoid both unwanted outcomes, try to focus everyone on the desired result—retaining as much valuable expertise as possible. And be sure to identify what's in it for both parties to participate. Then challenge both experts and novices to test their own assumptions about each other's knowledge, instead of acting based on untested beliefs. Only then can they design transfer tactics focused on more important organizational needs.

The U.S. Army Communications-Electronics Command (CECOM) found a tactic that helped circumvent the problem of valuing knowledge differently as it tried to develop its next generation of acquisition workers. CECOM had the consulting firm SAIC train 20 of its less experienced employees as "knowledge harvesters," so they could interview procurement experts. There were several benefits in having CECOM's junior people work alongside SAIC consultants while conducting interviews to capture the experiential knowledge of veteran procurement officers. "We had novices work with us as knowledge harvesters," said SAIC's Kent Greenes. "That way they could learn the knowledge elicitation methodology for future use. But we also greatly accelerated their own learning about the procurement process as they helped us do knowledge retention work." By creating a semi-structured process for knowledge acquisition, CECOM was able to jump start the knowledge base of its less experienced people and help them develop productive relationships with procurement experts that would be very valuable in the future.

Social Context for Transfer Is Unstable

One thing that makes it so challenging to design effective approaches for retention is that the social context for transferring experiential knowledge is in a state of flux. One older scientist commented: "Mentoring is up in the air now. As a mentor, I can't tell junior people what to do. The hierarchy is no longer critical to imparting knowledge. And it's not just that old people are leaving. There are no expectations that they will pass their knowledge along and that younger people will get it."

This statement reflects the instability felt in many organizations where jobs are continually restructured and technical knowledge becomes more complex. As a result, management has become more disconnected from the daily work of technical and scientific professionals. Frequent reorganizations have conditioned younger employees not to consider long-term careers in many settings. "You're losing the farm system where people used to come in at entry level and move through management training," said one retiring aerospace executive. "There's no more career path for the average person." One result of this turbulence is that norms about sharing knowledge have been disrupted.

Probably the biggest factor affecting the social context for knowledge transfer is the increased reliance on computers, particularly among younger workers, as a way of acquiring and accessing knowledge. One dramatic illustration of this is the increased reliance among nuclear weaponeers on computer simulations as the only way of "knowing" about the performance of nuclear weapons. The United States has not tested an atomic bomb in over a decade. Thus, the experiential knowledge of older weapons designers is rapidly leaving the nuclear weapons establishment. Younger scientists and engineers are enthusiastic about the value of computer models, but veterans of the nuclear weapons program insist there is only so much that can be simulated. "You can do computer simulations to an extent," said Dr. John Mansfield, a member of the Defense Nuclear Facilities Safety Board. "But you can't get everything. For example, it's very difficult to see if you're computing turbulence right. You need to do tests to check it."

The point is the role of computers in helping to develop, store, and access knowledge has disrupted many traditions of transferring knowledge across generations. To take a different type of example, when was the last time you communicated through a long handwritten letter? The technology has also created new questions, as noted by one senior scientist:

> Young people today are very facile with advanced technology tools, but that doesn't mean they have the content expertise they need to use them well. Good research requires deep knowledge on a relatively narrow topic. But how do you transfer this deep knowledge usefully when we know that the research methodologies enabled by new computer systems are going to be quite different?

In other words, the challenge of retaining knowledge is happening at the same time the context for learning has changed due to new technologies. There is no easy way around the fact that the social environment that shapes knowledge transfer is changing. As a leader, the first thing you can do is to be aware of the impact these shifts are having on your own situation. For example, how have reorganizations and layoffs disrupted traditional behaviors of passing knowledge on to successors? To what extent are younger employees constantly worried about being laid off? How are these feelings realistically going to affect your ability to develop workforce capabilities in the future? To what extent are employees' new behaviors inevitable or acceptable, given your retention needs? And, given that computer tools are changing the way much knowledge is being created and stored today, particularly by younger employees, how much danger is there that certain mission-critical human knowledge is going to be lost? There are no easy solutions to the problems these questions are likely to surface. But you have zero chance of solving them until they are at least put on the table and discussed by the organization's leaders. An important next step is evaluating the effects of the problems identified on your organization's strategic objectives.

New Types of Knowledge Pose Problems

Finally, another factor that complicates the quality of interpersonal knowledge sharing is the new types of knowledge that need to be transferred from experts to novices. Some kinds of intellectual capital can be transferred more readily than others. But, with advances in science and technology combined with globalization and the increased integration of work processes, new types of knowledge are routinely being created today. For example:

- Knowledge of how database processes work, how computer data is structured, and the rules for linking specific data elements is extremely complex and abstract. One supervisor for a credit card database explained:

    Every type of activity on the database has its different characteristics which determine how it is updated, how it is built and constructed, the type of data it contains, the source of data it comes from—because a lot of the activities just come from totally different sources.

    . . . There are 40 different types of activities and I probably know ten very well. That means I'm familiar with how the data is stored, the types of data fields in the event, how it is updated, and the nuances. . . . Is this field reliable, for example? Is it something that's populated? Some of these fields are found in more than one place in the database. For instance, by looking at the Address Change activity you can tell whether a credit card is active or canceled. And by looking at a field in the Master Record called "active or canceled" you can also tell. But which one is more reliable, since they sometimes conflict?[10]

This type of knowledge about the internal structure of a database can only be acquired through experience in using it. This knowledge is tacit, changeable, and idiosyncratic. In another example mentioned earlier, cornea transplants were relatively rare 30 years ago. Today they are routine. But every transplant, now possible because of medical advances, heals differently. And the only way to learn how to correct a patient's vision after surgery is to see hundreds or thousands of these cases to acquire experiential knowledge about what works in different situations.

• Cross-disciplinary knowledge is also increasingly important. Take John Mansfield, a veteran member of the Defense Nuclear Facilities Safety Board, for example. Dr. Mansfield is a Harvard-trained physicist who has held posts in the U.S. Defense Intelligence Agency, the Defense Nuclear Agency, and the Defense Advanced Research Projects Agency, where he was director of the strategic technology office. He has also had two stints on Capitol Hill as a congressional staffer for both the Senate and House Armed Services Committees, and along the way he was an associate administrator at NASA. Do you think this guy has a big Rolodex? Mansfield's experiential knowledge of the science and technology underlying nuclear weapons, along with his understanding of the inner workings of Capitol Hill and the executive branch, gives him a rare combination of expertise that is ideal for overseeing the safety practices of the nuclear weapons establishment. When he retires, that multidisciplinary knowledge will be almost impossible to replace.

New knowledge created as a result of increasingly complex work environments is often abstract, conceptual, and interdisciplinary. Equally important, it is best acquired only through experience, which is frequently driven by a passion for solving difficult problems. For example, Dick Ludwig is a retired DuPont chemist, who helped in the market development of Tyvek,[11] the non-woven plastic product that has dozens of uses. For example, you see it wrapped around buildings on just about every construction site you drive by. Early in his career at DuPont, Ludwig got interested in the tricky problem of printing on Tyvek. Solving this could open up all kinds of new markets for the product. "Initially, I thought I would work on printing for two years, but I became intrigued," he recalled. "And after four years I was treating it like a hobby. I would visit different printers in my spare time just to see how they did things. I was always excited about it." Not surprisingly, Ludwig became a leading expert about printing on Tyvek. In his 70s now, DuPont still calls on him to consult when difficult problems arise in this area, even though he has tried to train numerous people about what he has learned.

In reality, we have precious little accumulated insight about how to transfer new types of experiential knowledge, such as maintaining critical historical knowledge about a complex technology system or operating in a cross-cultural global sales environment. One recently retired global director of purchasing for a major oil company said, for example:

> There aren't many people who can quickly pick up knowledge about doing business in different cultures. It's hard to transfer that. In some cultures, until they believe you are honorable, people will negotiate differently with you. I had one major Israeli supplier where it took me years to establish a fairly open relationship. At one point they accused me of shopping their prices around. When they finally realized I hadn't done that, I had good credibility. But my replacement won't have that trust because they're always suspicious you're taking advantage of them. It's hard to transfer that credibility to anyone. And if I was bitter about leaving my company, a couple of words to the supplier's CEO and it would take years to rebuild that relationship.

Given that new types of experiential knowledge are both critical and extremely hard to replicate, what effective actions can you take to transfer at least some of what is known? First, as noted in the previous chapter, try to pinpoint and prioritize the most critical knowledge at risk. This means telling the truth about where you could be hurt the most. Is it losing cross-cultural knowledge about global operations? Is it knowledge about the vulnerabilities of your technology infrastructure? Or is it insights about solving cross-disciplinary problems? Where are the risks greatest?

One way to generate productive discussions about these threats in your organization is to use a technique called scenario planning. Generating plausible alternative outcomes if certain experts leave can be an effective tool for managing the uncertainties that surround looming threats of lost knowledge. The scenarios can provide managers with a tool for systematic evaluation of potential lost knowledge threats, as well as a method for assessing the payoff of proposed retention initiatives. Scenario planning can help make explicit the details about different types of experiential knowledge that may be lost. But most important, it connects these threats back to your strategic objectives so they can be prioritized.[12]

Another productive step is to recognize that despite all of the intense pressures posed by your growth objectives and the "speed is God" mantra, transferring experiential knowledge that can actually be used takes time. There are some short cuts, but they are few. And you should be skeptical of promises made by consultants and vendors in this area. One retiring sales executive for a global manufacturer recalled how he passed on key know-how and social knowledge. "I had an unusually long time to transfer knowledge to my successor," he said. "I spent two months in Europe and North America taking my replacement into 25 companies talking to senior level management. And we spent equal time on planes and in the office transferring knowledge. We scheduled time and made an honest effort to do it, which usually doesn't happen, especially when people are forced out."

In the end, face it, a lot of experiential knowledge is going to be lost to the next generation in your organization. There is only so much knowledge that can be passed on. It's always been that way. But what has changed is there are many new types of complex knowledge that have become vital to organizational success. And if intellectual capital is recognized as a critical asset, then it becomes more worthwhile than ever for leaders to understand the interpersonal dynamics between experts and novices that may be blocking whatever productive knowledge sharing is possible.

Organizational Paradoxes Undermine Knowledge Sharing

Improving the quality of interactions between employees isn't the only thing that has to change. Stemming the flow of lost knowledge also means confronting a variety of management dilemmas that undermine knowledge retention. For example:

- Many leaders are focused primarily on controlling operational costs, but it takes time and resources to transfer expert knowledge.
- Strong performance management systems require regular evaluation of how individuals are contributing to organizational objectives, but knowledge sharing can be promoted only by maintaining authentic communications and positive long-term relationships between employees and their managers.
- Given the strong socialization in professions and disciplines, such as chemistry and engineering, can employees also be expected to develop equal commitment to the long-term success of their organization? This identity with organizational objectives is needed to support knowledge sharing.

New approaches are needed to reconcile the conflicting values related to knowledge. Complex work environments inevitably consist of competing objectives, such as the need to cut costs while simultaneously training new employees for sophisticated roles. In these situations, effective knowledge retention comes not by choosing between alternatives, but by integrating competing needs into an approach that serves both goals.[13]

Current shifts in workforce demographics combined with the changing nature of knowledge in the workplace are presenting leaders with a series of opposing demands (e.g., cut costs but transfer knowledge). Successfully confronting these dilemmas is both very difficult and potentially very rewarding. But ignoring or denying their presence can paralyze the organization to inaction. As Charles Hampden-Turner has noted, "If you duck the dilemma you also miss the resolution. There is no cheap grace."[14]

This section will show how change leaders can approach dilemmas differently by designing knowledge retention initiatives that seek to create congruence between conflicting priorities. An example of these conflicts was evident in the comments of an executive in one aerospace firm:

> The biggest challenge is that our managers don't have knowledge retention as a core part of the way they operate. Most managers are still driven by yearly cycle results. The focus is more tactical, that is meeting the numbers today versus being concerned about a long-term knowledge strategy as the way you operate.
>
> Ideally, if managers are responsible for a key knowledge area, they would first understand how many people they have with those skills. If they're only one or two deep, then they need to hire in someone and mentor them, or rotate mid-level people into that job and get them trained. But if you're just focused on delivering numbers at the end of the year, then you're not going to do those things, even if you're just one person deep in a critical area. All of a sudden an area can go from being a top-performer to being in trouble, and management just says it's because we've lost all of our talent.

Charles Hampden-Turner describes a five-step process for reconciling dilemmas like the ones that are likely to block your efforts at knowledge retention.

Step 1: Mapping Dilemmas

Surface and map the conflicts that are holding your organization back. Say, for example, it is the dilemma described above by the aerospace executive. To simplify this conflict slightly, let's frame it as cost control versus employee development, which can be a proxy for knowledge retention.

Ask key stakeholders to locate the organization's current priorities on a chart like figure 11.3 and they might describe one of four conditions: (1) intense cost focus; (2) intense employee development focus; (3) oscillation between the two competing objectives because of adversarial relationships between key stakeholders advocating both positions; (4) a lackluster compromise designed to reduce tensions among adversarial stakeholders.

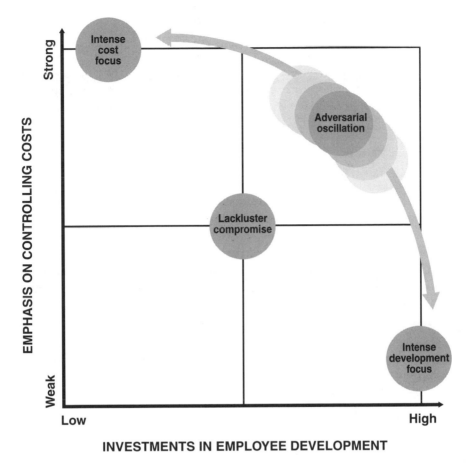

FIGURE 11.3. **Mapping an Organizational Dilemma**
The first step in addressing competing objectives that hinder knowledge retention is to locate the organization's current emphasis and approach. The competing issues of employee development and cost control provide an example here. *Source*: Adapted from Hampden-Turner, 1990.

Once you have located your organization between the axes that represent conflicting objectives, you are in a position to try to reconcile these differences.

Step 2: Convert to Process

Next convert the competing objectives, currently described as nouns or things, into more fluid processes. This is done by recasting objectives into present participles. (For those of you who slept through seventh-grade English class that means adding "-ing" to create a verb form.) Thus, cost containment and employee development become "containing costs" and "developing employees." This simple framing reduces the hard-edged oppositional quality of these apparently conflicting concepts. Suddenly, solid-sounding things become more fluidlike processes. Hampden-Turner points out, "It's no coincidence that the word 'solution' means both reconciling and a liquid."[15]

Step 3: Reframing and Contextualizing

Opposing values can be integrated by locating them in a figure/ground relationship, as shown in figure 11.4. Reconciling conflicting processes like these can be expressed by putting them in a picture surrounded by a frame and then having the frame change places with the picture. With this technique each value is *contained within* and *constrained by* its opposite. Now the two processes can be thought of as interwoven instead of mutually exclusive.

Thus, developing employees is both contained within and constrained by processes of containing costs. Development processes should not damage the cost-sensitive environment in which they are applied. At the same time, processes for containing costs exist in an environment that also needs to develop employee capabilities. When employee development processes are hurt by containing costs, then the former are not strong enough. And when employee development undermines cost containment activities, then the latter need to be strengthened. Cost-effective workforce development will only

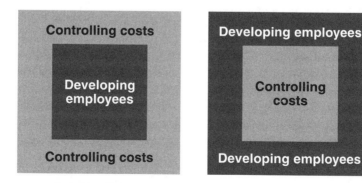

FIGURE 11.4. **Contextualizing Dilemmas**
Dilemmas that inhibit knowledge retention can be resolved by framing competing needs as both figure and ground. In this example, investments in employee development are both contained within and constrained by the competing need to control costs. This approach frames the two objectives as interdependent instead of mutually exclusive. *Source*: Adapted from Hampden-Turner, 1990.

occur where the two processes are interwoven but also retain their integrity and strength.

Step 4: Sequencing Actions

Ignoring the variable of time is one of the main reasons we feel trapped in dilemmas. Competing values, such as controlling costs and developing employees, often seem to be in conflict because they are implicitly being dealt with at the same time. But it is pretty hard to simultaneously teach someone and focus on the cost of their learning. The solution is to use time to mediate these apparent conflicts by dealing with competing values sequentially. This is why timing is an essential part of strategy implementation. Executives, for example, do something first to create the context or infrastructure for what is done second. These sequences are very purposeful and meaningful.

Often, there are preferred sequences and the trick is identifying them. For example, an emphasis on developing employees can be followed by cost-control activities, or vice versa. Hampden-Turner recommends starting a sequence with whichever of the two objectives is currently most neglected. Thus, leaders concerned with knowledge retention might have different operating units pilot a series of relevant employee development initiatives and then bring them to top management for review and decisions about additional funding to control development costs.

Here is another example of how sequencing works in the apparent conflict between relationship building and evaluating employee performance. A manager must spend considerable time building relationships with employees before evaluating them. If this relational work has been done first, then evaluating takes place in the context of relating. But if no such relationship has been created over time, then the chances of providing effective feedback are much less likely. "Indeed, elapsed time can be a good measure of how seriously values are taken in an organization," said Hampden-Turner. "If a supervisor has spent ten minutes in a year relating to a subordinate and now expects to evaluate him or her in another ten minutes, then the relationship is unlikely to survive the evaluation."[16] And meanwhile, the context for subsequent knowledge sharing has been undermined.

Step 5: Cycling between Objectives

To alternately emphasize conflicting objectives in sequence implies that they resemble a waveform moving between the axes of a dilemma. For example, units may first propose employee development initiatives and then leaders decide which proposals the organization can afford, given the need to control costs. Thus begins a wave encompassing both development and cost control.

Multiple units may initiate many retention-related pilots, and later leaders will identify which to fund more fully and which to cut. If units, in turn, try approved programs and provide feedback to top management, then over time the wave becomes part of a larger cycle (see figure 11.5).

Ideally, the conflicting objectives will balance each other out. But, in practice, one value in a dilemma is often more dominant than the other in a particular organization. For example, advocates for controlling costs are likely to have more influence than those supporting employee development. Unless, there is some way to correct the balance of influence, both values will

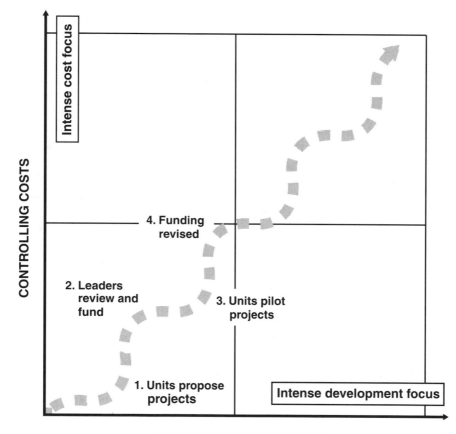

DEVELOPING EMPLOYEES

FIGURE 11.5. Cycling between Competing Objectives
Confront dilemmas that hinder knowledge retention by moving back and forth between conflicting needs. The resulting wave-form accommodates both objectives by recognizing the importance of sequencing activities. *Source*: Adapted from Hampden-Turner, 1990.

not be able to provide feedback to correct each other's potential excesses. When this happens, untempered cost controls, for example, become overly rigid and out of touch with the changing environment. One result has been described as the "capability trap." Even when intermittent employee development programs yield positive results, the mantra of "cost control" is likely to encourage management to downsize or find other ways to drain resources away from the improvements. Thus, the new employee capabilities stall or even decline, leading management to exhort its staff to work harder in hopes of controlling costs, while also maintaining performance levels.[17]

Repenning and Sterman suggest that when one value, such as controlling costs, becomes dominant for too long the best way to rebalance what should be competing objectives is to take counterintuitive action. This might mean temporarily letting performance deteriorate even faster, while increasing investments in employee development to rebuild capabilities.

Organizations won't significantly improve knowledge retention without confronting dilemmas that threaten to sustain the status quo and promote lost knowledge. It may be a conflict between controlling costs and developing employees, or between your employees' professional identifies and their commitment to the organization's mission. Whatever the conflict that prevents knowledge transfer, managing these competing values is difficult. Pursuing a single objective would seem seductively simpler at times, but it's actually more dangerous in the long run. "There are always *two* opposed ways of wrecking the ship," notes Hampden-Turner. "You can sacrifice it to something hard, unambiguous, precise, detailed, and definite; or to something soft, vague, general pervasive, and indefinite."[18] Thus, plotting a course that balances conflicting values to synthesize their valuable qualities gives you the best chance of succeeding in the long run.

The Psychological Trap of "Competing Commitments"

"We've got to stop letting knowledge walk out the door!" That's a phrase you're going to hear a lot as more baby boomers retire. Managers may mean it, but still nothing happens. Sometimes it is not a matter of expert/novice dynamics or organizational dilemmas. Sometimes the barrier is more psychological. Many leaders know they have performance problems related to knowledge loss, and they sincerely want to do something. Just like those New Year's resolutions to start exercising, however, the intention to take action usually gets sidetracked.

Organizational psychologists Robert Kegan and Lisa Lahey would argue that the manager's "We've got to stop . . ." admonition is symptomatic of a very profound barrier to change. Kegan and Lahey contend that even when individuals or groups sincerely want to change, they often unconsciously invest energy in hidden competing commitments. The resulting dynamic, which produces an inexplicable lack of progress, actually creates an "immunity" to change. For example, you may find that the expert who won't collaborate to share knowledge, despite a sincere commitment to being a team player, is equally dedicated to not losing the security that comes with being the recognized guru in a particular area.[19]

By "competing commitments" we're not talking about all those other appointments, project meetings, and kid's soccer games that clog your calendar. This is, rather, a psychological notion that describes hidden assumptions that individuals and groups have that undermine the achievement of their stated objectives. This dynamic is particularly relevant when it comes to retaining knowledge because, like it or not, we often have very mixed feelings about what other people know. Kegan and Lahey would argue that it is these hidden and undiscussable beliefs most of us hold that will actually prevent us from taking effective action to retain knowledge, even when we know it is essential to the organization's survival. The first step to short-circuiting this dynamic is understanding how it works.

For example, one group used a "competing commitments" exercise to diagnose what would block their change efforts when confronted with a typical lost knowledge scenario. A considerable number of veteran employees were scheduled to retire in the next few years and management had been talking about succession planning and trying to transfer vital knowledge for some time. But there had been no meaningful action. Given pending retirements, there was general consensus that change was needed, as reflected in commonly heard statements such as:

- "We've got to do more about succession planning."
- "The problem is no one around here shares knowledge."
- "Why can't we get better at capturing people's knowledge so others can use it?"
- And, of course, the ever-popular: "We've got to stop all this knowledge from walking out the door."

These comments represent what Kegan and Lahey call the "culture of complaint." Often dismissed as useless whining, comments like these are actually a useful window into the things that people really care about. In general, we complain the loudest about the things we most value. But the trick is to translate these gripes into something more useful. In other words, what values are hidden in these complaints? *Or, what commitments are implied by our complaints about lost knowledge?* Based on the complaints listed above, the team doing this exercise agreed they really cared about:

- Keeping critical knowledge in the organization.
- Investing in programs and processes to support knowledge sharing and the faster development of workforce capabilities.
- Creating an environment where employees are motivated to share.
- Developing systems to better capture and organize document-based knowledge.

At the same time, this group of managers was frustrated because they seemed unable to make any progress on these objectives. Lots of knowledge was still being lost. So the group was asked: *"What are you doing, or not doing, that is keeping your commitments from being more fully realized?"* The answers to this question took a little longer, but soon the managers agreed that they were focusing too much on cutting costs and creating efficient operations. And they also admitted to:

- Not identifying what critical knowledge had to be retained.
- Not developing sufficient sponsorship to support new initiatives.
- Not implementing effective programs and processes explicitly designed to support knowledge transfer.
- Not taking into account the emotional and career development needs of individual employees, which was necessary, they said, to motivate sharing.

These behaviors are puzzling, although fairly typical. The group said they wanted to retain knowledge, yet they behaved in ways that continued to encourage its departure. One way to understand this problem is as an organizational dilemma as described in the previous section. Yet, in situations like this managers also need to explore why they behave in ways that undermine what they are committed to. That's where the approach developed by Kegan and Lahey is helpful. Instead of jumping into designing new action plans to change the unproductive behaviors that were promoting knowledge loss, the management group considered another question. They were asked to reflect on the consequences of the actual behaviors they had listed. They did this by answering an unusual question: *"If you imagine doing the opposite of the undermining behavior, can you detect in yourself or the group any discomfort, worry, or vague fear?"* In other words, if they actually identified critical knowledge, or developed strong sponsorship, or implemented effective programs, is there something they are afraid would happen? Managers thought about this question and then one-by-one made comments like:

- "If we actually identified critical knowledge, I'm afraid we'd find out there's certain knowledge we absolutely can't retain, which makes us more vulnerable than we dare to admit."

- "I'm afraid if we implement them we'll discover programs and processes don't transfer knowledge the way we want them to."
- "If we developed the champions we want for these initiatives, then we'd really be accountable for producing results. Frankly, it's easier to just complain about the problem."
- "If we developed a knowledge-sharing culture, more 'old-timers' knowledge will be available for reuse, which means I wouldn't get as much credit for my own knowledge. I want to develop my own capabilities. That's what I get rewarded for."
- "If we focused less on cost control and more on being innovative, we'd discover we don't have the skills we need to be really creative."

It's an important step to identify fears such as feeling real vulnerability to lost knowledge, being held accountable for knowledge retention, feeling your own knowledge has been devalued, or realizing you don't have what it takes to be really innovative. But to understand their impact these passive fears need to be translated into proactive commitments that are actually blocking knowledge retention. To better articulate the competing commitments that were actually supporting knowledge loss, the management group answered another question: *By engaging in these undermining behaviors (e.g., not identifying critical knowledge), what unpleasant outcome are you trying to prevent?* Slowly and sometimes emotionally members of the management group made observations such as:

- "I think we're committed to not confronting the fact that there is vital knowledge the organization is definitely going to lose."
- "We're committed to not being put in a position where we fail to deliver for senior management on this problem."
- "I'm committed to being valued for my own knowledge, and not having to rely on what some old-timer knew just because it's available to us."
- "I'd say we're committed to not finding out we don't really have what it takes to be innovative."

These comments represent commitments held in the group, which lay at the heart of their inability to create the organizational changes needed to retain knowledge. Uncovering these hidden beliefs can be difficult and sometimes embarrassing. We are likely to view them as character weaknesses, but in reality, Kegan and Lahey argue, they represent a form of self-protection, guarding us from deeply held beliefs that we don't want to confront. In this case, the competing commitments described above go a long way toward explaining why this group of managers behaved in ways that undermined their seemingly more noble commitment to knowledge retention. The final question, of course, is what hidden beliefs are driving this behavior? Once the managers had identified their competing commitments, they were asked to first create the beginning of a sentence by inverting the competing commitment (e.g., "I assume that if we did X, then . . ."), and then filling in the blank. This revealed the following beliefs:

- "I assume that if we did confront the fact that the organization is definitely going to lose vital knowledge, we would be paralyzed by the feeling of vulnerability and powerlessness that would result."
- "I assume that if we were put in a position where we failed to deliver on this problem for senior management, then they would see we are incompetent."
- "If I had to rely on some old-timer's knowledge because it was available to me, people would realize how little knowledge I actually had, and I'd never get promoted."
- "I assume that if they found out I really don't have the ability to be innovative, then I'd be fired."

Kegan and Lahey call these four statements "big assumptions" (see figure 11.6). These are deeply rooted beliefs we have about ourselves and how the world works. They include well disguised feelings of vulnerability, in-

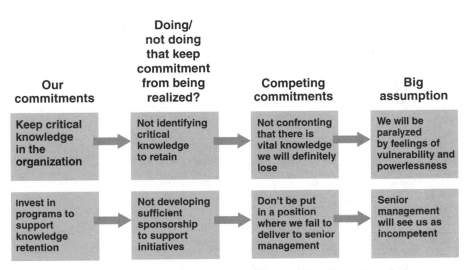

FIGURE 11.6. Identifying Competing Commitments That Block Knowledge Retention

This chart illustrates two competing commitments and the underlying big assumptions that can unconsciously keep managers from even trying to retain critical knowledge. *Source*: Adapted from Kegan and Lahey, 2001.

competence, powerlessness, and low self-worth. These big assumptions produce the competing commitments that in turn lead to behaviors that undermine our stated objectives. Revealing big assumptions can feel embarrassing
because they expose vulnerabilities that we think will change how people
view us. We would prefer to keep our big assumptions hidden, but as long
as we do, meaningful change is difficult.

Once you have identified the big assumptions held by you or your group,
the logical step is to take actions that will alter this dysfunctional dynamic
blocking change. The first step is just to become aware of your actions that
seem related to your big assumptions. For example, the group described
above could explore whether there are particular ways in which their feelings
of vulnerability and powerlessness influence their inaction. (Of course, you
and the groups you work with may have a completely different set of competing commitments and big assumptions. These are just for illustration.) For
example, the group of managers could discover that their fear of feeling vulnerable actually kept them from explicitly discussing the likely effects of losing several experts from a key department.

Step two is to actively look for evidence that contradicts your big assumption. Kegan and Lahey point out:

> Because big assumptions are held as fact, they actually inform what
> people see, leading them to systematically (but unconsciously) attend to
> certain data and avoid or ignore other data. By asking people to search
> specifically for experiences that would cause them to question their big
> assumptions, we help them see that they have been filtering out certain
> types of information—information that could weaken the grip of the
> big assumptions.[20]

When addressing knowledge retention, if a manager was avoiding the
issue to keep from feeling vulnerable, one strategy might be to talk with executives in other units who had already lost key people to see how they had
fared. For example, a number of organizations studied for this book, such as
TVA and Northrop Grumman, have found that explicitly confronting attrition and its potential impact on workforce capabilities, has actually reduced
management's anxiety about the effects of lost knowledge on performance.
Insights like this can help reduce the power of hidden assumptions that are
blocking action.

Another important step is to design a small test of your big assumption.
For example, managers who worry about feeling powerless could decide to
confront the problems caused by turnover in a small part of their organization. This test might include identifying the explicit knowledge at risk and
then designing the best possible transition options.

The last step would be to evaluate the results of this test. Learning would come from reflecting on the experience and how it did or did not support the fear of feeling powerless in that situation. New tests could then be designed and run to continue questioning big assumptions that are blocking change. Of course, testing these hidden assumptions doesn't mean they will be proved totally false. Indeed, some managers may feel quite vulnerable once they know the explicit risks of lost knowledge. But people can usually find more productive ways to respond once they are conscious of previously hidden fears.

Working through hidden assumptions that are blocking change is an ongoing process. Surfacing these beliefs and confronting them head-on can be challenging. But at least it gives leaders a clearer understanding of why employees, who seem genuinely committed to sharing knowledge, actually behave in ways that undermine knowledge transfer. Surfacing competing commitments can be critical in helping employees recognize their contradictory feelings about knowledge retention. And making these conflicts discussable is essential for achieving the organization's goal of sustaining and improving overall performance.

If this exercise seems that it would take too much time and be a little too "touchy feely"—then just reflect on how successful you have been so far in your knowledge retention efforts. If they're going well and truly having an impact on the organization, then count yourself lucky. If not, this exercise can help you get more traction as you confront threats of lost knowledge. That's because not much is going to happen until managers and professionals confront their own ambivalence about retaining knowledge. The problem with delaying this challenging work is that those retirement dates aren't getting any further away.

Conclusion

Pretending there is a single approach to managing the organizational change needed to improve knowledge retention greatly underestimates the complexity of the problems you are facing. This chapter's approach to change implementation may seem complex and time-consuming to those seeking a single, structured formula for change management. But to effectively implement changes that improve retention you must view the obstacles through multiple lenses. Analyzing barriers to change through the different frameworks provided here will give you a deeper understanding of the challenges you face in altering processes and behaviors to reduce the costs of lost knowledge. That's because variety is a strength when making decisions in complex situations.[21] Also leaders need different tools to create a customized change strategy given their particular situations, objectives, and management styles. Thus, ultimately you and your colleagues must decide which of the frameworks presented here (or other ones you can draw on) are most useful for taking action in your situation.

12

Creating the Future
Thinking Strategically about
Knowledge Retention

Of course, where and how you focus your knowledge retention efforts depends on where the sponsors are in your organization. Knowledge retention can be a corporate-wide, operating unit, functional, or group-level initiative. After identifying the knowledge most at risk, a plant manager is more likely to concentrate resources on improving knowledge-transfer practices and using retirees, while a corporate executive might concentrate on succession management, building an information technology infrastructure that supports knowledge sharing, and creating a more retention-oriented culture. But no matter where lost knowledge is seen as a threat in your organization, thinking strategically about the solution will determine whether or not you are successful in the long term. This means doing at least five things right.

Link Knowledge Retention Initiatives
to the Organization's Strategy

If the experience with knowledge management is any indicator, this will be a frequently violated principle.[1] Managers seeking to apply knowledge resources more effectively have consistently ignored this maxim, preferring instead to build "knowledge bases" that support marginal functions or to pursue unfocused initiatives, such as launching new communities of practice in an IT or sales department with only vague objectives.

You can use the framework of strategic impacts described in chapter 2 to identify where lost knowledge might impact the performance of your core strategic processes. Figure 12.1 can help generate questions that should be asked before trying to decide where to focus. Of course, the labels on the horizontal axis should be changed to suit your organization's particular context and the level at which the analysis is being conducted (e.g., organization-wide, operating unit, department).

When exploring risks posed by lost knowledge, different business strategies will, of course, create more vulnerability in certain processes. Firms placing a priority on innovation capabilities will probably want to look first at R&D processes, while those pursuing a growth strategy might be more

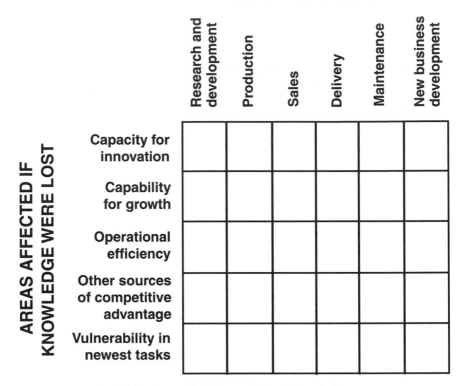

FIGURE 12.1. Identifying Strategic Threats of Lost Knowledge

concerned with production and sales. A low-cost strategy will put an emphasis on sustaining production and maintenance capabilities. And when evaluating capabilities relative to competitors, retaining knowledge in R&D, sales, and delivery processes will be of most concern.

One insidious characteristic of lost knowledge is that, when taking a strategic perspective, management can easily overlook threats that could undermine core operational processes. For example, when a technician retired from a radar equipment assembly line at Texas Instruments, the quality problems resulting from the undocumented knowledge she took with her cost the company over $200,000. The performance of this core assembly process was probably taken for granted by management and would not have been considered in a strategic analysis of lost knowledge threats.

Focus on Reducing Uncertainty Created
by the Threat of Lost Knowledge

Changing workforce demographics and the attendant potential loss of organizational capabilities creates additional uncertainty for executives who are
already operating in dynamic and volatile competitive environments. The
loss of experiential knowledge increases risks for management, making some
decisions and situations seem even more complex and uncertain.[2] For example, the risk for development projects in oil exploration is greatly increased
by the lack of experienced personnel because a 5 percent deviation in project
timing or cost can reduce a project's overall NPV by 10 percent.[3] Lost knowledge also increases risks in production and maintenance processes because
when things go wrong decision making may be slower due to lack of experience.

Management's ability to handle the uncertainty created by changing
workforce demographics will be a key to its strategic effectiveness. Strategic
planners have historically treated human capital as certain and, thus, predictable, or uncertain and, therefore, completely unpredictable.[4] But this sets
up a dangerous binary view of workforce capabilities. The impact of lost
knowledge is neither completely certain and predictable, nor is it entirely
uncertain and unpredictable.

An important task, then, in clarifying this uncertainty is to identify any
clear trends in your workforce demographics that will influence the organization's ability to create, produce, and deliver future products or services.
Depending on the industry, gaps may show up in the number of geophysicists needed for global oil exploration, aviation mechanics needed to service
commercial jets, or nurses needed to staff hospital operating rooms.

As the saying goes, you have to know where the organization is headed
before you can take action to avoid going there.[5] These projections about the
future can be created by using several "no change" assumptions. (1) What if
the competitive environment changes only as we expect it to? (2) What will
happen to our performance capabilities in the future if there are no changes
in our expected attrition rates, recruiting plans, or employee retention practices? The scenario described by your answers to these questions assumes the
organization will make no attempt to adapt even to the environment expected in the future, which is very unlikely to be as stable as anticipated.[6]

Once critical gaps become evident, for example, not enough geophysicists, then you need to identify the key variables that will determine future
capabilities in this function or unit. What are projected attrition rates? How
many have you been able to hire? What is the time-to-competence? After
identifying ranges for these variables, you can then define potential outcomes
that lie along a continuum. The resulting scenarios will supply considerable

new information that will help reduce the uncertainty that makes it very difficult to act on the problem. For example, once it recognized a looming HR crisis, the Tennessee Valley Authority surveyed its employees to collect more accurate data about retirement plans in critical areas. Then management polled supervisors for a detailed assessment of who the real "irreplaceable experts" were. Finally, knowing the capabilities of successors in the pipeline enabled TVA management to do more detailed succession planning. In the process, they have greatly reduced the uncertainty surrounding the jump in retirements expected in the years ahead.

Take a Systemic Approach to Addressing Workforce Capability and Knowledge Retention Problems by Integrating Four Perspectives

The threat of lost knowledge that results from changing workforce demographics represents what Ackoff calls a "messy problem." This means people will have very different views on whether there is a problem. And, even if they agree something is wrong, they may not agree on what the problem is.[7]

Because they are so messy, lost knowledge problems are likely to generate narrow pragmatic solutions, for example, "let's build a knowledge base to capture retirees' expertise" or "let's reinvent our recruiting process." Or they lead to vague, unfocused solutions, such as "we must become a learning organization."

In order to avoid these common mistakes, recognize that lost knowledge almost always represents a complex problem. Therefore, it cannot be solved by isolating it from the organizational system that produced the lost knowledge. And this system can only be understood in the context within which it is embedded. For example, instead of trying to solve a specific instance of lost knowledge due to attrition, management needs to examine the systems creating the result that is blamed on lost knowledge. When an alienated R&D manager retired from a pharmaceutical firm, he took with him many years of valuable experiential knowledge that immediately decreased the effectiveness of this R&D group. In this situation, the useful diagnostic question is not what should we have done to capture that guy's knowledge before he left? The right issues to raise are more likely to be: What is it about our career development process, our performance management system, our retirement policies, our job design, our culture, and our knowledge-sharing practices that produced such an alienated employee who was not motivated to share his knowledge long before his departure was announced? And what is it about these organizational systems that are likely to produce more people like that? In other words, when designing solutions to reduce the problematic conditions that create lost knowledge, you need to examine the situation from at least four perspectives (see figure 12.2).

For example, General Mills says each time it loses a product marketing manager, it costs the company more than $1 million in sales. To address this problem effectively, four perspectives should be taken into account.

The operational or content perspective is held by those closest to the activity where the knowledge is used. It tells us specifically what essential systems the knowledge affects. For example, the marketing manager's knowledge of customers affects decision making about where, when, and how to market a product, which directly influences sales. The strategic view locates the knowledge in a larger organizational context. We may find these marketing managers are working on products that are strategically important to the company, or they may be relatively unimportant to future objectives. Thus, this perspective, usually held by senior executives, determines whether the potential lost knowledge has implications for the firm's ability to implement its strategy. A knowledge management view of turnover among marketing managers will provide insights on how their knowledge relates to the organization's overall knowledge base. Is it unique? What type of knowledge is it? How could it be better transferred or re-created? How could it be shared

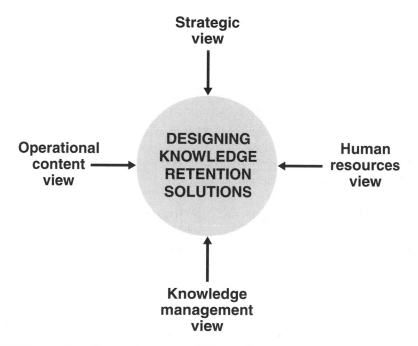

FIGURE 12.2. Four Perspectives on Lost Knowledge

or stored better to reduce the firm's vulnerabilities? For example, with the marketing manager, the first step is understanding the types of knowledge essential for decision making. Then, where did it come from? Is it only acquired through years of experience talking to customers and analyzing market data? Is any of it documented? Do others in the organization have the same knowledge? What systems, processes, or practices currently determine how this knowledge is passed on to a marketing manager's successor? How are these mechanisms, or the lack of them, contributing to the problem?

Finally, the HR perspective looks at the larger environment in which the knowledge holder operates. It explores how knowledge holders are recruited, developed, why they leave, and how their replacements are recruited. The HR view provides a contextual or larger systems perspective on the environment that has shaped the knowledge holders. For example, how are marketing managers recruited? What are their career paths—official and actual? What does the culture do to encourage turnover? How does compensation affect knowledge sharing?

An effective knowledge retention solution requires understanding and integrating all four of these perspectives to implement initiatives that will resolve the systemic factors that created the lost knowledge problem in the first place. Of course, when lost knowledge becomes an immediate threat to ongoing operations, there isn't time to include all four perspectives in designing a larger systemic solution. In late 2001, when Delta Air Lines faced the loss of many veteran aviation maintenance technicians within two months, management wanted to capture some of that knowledge fast! A larger system-wide solution would have to wait.

But when trying to minimize the future costs of lost knowledge because of looming retirements or other major changes, all four perspectives should be included to design effective strategies for improving knowledge retention.

View Existing Knowledge as a Resource for Learning from the External Environment

The idea that knowledge underlies the critical capabilities necessary to achieve most organizational objectives is intuitively obvious. Thus, changing workforce demographics will encourage a lot of executives to focus on what knowledge they need to hold onto in order to sustain performance. But simply thinking of intellectual capital as an asset to be protected is a dangerously narrow approach because it can overlook important impacts of lost knowledge. A strategic perspective must also consider how knowledge affects an organization's capacity for learning and change.

In the digital economy, "learning is the new form of labor," said Shoshanna Zuboff.[8] Scores of books and articles in recent years have promoted the importance of individual and organizational learning to continually improve performance. But make no mistake about it. Losing extensive experiential knowledge related to strategically important activities will degrade your organization's ability to learn from the external environment. Toward the end of his career one of Corning's senior scientists was assigned to travel the world just to listen to customers. In one such meeting, executives from the British Post Office said they needed more bandwidth than copper could provide to support emerging communication technologies. The veteran scientist brought these ideas back to the lab and they led to the development of fiber optics. Experiential knowledge is a key component in interpreting inputs from the environment and helping the organization to respond effectively.

Sometimes called "absorptive capacity," researchers have argued that the ability of an organization "to recognize the value of new, external information, assimilate it, and apply it" is largely a function of the entity's existing related knowledge.[9] The absorptive capacity of any unit depends on the ability of the key boundary spanners or gatekeepers to identify potentially valuable external information, interpret it, and bring it into the organization. Internal communication networks, processes, and cultural norms are also necessary to help assimilate and disseminate the new knowledge so it can be applied.[10]

In practice, executives will face three different scenarios where levels of knowledge influence the capacity for learning and change. First, managers may attempt to retain knowledge without concern for its impact on subsequent learning and innovation. This is what happens when existing operations are immediately threatened by lost knowledge, such as the running of a complex database update process that must be transferred from one person to another, or by the unexpected departure of highly specialized nuclear weapons designers.

Second, executives will seek to retain knowledge because they implicitly recognize its value for organizational learning and potential innovations. A common example would be keeping a senior sales or technical executive on a consulting retainer after retirement because of his or her extensive customer relationships and industry contacts. Losing this knowledge clearly diminishes the firm's capacity for learning about customers and competitors.

Third, sometimes losing knowledge is seen as a necessary trade-off for facilitating change. In the past 20 years endless rounds of downsizing and reorganizations have encouraged early retirements and other departures to enable changes deemed essential by leadership (e.g., cutting costs, changing culture, pursuing new business opportunities). But these decisions have left many organizations dangerously thin in many areas of expertise. Managers can no longer afford to ignore the impacts their personnel decisions have on the unit's absorptive capacity. If your organization is committed to improving its learning capabilities, you must be explicit in your consideration of the trade-offs between personnel changes (e.g., layoffs, reorganizations) and the impact of lost knowledge on learning and innovation.

In most cases, creating new strategic competencies involves some combination of fundamentally extending the organization's existing knowledge and at the same time developing new capabilities and market knowledge.[11] Thus, an important question is what existing experiential knowledge is needed to acquire new capabilities? This is knowledge that needs to be retained because, ultimately, strategic advantage comes from being able to absorb external knowledge and integrate it with internal capabilities so the organization learns faster than the competition.[12]

Take a Long-Term Perspective on the Problems of Lost Knowledge

While short-term threats of knowledge loss will increasingly plague organizations, a strategic perspective means viewing knowledge retention as a long-term effort. This must become a way of thinking for management, if organizations are to sustain workforce capabilities in the face of shifting demographics and looming shortages of skilled workers.

There is no standard format or formula for knowledge retention strategies. Every organization is going to have to define the problem and solution for itself, based on its own unique situation and the perspectives of its leaders. At the World Bank, for example, it appears knowledge retention will primarily be addressed in the context of the larger knowledge management strategy, which is closely aligned with strategic objectives for becoming a "knowledge bank." For the McLane Company, on the other hand, knowledge retention is a key driver behind the company's leadership development program, given the pending retirement of key executives.

One rule of thumb is that any knowledge retention strategy should map to the organization's strategic planning approach. Large bureaucratic organizations that pursue a "rationally deliberate" strategic planning process are going to be comfortable with a more formalized approach to planning for knowledge retention. On the other hand, smaller, more dynamic organizations that use an "adaptively emergent" planning process will be better served by an approach that supports a more flexible portfolio of projects.[13] Regardless of the planning approach used, when it comes to implementation, knowledge retention action plans should integrate seamlessly into key operational, HR, and knowledge management activities. Initiatives that burden employees with additional tasks are doomed to fail.

Because knowledge retention initiatives are addressing complex problems, they should be designed for ongoing modifications to react to changes in the operating environment. This requires built-in feedback systems to continually assess the performance of the solution.[14] For example, the McLane Company introduced a software tool intended to develop more effective operational problem-solving skills in its employees and also to capture their solutions for future use. The system was designed so McLane's top management could monitor its use. When feedback showed that the system was having little real impact on problem-solving behaviors, management killed the rollout of the system, redesigned it, and reintroduced it with more comprehensive training and support.

Part of the long-term perspective is also recognizing that your thinking about knowledge retention solutions will evolve. This will happen, in part, out of experience as your organization takes action to survive threats of lost knowledge too serious to ignore. Your understanding of knowledge retention solutions can also grow through "collective contacts" with other organizations where you can learn and borrow ideas.[15] For example, one such innovative project is the inter-company network based in Europe founded by Siemens and BMW to address the challenges of losing expertise through retirement and attrition. One of the primary goals of the "Leaving Experts" community of practice described in chapter 6 is for members to collect and exchange information about the knowledge-transfer methods they are using.

Another example of collective learning comes from the American Productivity & Quality Center, which sponsored a research consortium that included more than 25 organizations ranging from Allstate Insurance Company to the U.S. Navy. These organizations shared the challenges they faced and lessons being learned in designing knowledge retention solutions.

Conclusion

Ultimately, taking a strategic approach to knowledge retention can help you manage the risks of lost knowledge by reducing costly surprises. It will also help develop more of a future orientation, which will be essential to address the challenges of sustaining workforce capabilities in the years ahead.

Retaining organizational knowledge is not just a short-term management problem. Like the quality movement, it represents a philosophical approach to business that will become a prerequisite for remaining competitive in the years ahead. Retaining knowledge to sustain performance in the face of changing workforce demographics is a management challenge that is here to stay for at least the next two decades. By then, with luck, we'll be back on the moon. And this time we won't forget how we got there!

Notes

INTRODUCTION

1. Harvey Rose, "Exit Strategies," *Knowledge Management* 4/11 (December 2001).

2. See, for example, Beverly Goldberg, *Age Works: What Corporate America Must Do to Survive the Graying of the Workforce* (New York: Free Press, 2000); Peter G. Peterson, *Gray Dawn: How the Coming Age Wave Will Transform America—And the World* (New York: Times Books, 1999); William K. Zinke and Susan Tattershall (eds.), *Working through Demographic Change: How Older Americans Can Sustain the Nation's Prosperity* (Boulder, Colo.: Human Resource Services, 2000); Ken Dychtwald, *Age Power: How the 21st Century Will Be Ruled by the New Old* (New York: J. P. Tarcher, 2000); and Paul Wallace, *Agequake: Riding the Demographic Rollercoaster Shaking Business, Finance, and Our World* (London: Nicholas Brealey, 2001).

3. Some of the best include: Chris Collison and Geoff Parcell, *Learning to Fly: Practical Lessons from One of the World's Leading Knowledge Companies* (Oxford: Capstone Publishing, 2001); Thomas H. Davenport and Laurence Prusak, *Working Knowledge* (Boston: Harvard Business School Press, 2000); Nancy Dixon, *Common Knowledge: How Companies Thrive by Sharing What They Know* (Boston: Harvard Business School Press, 2000); and Dorothy Leonard-Barton, *Wellsprings of Knowledge* (Boston: Harvard Business School Press, 1995).

CHAPTER 1

1. Michael D. Griffin, Testimony to House Science Committee, "Hearings on Perspectives on the President's Vision for Space Exploration," Washington, D.C. [Online] March 10, 2004. Available: http://www.house.gov/science/hearings/full04/mar10/griffin.pdf [March 30, 2004].

2. Geof Petch, "The Cost of Lost Knowledge," *destination KM.com*. [Online] January 31, 2001. Available: http://www.destinationkm.com/articles/default.asp?ArticleID=513&KeyWords−petch [March 26, 2004].

3. Petch, "The Cost of Lost Knowledge."

4. Thomas A. Stewart, *Intellectual Capital: The New Wealth of Organizations* (New York: Doubleday, 1997); W. Chan Kim and Renee Mauborgne, "Strategy, Value Innovation, and the Knowledge Economy," *Sloan Management Review* (Spring 1999).

5. Dates used to define generations vary somewhat, but the overall demographic patterns do not change. My numbers come from Lynne C. Lancaster and David Stillman, *When Generations Collide* (New York: Harper Business, 2002), 13.

6. Of course, it is difficult to draw comparisons among countries because of the

tremendous differences in political and economic circumstances. For example, while many European countries have aging workforces, they also have much higher unemployment than the United States, and they also have much less flexible labor markets and more stringent retirement policies. Japan also has virtually no history of immigration, which might be used to help relieve labor shortages. Thus, from a workforce planning perspective, the options facing executives and policy makers vary widely, given the local political and economic context.

7. Arlene Dohm, "Gauging the Labor Force Effects of Retiring Baby Boomers," *Monthly Labor Review* (July 2000): 17; Mitra Toossi, "Labor Force Projections to 2012: The Graying of the U.S. Workforce," *Monthly Labor Review* (February 2004).

8. Among those who have provided more optimistic views about the impact of the aging workforce on the U.S. labor supply are: Peter Cappelli, "Will There *Really* Be a Labor Shortage?" *Organizational Dynamics* 32/3 (2003): 221–233; and Howard N. Fullerton, Jr. and Mitra Toossi, "Labor Force Projections to 2010: Steady Growth and Changing Composition," *Monthly Labor Review* 124 (November 2001). Those predicting serious labor shortages include: Roger Herman, Thomas Olivo, and Joyce Gioia, *Impending Crisis: Too Many Jobs, Too Few People* (Winchester, Va.: Oak Hill Press, 2002); Peter G. Peterson, *Gray Dawn: How the Coming Age Wave Will Transform America—And the World* (New York: Times Books, 1999).

9. Derek Burleton, "The Demographic Challenge: Slowing Population, Aging Workforce Trends More Severe in Canada Than in the U.S." Paper prepared for the Toronto Dominion Bank Forum on Living Standards. [Online] July 2002. Available: http://www.td.com/economics/standard/full/Burleton.pdf[April 11, 2004]. "The Aging Workforce Conference," Health, Safety and Industrial Relations Training Fund, Communication, Energy and Paperworkers Union of Canada. [Online] April 2002. Available: http://www.cep.ca/health_safety/files/aging_e.pdf [April 11, 2004].

10. "World Population Prospects: The 2000 Revision," United Nations Department of Economic and Social Affairs, Population Division. [Online] Available: http://www.un.org/esa/population/publications/wpp2002/WPP2002 -HIGHLIGHTSrev1.PDF [April 15, 2003].

11. Martin Mühleisen and Hamid Faruqee, "Japan Population Aging and the Fiscal Challenge," *Finance & Development* 38/1. [Online] March 2001. Available: http://www.imf.org/external/pubs/ft/fandd/2001/03/muhleise.htm [March 26, 2004].

12. Axel Böersch-Supan, "Aging and Its Implications for Business," Discussant Remarks, CSIS Policy Summit on Global Aging. [Online] January 25, 2000. Available: http://www.csis.org/gai/Graying/speeches/axel.html [April 11, 2004].

13. Sources for these numbers are: Lawrence P. Farrell, "Acquisition Workforce Nears Crisis Point," President's Corner. [Online] May 2002. Available: http://www.ndia.org/Content/NavigationMenu/Resources1/Presidents_Corner2/May_2002.htm [March 26, 2004]; Christopher Lee, "NASA Official Warns of Aging Workforce," *Washington Post* (March 7, 2003): A31; and "Brain Drain: Retaining Intellectual Capital in the Energy Industry," Sapient. [Online] Available: http://www.sapient.com/pdfs/industry_viewpoints/sapient_braindrain.pdf [April 8, 2004].

14. "The Demographic Wall," *Cambridge Energy Research Associates, Inc.* (February 2001); Jonathan D. Krome and Jay W. Survant, "Practical Preparations for the

Big Crew Change," paper presented at the Society of Petroleum Engineers Annual Technical Conference, San Antonio, Tex., September 29–October 2, 2002; "Brain Drain: Retaining Intellectual Capital in the Energy Industry."

15. Mary B. Young, "Holding On: How the Mass Exodus of Retiring Baby Boomers Could Deplete the Workforce How Employers Can Stem the Tide," *The Linkage Learning Network*. [Online] March 2002. Available: http://www.cfor.org/services/ars_studies/Final%20Holding%20On-White%20Paper%207.30.pdf [April 11, 2004].

16. NPV (net present value) as used in this context implies that because of the expected turnover in its aging workforce management should not assume as great a return on its human capital. This is because its less experienced employee base will create opportunity costs in the future.

17. "The American Workplace Report 2001: Building America's Workforce for the 21st Century, 2001," *Employment Policy Foundation*. [Online] Available: http://www.epf.org/labor01/getpdf01.asp [April 11, 2004]; Young, "Holding On"; and Dohm, "Gauging the Labor Force Effects of Retiring Baby Boomers."

18. Some economists (see Cappelli, "Will There *Really* Be a Labor Shortage?") argue that the chances of long-term labor shortages in specific occupations are slim because if the demand is there wages will rise until supply and demand are brought back into balance. But this long-term macroeconomic view, even if true, is not helpful to the manager looking to hire a skilled professional next quarter. It might take years to adequately train replacements once the market reacts to occupational shortages. That kind of delay can be very costly for individual organizations.

19. Aaron Bernstein, "Too Many Workers? Not for Long," *Business Week* (May 20, 2002): 126; Michelle Moon Reinhardt, "Labor Shortage Looms Even as Layoffs Rise," *Austin Business Journal* (January 31, 2003).

20. Gloria Mark, "Extreme Collaboration," *Communications of the ACM* 45/6 (June 2002); Frank Mueller and Romano Dyerson, "Expert Humans or Expert Organizations," *Organization Studies* 20/2 (1999); Richard Boland and Ramkrishnan Tenkasi, "Perspective Making and Perspective Taking in Communities of Knowing," *Organization Science* 6/4 (July–August 1995); Janice Klein and Patrick Maurer, "Integrators, Not Generalists, Needed: A Case Study of Integrated Product Development Teams," in *Advances in Interdisciplinary Studies of Work Teams*, Volume 2 (Greenwich, Conn.: JAI Press, 1995).

21. Jurgen Drews, "Drug Discovery: A Historical Perspective," *Science* 287/5460 (March 17, 2000); Boland and Tenkasi, "Perspective Making and Perspective Taking in Communities of Knowing."

22. Names in this story are disguised.

23. Stone Giant Consulting, "Knowledge Management Infrastructure." [Online] Available: http://stonegiant.com/prod03.htm [January 19, 2004].

24. Jeff Bond, "In the Eye of the Storm," *Washington CEO* (October 1998).

25. Leonard H. Lesko, "Hieroglyphics," in *World Book Online Americas Edition*. [Online] Available: http://www.worldbookonline.com/ar?/na/ar/co/ar256100.htm [April 17, 2004].

26. Erling Hoh, "Modern Egypt Revives Ancient 'Great Library,' " *Insight on the News* 17/24 (June 25, 2001): 28.

27. Hoh, "Modern Egypt Revives Ancient 'Great Library' "; Lionel Casson, *Li-*

brarians in the Ancient World (New Haven, Conn.: Yale University Press, 2001); "Museum: Ancient Knowledge," *Applied Knowledge Research Institute.* [Online] Available: http://www.akri.org/museum/ancient.htm [April 15, 2004].

28. J. D. Verhoeven, A. H. Pendray, and W. E. Dauksch, "The Key Role of Impurities in Ancient Damascus Steal Blades," *Journal of Metals* 50/9 (1998): 58–64; Oleg D. Sherby, "Damascus Steel—A Rediscovery," *R&D Innovator* 3/10 (October 1994); Jeremy Manier, "Damascus Steel's Lost Secret Found," *Chicago Tribune* (August 13, 2001); Anna Feuerbach, "Crucible Damascus Steel—Historical Analysis and Replication Experiments." [Online] Available: http://home.att.net/~moltenmuse/ replications.htm [April 17, 2004].

29. Colin Gough, "Science and the Stradivarians," *Physics World.* [Online] April 2000. Available: http://physicsweb.org/article/world/13/4/8/1 [April 17, 2004]; Bruce Weber, "Seeking a Violin's Secrets with a CAT Scan," *New York Times* (December 12, 1997): E1.

30. For an in-depth discussion of "knowledge" and "knowing" in an organizational context, see J. C. Spender, "Organizational Knowledge, Learning and Memory: Three Concepts in Search of a Theory," *Journal of Organizational Change Management* 9/1 (1996): 63–78; Wanda Orlikowski, "Knowing in Practice: Enacting a Collective Capability in Distributed Organizing," *Organization Science* 13/3 (May–June 2002): 249–273; Markus Venzin, Georg von Krogh, and Johan Roos, "Future Research into Knowledge Management," in *Knowing in Firms: Understanding, Managing and Measuring Knowledge,* ed. Georg von Krogh, Johan Roos, and Dirk Kleine (Thousand Oaks, Calif.: Sage Publications, 1998), 26–66.

31. John Fialka, "Cold Warheads: Los Alamos Lab Tries to Stem the Decline of Bomb Know-How," *Wall Street Journal* (August 2, 2000): A1.

32. Lancaster and Stillman, *When Generations Collide.*

33. Thomas H. Davenport and Laurence Prusak, *Working Knowledge: How Organizations Manage What They Know* (Boston: Harvard Business School Press, 1997).

34. For some excellent research about the transfer of best practices, see Gabriel Szulanski, *Sticky Knowledge: Barriers to Knowing in the Firm* (Thousand Oaks, Calif.: Sage Publications, 2003); and Nancy Dixon, *Common Knowledge: How Companies Thrive by Sharing What They Know* (Boston: Harvard Business School Press, 2000).

35. For example, see Donald Marchand, "Competing with Intellectual Capital," in *Knowing in Firms: Understanding, Managing, and Measuring Knowledge,* ed. Georg von Krogh, Johan Roos, and Dirk Kleine (Thousand Oaks, Calif.: Sage Publications, 1998); and Verna Allee, *The Knowledge Evolution: Expanding Organizational Intelligence* (Boston: Butterworth-Heinemann, 1997).

36. There is no widely accepted definition of "knowledge," particularly in organizational research. My typology is based on an extensive review of the literature and recognition that practitioners need to understand the concept of knowledge in a way that is actionable. Some of the ideas in this section first appeared in David W. DeLong and Liam Fahey, "Diagnosing Cultural Barriers to Knowledge Management," *Academy of Management Executive* 14/4 (2000): 113–127. Among those who have most influenced my thinking on this subject are: Frank Blackler, "Knowledge, Knowledge Work and Organizations: An Overview and Interpretation," *Organization Studies* 16 (1995): 1021–1046; Spender, "Organizational Knowledge, Learning and Memory," 63–78; Orlikowski, "Knowing in Practice: Enacting a Collective Capability in Distributed Organizing," 249–273.

37. "Tacit" knowledge is knowledge that an actor or group is not consciously

aware of applying. It is often described as what we know but cannot communicate. In practice, knowledge is often tacit by degree. There are things an expert knows how to do that are almost impossible to articulate (e.g., how a top salesperson closes a complex deal). There are many other things individuals know that they could easily articulate if they were just reminded that they were of interest. This is often labeled as tacit knowledge, but it is more usefully called "implicit knowledge" by Carl Frappaolo in *Knowledge Management* (Oxford: Capstone Publishing, 2002). For more on tacit knowledge, see Spender, "Organizational Knowledge, Learning and Memory"; M. Polanyi, *Tacit Dimension* (New York: Doubleday, 1967).

38. Many researchers have made this distinction between knowledge that is more cognitive and knowledge that is more physical. Two examples are Shoshana Zuboff, *In the Age of the Smart Machine: The Future of Work and Power* (New York: Basic Books, 1988); and Blackler, "Knowledge, Knowledge Work and Organizations."

39. For more on social capital, see J. S. Brown and P. Duguid, "Organizing Knowledge," *California Management Review* 40/3 (1998): 90–111; J. Nahapiet and S. Ghoshal, "Social Capital, Intellectual Capital, and the Organizational Advantage," *Academy of Management Review* 23 (1998): 242–266; Don Cohen and Laurence Prusak, *In Good Company: How Social Capital Makes Organizations Work* (Boston: Harvard Business School Press, 2001).

40. For more on cultural knowledge, see W. G. Ouchi, "A Conceptual Framework for the Design of Organizational Control Mechanics," *Management Science* 25/8 (1979): 833–847; Spender, "Organizational Knowledge, Learning and Memory"; Sonja A. Sackman, *Cultural Knowledge in Organizations: Exploring the Collective Mind* (Newbury Park, Calif.: Sage Publications, 1991).

41. For an excellent description of structured knowledge and the evolution of its use in industrial organizations, see Zuboff, *In the Age of the Smart Machines.*

42. This definition is adapted from James P. Walsh and Gerardo Rivera Ungson, "Organizational Memory," *Academy of Management Review* 16/1 (January 1991): 57–91.

43. Walsh and Ungson, "Organizational Memory," 57–91.

44. For other studies on organizational memory, see, for example, Spender, "Organizational Knowledge, Learning and Memory"; Linda Argote, *Organizational Learning: Creating, Retaining and Transferring Knowledge* (Norwell, Mass.: Kluwer Academic Publishers, 1999); Fernando Olivera, "Memory Systems in Organizations: An Empirical Investigation of Mechanisms for Knowledge Collection, Storage and Access," *Journal of Management Studies* 37/6 (September 2000); Arnold Kransdorff, "Fighting Organizational Memory Lapse," *Workforce* 76/9 (September 1997).

45. Walsh and Ungson, "Organizational Memory," 57–91.

46. Mark S. Ackerman and C. A. Halverson, "Reexamining Organizational Memory," *Communications of the ACM* 43/1 (January 2000).

CHAPTER 2

1. Diane Vaughn, *The Challenger Launch Decision* (Chicago: University of Chicago Press, 1996), xv.

2. J. J. Fialka, "Nuclear-Site Cleanup Faces First Big Test," *Wall Street Journal* (February 3, 2003): A4.

3. J. Storck and L. Donnelly, "Leveraging Expertise at Oil Company (A): Nolan's Nightmare," Case Study (Boston: Boston University School of Management, 1997).

4. Reva Berman Brown and Martyn J. Woodland, "Managing Knowledge Wisely: A Case Study in Organisational Behaviour," *Journal of Applied Management Studies* 8/2 (December 1999): 175.

5. Rob Cross and Lloyd Baird, "Technology is Not Enough: Improving Performance by Building Organizational Memory," *Sloan Management Review* 41/3 (Spring 2000).

6. Some of the ideas in this section first appeared in David W. DeLong, "Uncovering the Hidden Costs of 'Lost Knowledge' in Global Chemical Companies," research note, *Accenture Institute for Strategic Change.* [Online] February 18, 2002. Available: http://www.accenture.com/xd/xd.asp?it=enweb&xd=_ins%5C researchnoteabstract_155.xml [March 26, 2004].

7. Michael H. Zack, "Developing a Knowledge Strategy," *California Management Review* 41/3 (Spring 1999): 125–145.

8. Aaron Bernstein, "Too Many Workers? Not for Long," *Business Week* (May 20, 2002): 126; Michelle Moon Reinhardt, "Labor Shortage Looms Even as Layoffs Rise," *Austin Business Journal* (January 31, 2003).

9. "Brain Drain: Retaining Intellectual Capital in the Energy Industry," Sapient. [Online] Available: http://www.sapient.com/pdfs/industry_viewpoints/sapient _braindrain.pdf [April 8, 2004].

10. Phill Trewyn, "Supply of Specialty Physicians Falls Short," *Business Journal of Milwaukee.* [Online] September 7, 2001. Available: http://www.milwaukee .bizjournals.com/milwaukee/stories/2001/09/10/focus1.html [April 8, 2003].

11. American Hospital Association, "A Looming Crisis in Care," Commission on Workforce for Hospitals and Health Systems. [Online] Available: http://www .aracnet.com/~oahhs/issues/workforce/ioho3crisis.pdf [April 11, 2004] and First Consulting Group, "The Healthcare Workforce Shortage and Its Implications for America's Hospitals." [Online] Fall 2001. Available: http://www .hospitalconnect.com/aha/key_issues/workforce/resources/Content/ FcgWorkforceReport.pdf [March 26, 2004].

12. Bob Violino, "The Best Cities to Work In," *Network Computing* 12/16 (August 6, 2001): 76.

13. Lynne C. Lancaster and David Stillman, *When Generations Collide* (New York: Harper Business, 2002).

CHAPTER 3

1. Adapted from Elizabeth Wolfe Morrison and Francis J. Milliken, "Organizational Silence: A Barrier to Change and Development in a Pluralistic World," *Academy of Management Review* 25/4 (2000): 706–725.

2. "Retaining Valuable Knowledge at Northrop Grumman Corporation—A Case Study," in Consortium Benchmarking Study, "Retaining Valuable Knowledge: Proactive Strategies to Deal with a Shifting Work Force" (Houston, Tex.: American Productivity & Quality Center, 2002).

3. The McLane Company became a subsidiary of Berkshire Hathaway in 2003.

4. Dorothy Leonard and David Kiron, "Managing Knowledge and Learning at NASA and the Jet Propulsion Laboratory (JPL)," Case No. 9-603-062 (Boston: Harvard Business School Publishing, 2002), 1.

5. John Aloysius Farrell and Glen Johnson, "Official Had Warned of NASA Safety Issues," *Boston Globe* (February 2, 2003): A1; "NASA Defends Use of Tiles on Columbia," *Associated Press* (February 5, 2003); "Paul Fischbeck's Study Alerted NASA That Disaster Could Result from Damaged Space Shuttle Tiles," *Carnegie Mellon News.* [Online] Available: http://www.cmu.edu/cmnews/extra/030212_nasa.htm [March 4, 2004]; Juliet Macur, "Critics Say NASA's Funds, Personnel Are Stretched Too Thin," *Dallas Morning News* (February 3, 2003).

6. William Fulmer, "The World Bank and Knowledge Management," Case No. 9-801-157 (Boston: Harvard Business School Publishing, 2001).

7. Fulmer, "The World Bank and Knowledge Management."

8. "Retaining Valuable Knowledge at The World Bank—A Case Study," in Consortium Benchmarking Study, "Retaining Valuable Knowledge: Proactive Strategies to Deal with a Shifting Workforce" (Houston, Tex.: American Productivity & Quality Center, 2002).

9. "Retaining Valuable Knowledge at Corning Incorporated—A Case Study," in Consortium Benchmarking Study, "Retaining Valuable Knowledge: Proactive Strategies to Deal with a Shifting Workforce" (Houston, Tex.: American Productivity & Quality Center, 2002).

10. "Retaining Valuable Knowledge at Best Buy Co., Inc.—A Case Study," in Consortium Benchmarking Study, "Retaining Valuable Knowledge: Proactive Strategies to Deal with a Shifting Workforce" (Houston, Tex.: American Productivity & Quality Center, 2002).

11. Till von Wachter, "The End of Mandatory Retirement in the US: Effects on Retirement and Implicit Contracts," Center for Labor Economics, University of California, Berkeley, Working Paper No. 49 (March 2002). [Online] Available: http://www.columbia.edu/~vw2112/papers/tvw_paper2.pdf [April 1, 2004]; "Gov't Forces Companies to Raise Retirement Age to 65," *Mainichi Daily News* (October 22, 2003). [Online] Available: http://mdn.mainichi.co.jp/news/archive/200310/22/20031022p2a00m0bu013000c.html [April 1, 2004].

12. For books on recruiting, see Lou Adler, *Hire with Your Head: Using POWER Hiring to Build Great Teams,* 2nd ed. (New York: John Wiley and Sons, 2002); Bradford Smart, *Topgrading: How Leading Companies Win by Hiring, Coaching and Keeping the Best People* (Upper Saddle River, N.J.: Prentice-Hall Press, 1999); Jim Harris and Joan Brannick, *Finding and Keeping Great Employees* (New York: AMACOM, 1999).

PART II INTRODUCTION

1. These questions were adapted from Jeffrey Pfeffer, *Competitive Advantage through People* (Boston: Harvard Business School Press, 1994), 227.

CHAPTER 4

1. Howard Muson, "Valuing Experience: How to Motivate and Retain Mature Workers," (New York: Conference Board, April 2003).

2. For details on creating a succession management system, see Jay A. Conger and Robert M. Fulmer, "Developing Your Leadership Pipeline," *Harvard Business Review* (December 2003).

3. Ron Elsdon, *Affiliation in the Workplace: Value Creation in the New Organization* (Westport, Conn.: Praeger, 2003), 150.

4. "Retaining Valuable Knowledge at Siemens AG—A Case Study," in Consortium Benchmarking Study, "Retaining Valuable Knowledge: Proactive Strategies to Deal with a Shifting Workforce" (Houston, Tex.: American Productivity & Quality Center, 2002), 11.

5. This company's name has been disguised.

6. Sandia is a multiprogram laboratory operated by Lockheed Martin Company for the U.S. Department of Energy's National Nuclear Security Administration.

7. Dorothy Leonard and David Kiron, "Managing Knowledge and Learning at NASA and the Jet Propulsion Laboratory (JPL)," HBS Case Study No. 9-603-062 (Boston: Harvard Business School Publishing, October 2002), 12.

8. One NASA Web site home page. [Online] Available: http://www.onenasa.nasa.gov/Onehome.htm [March 26, 2004].

9. This discussion of the dynamics of culture and culture change was significantly informed by Larry E. Senn and John R. Childress, *The Secret of a Winning Culture: Building High-Performance Teams* (Los Angeles: Leadership Press, 2002). Other valuable sources are: Edgar H. Schein, *The Corporate Culture Survival Guide* (San Francisco: Jossey-Bass, 1999) and Kim S. Cameron and Robert E. Quinn, *Diagnosing and Changing Organizational Cultures* (Boston: Addison-Wesley Publishing Co., 1999).

10. C. A. O'Reilly III and J. Pfeffer, *Hidden Value: How Great Companies Achieve Extraordinary Results with Ordinary People* (Boston: Harvard Business School Press, 2000).

11. "Leader Success Stories: Generating Change at TVA," Senn–Delaney case study. [Online] Available: http://www.sdlcg.com/sdlsite/stories/TVA/storytva.htm [April 1, 2004].

12. Muson, "Valuing Experience."

13. Glenn McEvoy and Mary Jo Blahna, "Engagement or Disengagement? Older Workers and the Looming Labor Shortage," *Business Horizon* (September 2001): 46.

14. The terms "consultant" and "contractor" are often used interchangeably today, although there are differences. Generally, consultants evaluate a client's problem and offer expert advice, while a contractor actually performs work-for-hire. The roles, however, often become blurred. The more meaningful legal distinction is between these two roles and workers who are considered "employees." See James F. Rogers, "Know the Difference between Contractors and Consultants," *CIO Magazine* (December 1, 2000). [Online] Available: http://www.itworld.com/Man/3859/ITW344/pfindex.html [April 1, 2004].

15. Muson, "Valuing Experience," 14; Rick Garnitz, "Semiretirement: A Practical Alternative for Boomers," *Employee Benefits Journal* (June 1, 2002).

16. Carolyn Hirschman, "Exit Strategies," *HR Magazine* (December 2001).

17. Garnitz, "Semiretirement," 51–53.

18. McEvoy and Blahna, "Engagement or Disengagement?"

19. The same kind of dialog (e.g., using focus groups, communities of interest, etc.) can be created with cohorts of new hires, as well, to surface and address their concerns.

20. For more detailed descriptions of the legal issues and pension regulations affecting phased retirement programs in the United States, Canada, and the United Kingdom, see William B. P. Robson, "Aging Populations and the Workforce: Challenges for Employers," British–North American Committee (October 2001), A BNAC Statement. [Online] Available: http://www.cdhowe.org/pdf/BNAC_Aging_Populations.pdf [July, 7, 2003]; for more on the U.S. legal situation, also see "Phased Retirement: It's Time Has Come," *Balancing Act Newsletter,* Employment Policy Foundation. [Online] April 15, 2003. Available: http://www.epf.org/research/newsletters/2003/ba20030415.pdf [March 26, 2004]; Donald J. Segal, "A Letter to the IRS from the Pension Committee on Implementing Phased Retirement Arrangements," *American Academy of Actuaries.* [Online] December 30, 2002. Available: http://www.actuary.org/pdf/pension/irs_30dec02.pdf [June 25, 2003]; and Anna Rappaport, "Employers Strategies for a Changing Workforce: Phased Retirement and Other Options," *Benefits Quarterly* (October 1, 2001).

21. Peter Cappelli, "A Market-Driven Approach to Retaining Talent," *Harvard Business Review* (January–February 2000): 103–111.

CHAPTER 5

1. Mike Burk, "Communities of Practice," *Public Roads* 63/6 (May 2000).

2. Of course, interviews can be a form of direct knowledge transfer, but in practice the ultimate recipients of the knowledge being transferred are often not present when debriefing interviews are conducted.

3. Nancy Dixon calls knowledge preservation within an existing group 'serial transfer.' As noted earlier, this book is not concerned with the transfer of 'best practices' across units because so many other variables are involved. For an excellent overview of "knowledge sharing," see Nancy Dixon, *Common Knowledge: How Companies Thrive by Sharing What They Know* (Boston: Harvard Business School Press, 2000).

4. Ikujiro Nonaka and Hirotaka Takeuchi, *The Knowledge-Creating Company: How Japanese Companies Create the Dynamics of Innovation* (New York: Oxford University Press, 1995).

5. Carl Frappaolo, *Knowledge Management* (Oxford: Capstone Publishing, 2002).

6. For more details, see Gabriel Szulanski, *Sticky Knowledge: Barriers to Knowing in the Firm* (Thousand Oaks, Calif.: Sage Publications, 2003).

7. Szulanski, *Sticky Knowledge,* 60.

8. Wayne E. Baker, "Teams as Networks: Using Network Analysis for Team Development," *Training Today* (March 1995).[Online] Available: http://www.humaxnetworks.com/teams.html [April 2, 2004].

9. "Configuration control" in this case means understanding all the modifications that have been made over the years to a building's systems, why the changes were made, and how they are supposed to work.

10. Harvey Rose, "Exit Strategies at the World Bank," *Knowledge Management* 4/11 (December 2001).

11. Jef Staes, "E-Learning and Knowledge Management, Symptoms of a New Siemens Reality," in *Knowledge Management Case Book,* ed. Thomas H. Davenport and Gilbert J. B. Probst, 2nd ed. (New York: John Wiley & Sons, 2002), 240–258.

12. Christina Bader-Kowalski and Antonie Jakubetzki, "The Siemens Management Learning Program," in *Knowledge Management Case Book,* ed. Davenport and

Probst, 228–239; "Retaining Valuable Knowledge at Siemens AG—A Case Study," in Consortium Benchmarking Study, "Retaining Valuable Knowledge: Proactive Strategies to Deal with a Shifting Workforce" (Houston, Tex.: American Productivity & Quality Center, 2002).

13. "Retaining Valuable Knowledge at Siemens AG—A Case Study," 10–11.

CHAPTER 6

1. This notion of control over knowledge transfer was adapted from David Snowden, "Narrative Patterns: The Perils and Possibilities of Using Story in Organizations," in *Creating Value with Knowledge,* ed. Eric Lesser and Laurence Prusak (New York: Oxford University Press, 2003).

2. Richard Stone, "How Storytelling Can Keep Your Organization on Track," *StoryWork Institute.* [Online] Available: http://www.storywork.com/orgontrack .html [March 26, 2004].

3. Philip J. Gill, "Once upon an Enterprise: The Ancient Art of Storytelling Emerges as a Tool for Knowledge Management," *destination CRM—Knowledge Management.* [Online] May 2001. Available: http://www.destinationcrm.com/ km/dcrm_km_article.asp?id=823&ed=5%2F1%2F01 [April 1, 2004].

4. Issues of ASK, which stands for Academy Sharing Knowledge, are available at http://www.appl.nasa.gov/ask.

5. For these stories, see David Collins, "When to Say No," *ASK Magazine.* [Online] January 2002. Available: http://appl.nasa.gov/pdf/48591main_ASK6.pdf [March 26, 2004]; and Jenny Baer-Riedhart, "Know Thyself—But Don't Forget to Learn about the Customer Too," *ASK Magazine.* [Online] September 2001. Available: http://appl.nasa.gov/pdf/48590main_ASK5.pdf [March 26, 2004].

6. "APPL Overview," *APPL.* [Online] Available: http://appl.nasa.gov/about/ overview/index.html [March 26, 2004].

7. Roy Malone, "Thank You Judy," *ASK Magazine.* [Online] Available: http:// appl.nasa.gov/ask/issues/11/stories/ask11_stories_thankyoujudy.html [March 26, 2004].

8. Kathy Sierra and Bert Bates, *Head First Java* (Sebastopol, Calif.: O'Reilly & Associates, 2003).

9. Charlotte Linde, "Narrative and Tacit Knowledge Exchange," *Journal of Knowledge Management* 5/2 (2001): 160–171; Walter Swap, Dorothy Leonard, Mimi Shields, and Lisa Abrams, "Using Mentoring and Storytelling to Transfer Knowledge in the Workplace," *Journal of Management Information Systems* 18/1 (Summer 2001); Stephen Denning, *The Springboard: How Storytelling Ignites Action in Knowledge-Era Orgs* (Boston: Butterworth-Heinemann, 2001).

10. *Callback* issues are available online at http://asrs.arc.nasa.gov/callback_nf .htm. Warning! This publication is not recommended for nervous flyers.

11. The concepts of mentoring and coaching are frequently used interchangeably, but they are not identical. Mentoring always involves coaching, but coaching does not necessarily involve a mentoring relationship. Coaching in the context of knowledge transfer is a more short-term, narrow activity focused on helping a less experienced individual learn how to do something more effectively by filling a specific knowledge gap. Mentoring, as a practice that supports knowledge retention, is a broader concept that implies more concern with the protégé's long-term development. It also includes passing on knowledge more indirectly related

to task performance. This section uses the term "mentoring," but recognizes that coaching is also an essential role in facilitating knowledge retention. For more on applying these two concepts in practice, see Lois J. Zachary, *The Mentor's Guide: Facilitating Effective Learning Relationships* (San Francisco: Jossey-Bass, 2000); James Hunt and Joseph Weintraub, *The Coaching Manager: Developing Top Talent in Business* (Thousand Oaks, Calif.: Sage Publications, 2002), and James Flaherty, *Coaching: Evolving Excellence in Others* (Boston: Butterworth-Heinemann, 1999).

12. This overview of mentoring is based on Swap, Leonard, et al.'s excellent review of the literature in "Using Mentoring and Storytelling to Transfer Knowledge in the Workplace."

13. Dorothy Leonard and David Kiron, "Managing Knowledge and Learning at NASA and the Jet Propulsion Laboratory (JPL)," HBS Case Study No. 9-603-062 (Boston: Harvard Business School Publishing, October 2002), 6.

14. Howard C. Fero and Jeanne Nakamura, "How Mentors Affect Workers' Interests and Involvement at Work" (2002), paper presented at the 17th Annual Conference of the Society for Industrial and Organizational Psychology, Toronto, Ontario, Canada.

15. Pamela Hinds and Jeffrey Pfeffer, "Why Organizations Don't 'Know What They Know': Cognitive and Motivational Factors Affecting the Transfer of Expertise," Graduate School of Business, Stanford University, Research Paper No. 1697 (Palo Alto, Calif.: Stanford University, July 2001); E. Finkel, C. Heath, and J. Dent, "Expertise and the Curse of Knowledge: The Communication Problems of Scientists," University of North Carolina at Chapel Hill, Working Paper (Chapel Hill: University of North Carolina, 2001).

16. Lessons in this section are adapted from Hinds and Pfeffer, "Why Organizations Don't 'Know What They Know' "; and Swap et al., "Using Mentoring and Storytelling to Transfer Knowledge in the Workplace."

17. Zachary, *The Mentor's Guide.*

18. For more details on conducting AARs, see Chris Collison and Geoff Parcell, *Learning to Fly: Practical Lessons from One of the World's Leading Knowledge Companies* (Oxford: Capstone Publishing, 2001); Gordon R. Sullivan and Michael V. Harper, *Hope is Not a Method* (New York: Times Business, 1996).

19. Rob Cross and Lloyd Baird, "Technology is Not Enough: Improving Performance by Building Organizational Memory," *Sloan Management Review* 41/3 (Spring 2000).

20. Nancy Dixon, *Common Knowledge: How Companies Thrive by Sharing What They Know* (Boston: Harvard Business School Press, 2000), 39.

21. Collison and Parcell, *Learning to Fly,* 50–53.

22. Ricci Graham, "Bikers Learn from the Army," *Knowledge Management.* [Online] January 16, 2001. Available: http://www.destinationKM.com/articles/default.asp?articleid=425 [December 17, 2003].

23. Two of the most important books describing communities of practice and their characteristics, benefits, and implementation issues are E. Wenger, R. McDermott, and W. M. Snyder, *Cultivating Communities of Practice: A Guide to Managing Knowledge* (Boston: Harvard Business School Press, 2002); and Hubert Saint-Onge and Debra Wallace, *Leveraging Communities of Practice for Strategic Advantage* (Boston: Butterworth-Heinemann, 2003).

24. For more on Shell's use of networks, see Wenger, McDermott, and Snyder, *Cultivating Communities of Practice.*

25. The challenges of connecting and supporting this community are described in an excellent book by Collison and Parcell, *Learning to Fly,* 130–139.

26. Details about Best Buy's CoP methodology are from "Retaining Valuable Knowledge at Best Buy Co., Inc.—A Case Study," in Consortium Benchmarking Study, "Retaining Valuable Knowledge: Proactive Strategies to Deal with a Shifting Workforce" (Houston, Tex.: American Productivity & Quality Center, 2002).

27. Adopted from Saint-Onge and Wallace, *Leveraging Communities of Practice for Strategic Advantage,* 141, 207.

28. "Retaining Valuable Knowledge at Siemens AG—A Case Study," in Consortium Benchmarking Study, "Retaining Valuable Knowledge: Proactive Strategies to Deal with a Shifting Workforce" (Houston, Tex.: American Productivity & Quality Center, 2002).

CHAPTER 7

1. This description of BP Connect was drawn largely from Chris Collison and Geoff Parcell, *Learning to Fly: Practical Lessons from One of the World's Leading Knowledge Companies* (Oxford: Capstone Publishing, 2001), 103–122.

2. Megan Santosus, "Underwriting Knowledge," *CIO Magazine* (September 1, 2002).

3. For a detailed description of the lessons learned from implementing the Navy's program management CoP, see W. Page Glennie and John Hickok, "Meeting Critical Defense Needs with CoPs," *KM Review* 6/3. [Online] July/August 2003. Available: http://www.tomoye.com/ourcompany/media/pdf/melcrum_article_july_2003.pdf [September 18, 2003].

4. Details of this U.S. Navy initiative were drawn from Josh Bersin, "Flag University Leverages Technology for Extensive and Deep Executive Education." [Online] August 2003. Available: http://www.bersin.com/tips_techniques/aug_mgt_flag.htm#top [September 16, 2003].

5. Josh Bersin, "Executive Education: The U.S. Navy Uses E-Learning to Expand Reach and Range" (August 2003). [Online] Available: http://www.bersin.com/tips_techniques/aug_mgt_flag.htm [April 2, 2004].

6. Ellen McCarthy, "RWD Helping Florida Promote Space Jobs," *Washington Post* (March 13, 2003): E05; Colleen O'Hara, "Filling the Pipeline: Online Learning Portal Targets Aerospace Industry," *Federal Computer Week* (November 4, 2002).

7. "Executive Guides: Knowledge Management." [Online] Available: http://guide.darwinmag.com/technology/enterprise/knowledge/index.html [July 25, 2004].

8. ClickFix application at DebTech described in Amy Casher and Eric Lesser, "Gray Matter Matters: Preserving Critical Knowledge in the 21st Century," Executive Brief, IBM Institute for Business Value (2003). [Online] January 30, 2004. Available: http://www-1.ibm.com/services/files/ibv gray.pdf [May 14, 2004]; also see Elizabeth Harding and Julie Lavallee, "Knowledge Retention Reduces Downtime at Diamond Mine," *Software Magazine* (June 2001): 9.

9. Dorothy Leonard and David Kiron, "Managing Knowledge and Learning at NASA and the Jet Propulsion Laboratory (JPL)," Case No. 9-603-062 (Boston: Harvard Business School Publishing, 2002), 9.

10. Larry Wash, "Case Study: Dow Chemical Implements Enterprise Content Management System from Xerox," *DM Review.* [Online] February 10, 2003. Avail-

able: http://www.datawarehouse.com/article/?articleId=3126&searchTerm=larry%20walsh [March 26, 2004].

11. Megan Santosus, "Case Files: Northrop Grumman: Thanks for the Memories," *CIO* (September 1, 2001).

12. "Berlex Laboratories: Empowering Employees across a Widely Dispersed, Diverse Enterprise," a Customer Success Story [Online] Available: http://www.documentum.com/customer_success/success/berlex_laboratories.htm [April 2, 2004].

13. For an overview of knowledge mapping, see Mark N. Wexler, "The Who, What and Why of Knowledge Mapping," *Journal of Knowledge Management* 5/3 (2001): 249–263.

14. Some managers and consultants prefer the term "organizational network analysis" or "knowledge network mapping" because they sound less academic.

15. For an excellent description of social network analysis, see Rob Cross, Stephen P. Borgatti, and Andrew Parker, "Making Invisible Work Visible: Using Social Network Analysis to Support Strategic Collaboration," in *Networks in the Knowledge Economy*, ed. Rob Cross, Andrew Parker, and Lisa Sasson (New York: Oxford University Press, 2003), 261–282.

16. Cross, Borgatti, and Parker, "Making Invisible Work Visible."

CHAPTER 8

1. While this section focuses on using retirees, it also pertains to using any mid-career employees, who leave voluntarily and take with them valuable expertise.

2. Study cited in William B. P. Robson, "Aging Populations and the Workplace." British–North American Research Association, *A BNAC Statement* 20. [Online] October 2001. Available: http://www.cdhowe.org/pdf/BNAC_Agining_Populations.pdf [October 1, 2003]. As noted in chapter 4, the terms "contractor" and "consultant" have become blurred and are often used interchangeably.

3. Alison Stein Wellner, "Tapping a Silver Mine," *SHRM Online* 47/3. [Online] March 2002. Available: http://www.shrm.org/hrmagazine/articles/0302/0302covstory_wellner.asp [April 28, 2004]; Leslie Haggin Geary, "Will You Ever Retire?" *CNN Money*. [Online] September 3, 2002. Available: http://money.cnn.com/2002/08/29/retirement/retirelate/ [March 26, 2004].

4. James Brian Quinn, "Strategic Outsourcing: Leveraging Knowledge Capabilities," *Sloan Management Review* 40/4 (Summer 1999).

5. Lisa Picarille, "Outsourcing for Strategic Value, Not to Cut Costs," *destination CRM*. [Online] September 29, 2003. Available: http://www.destinationcrm.com/articles/default.asp?articleid=3515 [October 1, 2003].

6. Rick Dove, "Outsourcing Knowledge Work—Why Not?" *Automotive Manufacturing and Production* 111/10. [Online] October 1999: 16. Available: http://www.parshift.com/Essays/essay057.htm [March 26, 2004].

7. Michael Schrage, "Don't Trust Your Code to Strangers," *CIO Magazine* (September 15, 2003): 42–44.

8. The need to regenerate lost knowledge, which is primarily the result of employee turnover, is not the same as the problem known as "reinventing-the-wheel" in knowledge management circles. This latter challenge refers to the tendency of working groups to create knowledge that already exists elsewhere in the organization. Failing to use knowledge that is available for adaptation and reuse

is a knowledge-sharing problem, which is caused by a lack of motivation and inadequate access to intellectual capital. On the other hand, the inability to access knowledge that was once known to exist within the organization is a lost knowledge problem. In this case, knowledge that a potential user would have once had access to is no longer available.

9. Andrew Hargadon and Robert I. Sutton, "Building an Innovation Factory," *Harvard Business Review* (May–June 2000): 160.

10. For an excellent description of how to conduct peer assists, see Chris Collison and Geoff Parcell, *Learning to Fly: Practical Lessons from One of the World's Leading Knowledge Companies* (Oxford: Capstone Publishing, 2001).

CHAPTER 9

1. Information describing Northrop Grumman was drawn from interviews, as well as "Retaining Valuable Knowledge at Northrop Grumman Corporation—A Case Study," in Consortium Benchmarking Study, "Retaining Valuable Knowledge: Proactive Strategies to Deal with a Shifting Work Force" (Houston, Tex.: American Productivity & Quality Center, 2002); and Megan Santosus, "Case Files: Northrop Grumman: Thanks for the Memories," *CIO* (September 1, 2001), 86–90.

2. Details in this section were drawn from interviews as well as an internal TVA document, "SHRM Innovative Practice Application—Knowledge Retention: Preventing Knowledge from Walking Out the Door," 2003.

CHAPTER 10

1. Adapted from Ron Elsdon, *Affiliation in the Workplace: Value Creation in the New Organization* (Westport, Conn.: Praeger, 2003), 119.

2. Howard Muson, "Valuing Experience: How to Motivate and Retain Mature Workers," (New York: Conference Board, April 2003).

3. Some of the ideas in this section were adapted from David DeLong, "Better Practices for Retaining Organizational Knowledge," research note, Accenture Institute for Strategic Change. [Online] November 2002. Available: http://www .accenture.com/xd/xd.asp?it=enweb&xd=_ins/researchreportabstract_178.xml [March 26, 2004].

4. Ideas in this section were adapted from the work of Jack Keen, president/cofounder of The Deciding Factor, Inc. (www.decidingfactor.com). See Jack M. Keen and Bonnie Digrius, *Making Technology Investments Profitable: ROI Road Map to Better Business Cases* (New York: John Wiley & Sons, 2003).

5. Elsdon, *Affiliation in the Workplace*.

CHAPTER 11

1. David W. DeLong, " 'My Job Is in the Box': A Field Study of Tasks, Roles, and the Structuring of Data Base-Centered Work" (doctoral dissertation, Boston University Graduate School of Management, 1997), 215.

2. These ideas were explored in detail in David W. DeLong and Patricia Seeman, "Confronting Conceptual Confusion and Conflict in Knowledge Management," *Organizational Dynamics* 29/1 (2000): 33–44.

3. William Fulmer, "The World Bank and Knowledge Management," Case Study No. 9-801-157 (Boston: Harvard Business School, January 5, 2001), 3.

4. The way SAIC helps clients choose projects raises a dilemma not unlike that experienced when investing in new sewer systems. There is never going to be anything sexy about these systems, but sooner or later you've got to invest in upgrading them. When it comes to making knowledge retention investments, sometimes the best choice is going to be as uninspiring as a new sewer line, but putting action off too long simply because the project does not inspire people could lead to very unpleasant results.

5. Steve Denning, "Storytelling to Ignite Change." [Online] Available: http://www.creatingthe21stcentury.org/Steve6_Pakistan.html [October 22, 2003].

6. Stephen Denning, *The Springboard: How Storytelling Ignites Action in Knowledge-Era Orgs* (Boston: Butterworth-Heinemann, 2001), 191.

7. Of course, the expert/novice dichotomy oversimplifies the many types of relationships you are likely to face when transferring knowledge. Often it will be more experienced versus less experienced employees. The expert/novice characterization just simplifies things for purposes of discussion.

8. Ron Zemke, Claire Raines, and Bob Filipczak, *Generational Work* (New York: AMACOM, 2000); Lynne C. Lancaster and David Stillman, *When Generations Collide* (New York: Harper Business, 2002).

9. Lancaster and Stillman, *When Generations Collide*.

10. DeLong, " 'My Job Is in the Box,' " 201.

11. Tyvek® is DuPont's registered trademark for its spun-bonded polyolefin.

12. An excellent resource on scenarios is Liam Fahey and Robert M. Randall, eds., *Learning from the Future: Competitive Foresight Scenarios* (New York: John Wiley, 1998).

13. Many of the ideas in this section are adapted from Charles Hampden-Turner, *Charting the Corporate Mind* (New York: Free Press, 1990); also see Fons Trompenaars and Charles Hampden-Turner, *21 Leaders for the 21st Century: How Innovative Leaders Manage in the Digital Age* (New York: McGraw-Hill, 2002) and Charles Handy, *The Age of Paradox* (Boston: Harvard Business School Press, 1994).

14. Hampden-Turner, *Charting the Corporate Mind*.

15. Hampden-Turner, *Charting the Corporate Mind*, 147.

16. Hampden-Turner, *Charting the Corporate Mind*, 125.

17. Nelson Repenning and John Sterman, "Nobody Ever Gets Credit for Fixing Problems that Never Happened: Creating and Sustaining Performance Improvement," *California Management Review* (Summer 2001).

18. Hampden-Turner, *Charting the Corporate Mind*, 203.

19. This section is adapted from the work of Robert Kegan and Lisa Lashkow Lahey, "The Real Reason People Won't Change," *Harvard Business Review* (November 2001); and *How the Way We Talk Can Change the Way We Work* (San Francisco: Jossey-Bass, 2001).

20. Kegan and Lahey, "The Real Reason People Won't Change," 90.

21. This approach has been characterized as "the multiple realities approach to knowing." See Ian I. Mitroff and Harold A. Linstone, *The Unbounded Mind: Breaking the Chains of Traditional Business Thinking* (New York: Oxford University Press, 1993).

CHAPTER 12

1. Michael H. Zack, "Developing a Knowledge Strategy," *California Management Review* 41/3 (Spring 1999): 125–145.

2. Lowell Bryan, "Just-in-Time Strategy for a Turbulent World," *McKinsey Quarterly* 2 (2002).

3. Jonathan D. Krome and Jay W. Survant, "Practical Preparations for the Big Crew Change," paper presented at the Society of Petroleum Engineers Annual Technical Conference, San Antonio, Tex., September 29–October 2, 2002.

4. Ideas here adapted from Hugh Courtney, Jane Kirklord, and Patrick Viguerie, "Strategy under Uncertainty," *Harvard Business Review* (November 1997).

5. Russell L. Ackoff, *Ackoff's Best: His Classic Writings on Management* (New York: John Wiley & Sons, 1999), 118.

6. Ackoff, *Ackoff's Best*.

7. Charles B. Keating, Paul Kauffmann, and David Dryer, "A Framework for Systemic Analysis of Complex Issues," *Journal of Management Development* 20 (2001): 772–784; Ackoff, *Ackoff's Best*.

8. Shoshanna Zuboff, *In the Age of the Smart Machine* (New York: Basic Books, 1988).

9. Wesley M. Cohen and Daniel A. Levinthal, "Absorptive Capacity: A New Perspective on Learning and Innovation," *Administrative Science Quarterly* 35/1 (March 1990).

10. Oswald Jones and Martin Craven, "Expanding Capabilities in a Mature Manufacturing Firm: Absorptive Capacity and the TCS," *International Small Business Journal* 19/3 (April–June 2001).

11. Peter J. Williamson, "Strategy as Options on the Future," *Sloan Management Review* (Spring 1999): 117–126.

12. Zack, "Developing a Knowledge Strategy."

13. Henry Mintzberg and Joseph Lampel, "Reflecting on the Strategy Process," *Sloan Management Review* (Spring 1999): 21–30.

14. Keating, Kauffmann, and Dryer, "A Framework for Systemic Analysis of Complex Issues."

15. Mintzberg and Lampel, "Reflecting on the Strategy Process."

Index

Italicized page numbers refer to figures.